AMAZING NORTHEAST

SIKKIM

AMAZING NORTHEAST

SIKKIM

Edited & Compiled by
Aribam Indubala Devi

Vij Books India Pvt. Ltd.
(Publishers, Dustributors & Importers)
4675-A, 21, Ansari Road, Darya Ganj,
New Delhi-110002

Published by
Vij Books India Pvt. Ltd.
(Publishers, Distributors & Importers)
4675-A, 21, Ansari Road, Darya Ganj,
New Delhi-110002
Phone: 91-11-65449971, 91-11-43596460
Fax: 91-11-47340674
E-mail: vijbooks@rediffmail.com

Copyright © Publishers

First Edition: 2010

ISBN: 978-93-80177-30-4

Contents

- -

Preface

In India, the Northeastern region is quite charming and interesting enough to be known about. Among the eight Northeastern States, Sikkim is a small hilly state, bound by vast stretches of Tibetan Plateaux in north, Chumbi Valley of Tibet and Kingdom of Bhutan in east, Kingdom of Nepal in west and Darjeeling (West Bengal) in south. The State has a total area of 7,096 sq km and is stretched over 112 km from north to south and 64 km from east to west. It lies in the northeastern Himalayas between 27 degree 00'46" and 28 degree-07'48" N latitude and 88 degree 00'58" to 88 degree-55'25" E longitude.

The early history of Sikkim started in 13th century with the signing of a bloodbrotherhood treaty between Lepcha Chief Thekong Tek and Tibetan prince Khye-Bumsa at Kabi Lungtsok in north Sikkim. This followed the historical visit of three revered Lamas to Yuksam in 1641 in west Sikkim, where they consecrated Phuntsog Namgyal, a sixth generation descendent of Khye-Humsa as the first Chogyal of Sikkim, thus heralding the beginning of the Namgyal dynasty in Sikkim. With the march of history, events in Sikkim saw the State pass through the process of democratisation and become an integral part of the Indian Union in 1975.

Sikkim is a blessed land, where people from all communities live in harmony. In spite of the fact that Sikkim comprises different people and is a multiethnic society. It is perhaps the most peaceful State of the Indian Union to promote communal harmony and human relations, a feat which is much expected in a plural society, like India.

This small but comprehensive and compact book on this northeastern state, offers all information, within one cover. Hopefully, it would serve all those working on or interested in knowing about northeastern India, be they scholars, researchers, journalists, students or general readers. This is in fact, 'Knowledge in Nutshell'.

— *Editor*

Sikkim

An Overview

Governor	:	Balmiki Prasad Singh
Chief Minister	:	Pawan Chamling
Speaker	:	D.N. Takarpa
Chief Secretary	:	T.T. Dorji
Capital	:	Gangtok
High Court	:	Gangtok

Brief Description

Sikkim lies between 27.04° to 28.07° North latitude and 80.00° to 88.55° East longitude. It is bound on the north by the Tibet plateau, on the east by Chumbi valley of Tibet and Bhutan, on the west by Nepal and on the south by Darjeeling district of West Bengal. It shares a 97.8 km long international boundary with Nepal, 30.90 km long border with Bhutan and a 220.35 km long border with Tibet. This State in the north-western Himalayan mountain ranges covers a total area of 7,096 sqe km constituting 0.22 per cent of India's geographical area and 2.7 per cent of the North-East.

Facts and Figures

- *Area:* 7,096 sq km (2.7% of total area of North-East)
- *Geographical Location:* Situated between longitude 88'E to 89'E & latitude 27'N to 28'N
- *Capital:* Gangtok
- *Population:* 5,40,493 (2001 Census) (1.4% of population of North-East)
- *Density of Population (per sq km):* 73 (National Figure: 324)
- *Male:* 2,88,217
- *Female:* 2,52,276

Contd...

The early history of Sikkim starts in the 13th century with the signing of a blood-brotherhood treaty between the Lepcha Chief Thekong Tek and Tibetan prince Khye-Bumsa at Kabi Lungtsok in North Sikkim. In 1641, the Namgyal dynasty was heralded in Sikkim. Subsequently Sikkim passed through a process of democratisation and became an integral part of the Indian Union in 1975. It became the 22 nd state of India on 26 April 1975.

According to Census 2001, Sikkim has a total population of 540,493. It constitutes 0.05 per cent population of India and 1.38 per cent of North-East. It is a multi-ethnic state comprising both tribal and non-tribal groups. The Lepchas are the original inhabitants of the state. The Sherpas are a marginal ethnic group in the state. The Bhutias and the Nepalese migrated to the state from Tibet and Nepal respectively. Nepalese, today are the dominant ethnic group in the state. The local language is Nepali. English is the official language. The rate of literacy in Sikkim is 69.68 per cent.

For administrative reasons, Sikkim is divided into four districts and each district has further been bifurcated into two subdivisions. The state has been further divided into 100 Zilla Panchayat wards, 166 Gram Panchayats and 454 Revenue Blocks. Capital of Sikkim is located at Gangtok, which is at an altitude of 1,780 m. It became a member of the North Eastern Council (NEC) in 2005.

- *Sex Ratio:* 875 females to 1,000 males (National figure: 933 females to 1,000 males)
- *Literacy Rate (2007):* 76.6% (National Figure: 67.6%)
- *Birth Rate (2006):* 19.2 (National Figure: 23.1)
- *Death Rate (2006):* 5.6 (National Figure: 7.4)
- *Infant Mortality Rate (2007):* 34 (National Figure: 55)
- *Per Capita Income (in Rs) (2006-07):* 29,521 (National Figure: Rs. 29,901)
- *Net State Domestic Product (NSDP) (Rs. in crore) (2007-08):* 1,990 (National Figure: 38,11,441)
- *Per Capita NSDP (2007-08):* Rs. 33,553 (National Figure: Rs. 33,283)
- *Per Capita GSDP (2004-05):* Rs. 26,215 (National Figure: Rs. 25,944
- *No. of Towns (as per 2001 Census):* 9
- *No. of Villages (as per 2001 Census):* 452
- *State Bird:* Blood Pheasant
- *State Animal:* Red Panda
- *State Flower:* Noble Orchid
- *Languages:* Nepali, English, Hindi, Bhutia (Sikkimese), Bhutia (Tibetan), Lepcha, Limboo
- *No. of Districts:* (04) North Sikkim, West Sikkim, East Sikkim, South Sikkim
- *Major Towns:* Gangtok, Namchi, Geyzing, Mangan, Pelling
- *Major Plantations:* Tea, Medicinal Plants
- *Major Fruits, Vegetables & Spices:* Cardamom, Orange, Ginger
- *Nearest Airport:* Bagdogra

Sikkim has been declared an industrially backward state. The economy of the state is primarily based on agriculture and animal husbandry. 56.34 per cent of the total working population depend on these for their livelihood. Most of the industries that exist in Sikkim are either small or medium scale. The per capita Gross State Domestic Product (GSDP) in 2004-05 is rupees 26,215 and the Net State Domestic Product (NSDP) in 1999-2000 is Rupees 13,356. Sikkim ranks 18th in the human resource development index and 17th in the poverty index in India.

Sikkim has become a major tourist attraction over the years and generates substantial revenue from this sector.

Area, Population and Headquarters of Districts

S.No.	District	Area (sq km)	Population	Headquarters
1	East Sikkim	954	1,78,452	Gangtok
2.	North Sikkim	4,226	31,240	Mangan
3.	South Sikkim	750	98,604	Namchi
4.	West Sikkim	1,166	98,161	Gyalshing

[Based on Latest Official Data Available]

(*xii*)

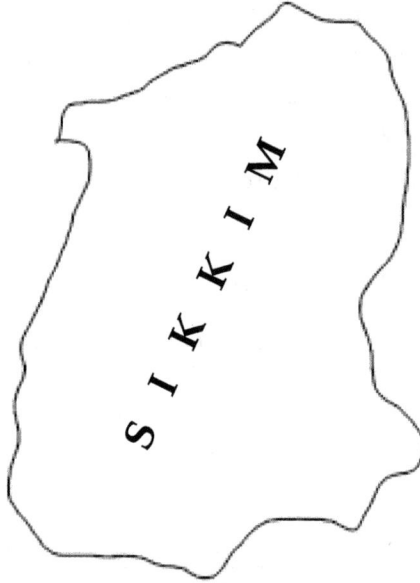

Sikkim

Outline Map

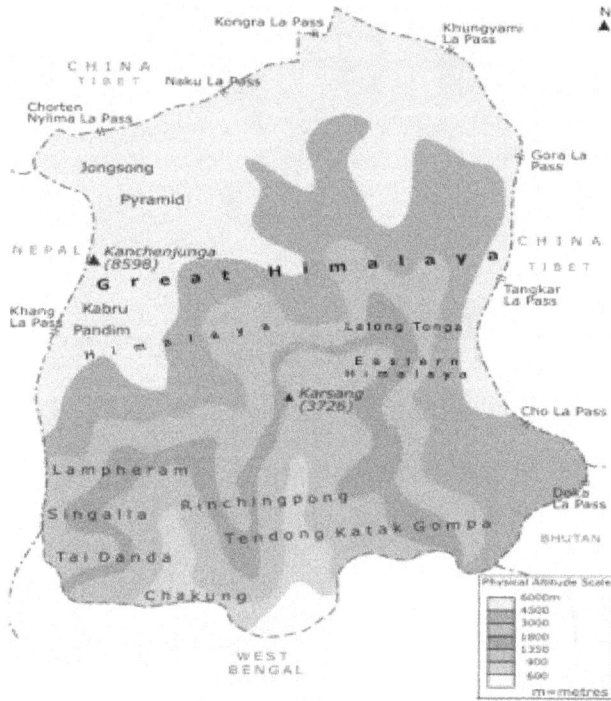

Geographical Map

(xii)

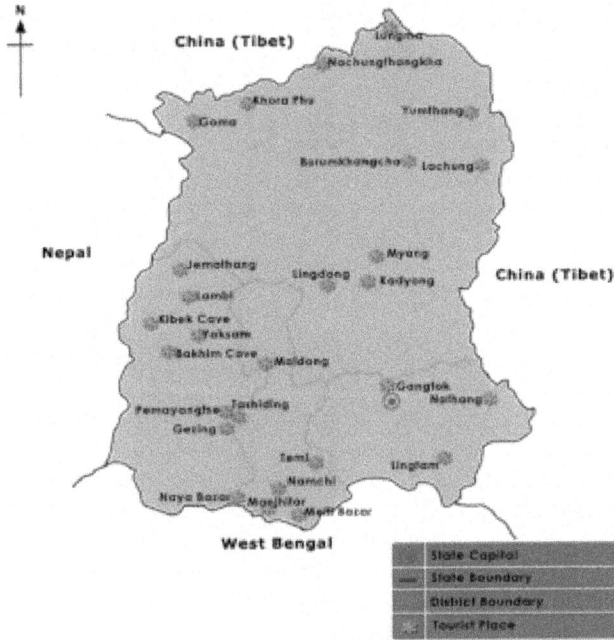

Tourist Map

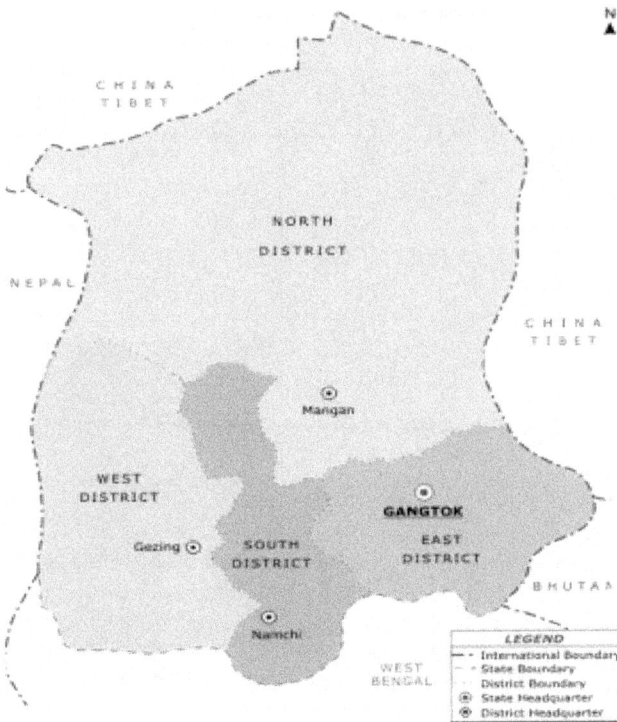

Districts of the State

Introduction

Sikkim is a landlocked Indian state nestled in the Himalayas. It is the least populous state in India and the second-smallest in area after Goa. The thumb-shaped state borders Nepal in the west, the Tibet Autonomous Region of China to the north and the east and Bhutan in the southeast. The Indian state of West Bengal borders Sikkim to its south. Despite its small area of 7,096 sq km (2,740 sq mi), Sikkim is geographically diverse due to its location in the Himalayas. The climate ranges from subtropical to high alpine. Kangchenjunga, the world's third-highest peak, is located on the border of Sikkim with Nepal. Sikkim is a popular tourist destination owing to its culture, scenic beauty and biodiversity.

Legend has it that the Buddhist saint Guru Rinpoche visited Sikkim in the 9th century, introduced Buddhism and foretold the era of the monarchy. Accordingly, the Namgyal dynasty was established in 1642. Over the next 150 years, the kingdom witnessed frequent raids and territorial losses to Nepalese invaders. It allied itself with the British rulers of India but was soon annexed by them. Later, Sikkim became a British protectorate and was merged with India following a referendum in 1975.

The official language of the state is English, but there is a sizable population that converses in Nepali (the *lingua franca* of the state), Lepcha, Bhutia, and Limbu. It is the only state in India with an ethnic Nepalese majority. The predominant religions are Hinduism and Vajrayana Buddhism. Gangtok is the capital and the largest town. Sikkim has a booming economy dependent on agriculture and tourism.

Toponym

The most widely accepted origin of the name Sikkim is that it is a combination of two words in the Limbu *Su*, which means "new", and *Khyim*, which means "palace" or house, in reference to the palace built by the state's first ruler, Phuntsog Namgyal. The Tibetan name for Sikkim is *Denjong*, which means the "valley of rice". The Lepchas, original inhabitants of Sikkim called it *Nye-mae-el* or *paradise*, and the Bhutias call it *Beymul Demazong*, which means *the hidden valley of rice*. In Hindu religious texts, Sikkim is known as *Indrakil*, the garden of Indra.

Historical Aspects

Not much is known about Sikkim's ancient history, except for the fact that the first inhabitants were the Lepchas or Rong (ravine folk). They were later encompassed and absorbed by other clans. Sikkim also finds its mention on many Hindu texts as Indrakil or *garden of Lord Indra*.

The Buddhist saint Guru Rinpoche is said to have passed through the land in the 9th century. According to legend the Guru blessed the land, introduced Buddhism to Sikkim and also foretold the era of the monarchy in the state, which would arrive centuries later. There are numerous stories regarding the migration of Tibetans into Sikkim and the establishment of the Sikkimese monarchy. The most popular states that in the 13th century, Guru Tashi, a Prince from the Mi-nyak House in Kham in Eastern Tibet, had a divine revelation one night instructing him to travel south to seek his fortunes. Guru Tashi settled down in the Chumbi Valley in Sikkim. In recent years a number of scholarly article have been written on the history of Sikkim, which cast doubt over the validity of these stories.

Kingdom of Sikkim

In 1642, the fifth generation descendant of Guru Tashi, Phuntsog Namgyal was consecrated as the first Denjong Gyalpo or the Chogyal (king) of Sikkim by the three great Lamas who came from the north, west and south to Yuksom Norbugang in West Sikkim. The event, *Naljor Chezhi*, was as predicted by Guru Rinpoche some eight hundred years before. This historical gathering of the three virtuous lamas is called Yuksom, which in Lepcha means the 'Three Superior Ones'. The chogyal, along with the three lamas proselytised the Lepcha tribes into Buddhism and annexed the Chumbi Valley, the present-day Darjeeling district and parts of today's eastern Nepal.

Invasion from Nepal

In 1700 the Nepalese Gurkha Army invaded Sikkim, and took the former capital Rabdentse by storm.

Phuntsog Namgyal was succeeded by his son, Tensung Namgyal in 1670. The reign of the chogyal was peaceful and saw the capital being shifted from Yuksom to Rabdentse. Chadok Namgyal, the King's second wife's son, took over the throne from him in 1700. This outraged his elder half-sister Pendiongmu, who ousted him with the help of the

Bhutanese. Chadok fled to Tibet where he remained in exile for ten years before returning and reclaiming his lost territory with the help of the Tibetans. His son Gurmed Namgyal succeeded him in 1717. Gurmed's reign saw many skirmishes between the Nepalese and Sikkimese. Phunstok Namgyal, the illegitimate child of Gurmed, succeeded his father in 1733. His reign was tumultuous as he was faced with attacks by the Bhutanese and the Nepalese who managed to capture the capital Rabdentse. Tenzing Namgyal, the next ruler of Sikkim, was a weak ruler, and his sovereignty saw most of Sikkim being appropriated by Nepal. The chogyal was forced to flee to Lhasa where he died in 1780. Tshudpud Namgyal, his son returned to Sikkim in 1793 to reclaim the throne with the help of China. Finding Rabdentse too close to the Nepalese border, he shifted the capital to Tumlong.

British Arrival

With the arrival of the British in neighbouring India, Sikkim allied itself with them as they had a common enemy – Nepal. The infuriated Nepalese attacked Sikkim with vengeance, overrunning most of the region including the Terrai. This prompted the British East India Company to attack Nepal resulting in the Gurkha War in 1814. Treaties signed between Sikkim and Nepal – the Sugauli Treaty and Sikkim and British India – Titalia Treaty, returned the territory annexed by the Nepalese to Sikkim in 1817.

Meanwhile the British were looking for a route to establish trading links with Tibet. An offshoot of the ancient Silk Road through Sikkim meant that the kingdom was ideal as a transit route. A secondary reason for the establishment of links was to quell the growing Russian influence in Tibet. However, ties between Sikkim and India grew sour with the taxation of the area of Morang by the British. In 1835, Sikkim was forced to cede the town of Darjeeling to the British on the condition that a compensation of Rs. 35,000 be paid to him.

Puppet State

In 1849, a pair of British doctors, Campbell and Hooker, ventured into the mountains of Sikkim unannounced and unauthorised by the Chogyal of Sikkim. The doctors were detained by the Sikkim government, which led to a punitive British expedition against the Himalayan Kingdom, in which the whole of Darjeeling district and Morang were annexed in 1861, although the kingdom continued to exist as an independent rump state centred around the capital at Gangtok. The old Chogyal was forced to abdicate in favour of his son, Sidekong Namgyal in 1863.

The Chogyals of Sikkim endeavoured to modernise their state in the succeeding decades, along with their army. A state visit to Darjeeling by Sidekong's half brother, Chogyal Thutob Namgyal in 1873 failed to yield such results, and he returned to Tumlong disappointed. In 1886, the British, interested in trade with Tibet, launched a brief expedition into Sikkim. The Tibetans occupied several of Sikkim's northern border forts, and the Chogyal and his wife were held prisoner by the British when they came to negotiate at Calcutta. In 1888, the Tibetans were defeated and northern Sikkim came under the rule of British India. The British established new landholdings in Sikkim, but released the Chogyal only to have him captured again in 1891. In 1894, the capital was shifted to Gangtok.

In 1895, the Chogyal was released, but the British governors in India reneged on an agreement – the Ten Clauses Agreement – which returned sovereignty to Sikkim. The governor of British India, Claude White, refused to return any sovereignty, and only let the Chogyal retain the judiciary of Sikkim.

In 1905, the Prince of Wales – the future King George V – arrived in Calcutta on a state visit during which he met the Chogyal. The two made an excellent acquaintance and the Crown Prince of Sikkim, Sidkeong Tulku was sent to study at Oxford University. When Sidkeong came to power, he arranged widened sovereignty for Sikkim from King George's government and endorsed sweeping reforms in his short rule as Chogyal, which ended in 1914. In 1918, Sikkim's independence in all domestic affairs was restored, and in the next decade she embarked on a policy to end social ills, outlawing gambling, child labour, and indentured service.

Independent Monarchy

Sikkim had retained guarantees of independence from Britain when she became independent, and such guarantees were transferred to the Indian government when it gained independence in 1947. A popular vote for Sikkim to join the Indian Union failed and Indian Prime Minister Jawaharlal Nehru agreed to a special protectorate status for Sikkim. Sikkim was to be a tributary of India, in which India controlled its external defence, diplomacy and communication. A state council was established in 1955 to allow for constitutional government for the Chogyal, which was sustained until 1973.

In 1962, India and the People's Republic of China went to war. Although Sikkim was an independent country, skirmishes occurred at the Nathula Pass between Indian border guards and the Chinese soldiers. After the war, the ancient pass was shut down (it reopened July 6, 2006).

The old ruler Tashi Namgyal died in 1963 after suffering from cancer. The last hereditary ruler, the Chogyal Palden Thondup Namgyal, ascended to the throne in 1965. Trouble began to brew for the crown even before the Chogyal assumed the throne, as Indian Prime Minister Nehru, who had carefully preserved Sikkim's status as an independent protectorate, died in 1964. His daughter Indira Gandhi, who became Prime Minister in 1966, would have little patience for maintaining an independent Sikkim or its monarchy. The chogyal, who responded to the increased pressure by drinking, was viewed by India as politically dangerous, especially after his wife, the American socialite

Hope Cooke, published a journal article advocating a return of certain former Sikkimese properties.

In early 1970, the anti-monarchy Sikkim National Congress Party demanded fresh elections and greater representation for the Nepalese.

In 1973, anti-royalty riots in front of the palace led to a formal request for protection from India. India worried that an unstable Sikkim would invite Chinese to act on its claims that Sikkim was part of Tibet, and therefore part of China. The Indian government appointed a Chief administrator, Mr. B. S. Das, who effectively wrested control of the country away from the Chogyal.

Frosty relations between the Chogyal and the elected Kazi (Prime Minister) Lhendup Dorji resulted in an attempt to block the meeting of the legislature. The Kazi was elected by the Council of Ministers which was unanimous in its opposition to the retention of the Monarchy. Matters came to a head in 1975 when the Kazi appealed to the Indian Parliament for representation and change of status to statehood. On April 14, 1975, a referendum was held, in which Sikkim voted to merge with the union of India. Sikkim became the 22nd Indian State on April 26, 1975. On May 16, 1975, Sikkim officially became a state of the Indian Union and Lhendup Dorji became head of State (chief minister). This was promptly recognised by the United Nations and all countries except China.

The position of Chogyal was thus abolished, ending the monarchy. In 1982, Palden Thondup succumbed to cancer in the United States.

As an Indian State

The 1979 assembly election saw Nar Bahadur Bhandari elected Chief Minister of Sikkim. Bhandhari held on to win again in 1984 and 1989. In 1994, Assembly politician Pawan Kumar Chamling became the Chief Minister of Sikkim. In 1999 and 2004, Chamling consolidated his position to sweep the polls.

Sino-Indian relations were somewhat bruised in 2000 by an event in Sikkim which challenged China's longstanding claim of Sikkim as an independent country. The unusual event was the escape of Ogyen Trinley Dorje from Tibet to Dharamsala, India. Ogyen Trinley Dorje is one of the two rival claimants who seeks recognition as the 17th Karmapa, the head of the Black Hat branch of Tibetan Buddhism. The two claimants did battle in the Indian court system for control of the considerable funds collected by the 16th Karmapa for the restoration and maintenance of Rumtek Monastery, located in Gangtok, Sikkim. The Chinese, who recognise Ogyen Trinley Dorje as the true Karmapa, were unhappy about the court outcome which awarded the monastery funds to the other rival. However, the Chinese government was in a quandary as to what to do about it, as any protest to India would mean an explicit endorsement that the high court of India holds jurisdiction over Sikkim.

In 2003, with the thawing of ties between the two nations, Sikkim was finally recognised to be a part of India by China. The two governments also proposed to open the Nathula and Jelepla Passes in 2005.

Geographical Aspects

Sikkim is a gorgeous and beautiful state nestled in the Himalayas. Sikkim is thumb-shaped and has a mountainous terrain. The state is hilly and as a result is unfit for agriculture. Certain hill slopes have been converted into farm lands using terrace farming techniques and is used for cultivation. The summit of the Kanchenjunga is the highest point in Sikkim. Numerous streams from the west and south of the state combine into the river Teesta and its tributary, the Rangeet. The Teesta is described as the "lifeline of Sikkim", which flows through the state from north to south.

The Himalayan ranges surround the northern, eastern and western borders of Sikkim in a crescent shape. The Lower Himalayas are the most populated areas. The state has 28 mountain peaks, 21 glaciers, 227 high altitude lakes including the Tsongmo Lake, Gurudongmar and the Khecheopalri Lakes, five hot springs, and over 100 rivers and streams.

Sikkim is connected to Tibet, Bhutan and Nepal by eight mountain passes. The hills of Sikkim mainly consist of gneissose and half-schistose rocks, making the soil poor and shallow. The soil contains large amounts of iron oxide, ranging from neutral to acidic and has poor organic and mineral nutrients. This type of soil tends to support evergreen and deciduous forests. A large portion of Sikkim is covered by the Precambrian rock. The rock consists of phyllites and schists and therefore are prone to weathering and erosion. This with intense rain, causes soil erosion and heavy loss of soil nutrients through leaching. As a result, landslides are frequent in the area.

Sikkim is famous for hot springs which have medicinal and therapeutic values. The most important hot-springs are at Phurchachu(Reshi), Yumthang, Borang, Ralang, Taram-chu and Yumey Samdong. All these hotsprings have high sulphur content and are located near the river banks. The average temperature of the water in these hot springs is 50°C. The climate ranges from sub-tropical in the south to tundra in the northern parts. The inhabited regions of Sikkim enjoys a temperate climate. The temperatures seldom exceeds 28°C in summer and is below 0°C in winter. The state enjoys five seasons as winter, summer, spring, autumn, and monsoon. The average annual temperature of Sikkim is around 18°C (64°F). Sikkim is one of the few states in India having regular snowfall. During the monsoon months, the state faces heavy rain fall that increases the number of landslides. The state has a record for the longest period of non-stop rain continiously for eleven days. In the northern region temperatures drop below -40°C in winter as a result of high altitude. Fog also affects most parts of the state during winter and the monsoons.

Geology

The hills of Sikkim mainly consist of gneissose and half-schistose rocks, making their soil brown clay, and generally poor and shallow. The soil is coarse, with large amounts of iron oxide concentrations, ranging from neutral to acidic and has poor organic and mineral nutrients. This type of soil tends to support evergreen and deciduous forests. Most of Sikkim is covered by Precambrian rock and is much younger in age than the hills. The rock consists of phyllites and schists and therefore the slopes are highly susceptible to weathering and prone to erosion. This, combined with the intense rain, causes extensive soil erosion and heavy loss of soil nutrients through leaching. As a result, landslides are frequent, isolating the towns and villages from the major urban centres.

Regions

Sikkim has four districts, each overseen by a Central Government appointee, the district collector, who is in charge of the administration of the civilian areas of the districts. The Indian army has control of a large territory, as the state is a sensitive border area. Many areas are restricted and permits are needed to visit them. There are eight towns and nine subdivisions in Sikkim.

The four districts are East Sikkim, West Sikkim, North Sikkim and South Sikkim. The district capitals are Gangtok, Geyzing, Mangan and Namchi respectively. These Four Districts are further divided into Subdivisions. "Pakyong" and "Rongli" are the subdivisions of the East District. "Soreng" is the subdivision of the West District. "Chungthang" is the subdivision of the North District. "Ravongla" is the subdivision of the South District.

Rivers

Tista or Teesta is the largest river of Sikkim. Winding its way through Sikkim the Teesta river divides the states into two parts. Teesta can be called as *Ganga* of the state of Sikkim as most of the Sikkim's settlements are found along the banks of this river. The Teesta comes out as a snout from the Zemu glacier above Lachen Gompha. It is joined by the Lhonk stream from the north. Another stream Lachung rises from Pauhunri and meets the Teesta at Chumthang. Rangit is another principle river.

Wildlife

Mountain slopes, foot -hills and valley walls covered with a variety of dense growth offer a natural habitat for many types of animals, birds and insects. About 500-600 species of birds and 631 species of butterflies alone are found in this small state. Orchids found in abundance attract several hundreds species of butterflies which can offer a lepidopterist a lifetime of work and delight. In forest surrounded valleys the butterflies are found inn swarming numbers.

The black and the dreaded brown bear are mostly found in forests located at heights ranging from 4,000 feet to 11,000 feet (1,250 metres to 3,453 metres) above sea level. Musk deer are quite common in areas with an average height of 9,000 feet (about 2,800 metres). Tiger, leopard, sambar, barking deer, leopard cat, marbed cat, squirrel are mostly confined to warmer areas. Yak, panda, otter, goral, wild bear, ovis, nahura, bhyang-lung (wild sheep) and Vyang-gra (wild goat) are other animals that can be seen in Sikkim. Otter is much prized for the brocaded fur caps worn by some Sikkimese. The tail-less mountain rats, rock Lizards and snow fox like predators are also found in high altitudes.

Numerous species of birds ranging from gigantic Imamergeyer to the miniscule flower pecker abound in the forests of Sikkim and are enough to make this land an Ornithologists paradise. Flamboyant pheasants, partridges, ducks, quails, teals, eagles, barbet, Himalayan cuckoo, Babblers and Thrushes are some of the birds found in Sikkim. The Tibetan black crow with rosy feet is also found in northern Sikkim. The bright red coloured Miniwet known as "Red King" in Nepal has also its habitat in Sikkim. Crap and Trout fish abound in the rivers and lakes of the state.

Climate

Though Sikkim is a small town, it has all the possible climate right from the tropical to the tundras. So much so, it is possible to drop from the arctic heights to the tropical lowlands within a matter of a couple of hours. On most parts of the northern, eastern and western borders the earth is blanketed with snow almost throughout the year because of high altitudes. Elevations of 6,000 metres, i.e. 19,900 ft and above remain snowbound throughout the year whereas places as low as 3,000 metres, i.e. 9,840 ft come within the snowline during the winters. In the southern border there can be found altitudes plummeting down to as low as sea level and also full of rich tropical forests. Even the climate on two opposite sides of a hill can vary considerably.

Temperature

The temperatures that a particular place experiences varies considerably with altitude. At places of low altitude, like Singtam, Rangpo and Jorethang, the temperatures vary between 4°C to 35°C. Whereas in the places like Gangtok with moderate altitudes of about 1800 metres, i.e. 6,000 ft experience temperatures between 1°C and 25°C. It can also be seen that at altitudes above 4,000 metres, i.e. 131,00 ft, the temperature never rises above 15°C and remains much below the freezing point during the winters and great part of the spring and autumn as well.

Rainfall

Sikkim is one of the rainiest regions in India. Most parts of the place experience torrential rains during summers. This happens because of the fact that the proximity of Sikkim to the Bay of Bengal and also the mountains of the state come directly in the path of the monsoon clouds,. So much so that even a small depression over the Bay of Bengal triggers off a downpour in Sikkim. Even during spring and autumn moisture laden clouds formed due to local evaporation. And these eventually continue to batter a greater part of Sikkim. It is only during October to March that there is hardly any rain and the weather remains more or less clear.

Rainfall however varies considerably from place to place because of the hill features. The northern border of Sikkim experiences comparatively low rainfall because the monsoon clouds dry out by the time they hit the northern barrier. For the sake of comparison, Gangtok registers an average of 325 cm rainfall per annum whereas Muguthang in the extreme north experiences an average rainfall of only 60 cm per annum. Most of Sikkim does not experience high intensity winds. However, at many hill tops and passes, winds and blizzards having considerably high speeds.

The rainfall would decrease at higher altitudes and so would the maximum-minimum temperature. Because of high humidity in this region, even a temperature of 30 C is considered to be uncomfortably hot.

Flora and Fauna

Sikkim is situated in an ecological hotspot of the lower Himalayas, one of only three among the Ecoregions of India. The forested regions of the state exhibit a diverse range of fauna and flora. Owing to its altitudinal gradation, the state has a wide variety of plants, from tropical to temperate to alpine and tundra, and is perhaps one of the few regions to exhibit such a diversity within such a small area. Nearly 81 per cent of the area of Sikkim comes under the administration of its forest department.

The flora of Sikkim include the rhododendron, the state tree, with a wide range of species occurring from subtropical to alpine regions. Orchids, figs, laurel, bananas, sal trees and bamboo grow in the lower altitudes of Sikkim, which enjoy a subtropical-type climate. In the temperate elevations above 1,500 metres, oaks, chestnuts, maples, birches, alders, and magnolias grow in large numbers. The alpine-type vegetation includes juniper, pine, firs, cypresses and rhododendrons, and is typically found between an altitude of 3,500 to 5,000 m. Sikkim has around 5,000 flowering plants, 515 rare orchids, 60 primula species, 36 rhododendron species, 11 oak varieties, 23 bamboo varieties, 16 conifer species, 362 types of ferns and ferns allies, 8 tree ferns, and over 424 medicinal plants. A variant of the Poinsettia, locally known as "Christmas Flower", can be found in abundance in the mountainous state. The orchid *Dendrobium nobile* is the official flower of Sikkim.

The fauna include the snow leopard, the musk deer, the Himalayan Tahr, the red panda, the Himalayan marmot, the serow, the goral, the barking deer, the common langur, the Himalayan Black Bear, the clouded leopard, the Marbled Cat, the leopard cat, the wild dog, the Tibetan wolf, the hog badger, the binturong, the jungle cat and the civet cat. Among the animals more commonly found in the alpine zone are yaks, mainly reared for their milk, meat, and as a beast of burden.

The avifauna of Sikkim consist of the Impeyan pheasant, the crimson horned pheasant, the snow partridge, the snow cock, the lammergeyer and griffon vultures, as well as golden eagles, quail, plovers, woodcock, sandpipers, pigeons, Old World flycatchers, babblers and robins. Sikkim has more than 550 species of birds, some of which have been declared endangered.

Sikkim also has a rich diversity of arthropods, many of which remain unstudied even today. As with the rest of India, the most studied group is that of the butterflies. Of approximately 1,438 butterfly species found in the Indian subcontinent, 695 have been recorded from Sikkim. These include the endangered Kaiser-e-Hind, Yellow Gorgon and the Bhutan Glory.

Social Aspects

People

Communities, cultures, religions and customs of different hues intermingle freely in Sikkim to constitute a homogeneous blend. Hindu temples coexist with Buddhist monasteries. Few Christian churches are also present in this place along with Muslim mosques and Sikh Gurdwaras. Although the Buddhists with monasteries all over the state are the most conspicuous religious group. They are in fact a minority constituting only 28 per cent of the population. The majorities that constitute 68 per cent profess Hinduism. The predominant communities can be named as the Lepchas, Bhutias and the Nepalis. In urban areas many plainsmen such as Marwaris, Biharis, Bengalis, South Indians, Punjabis, etc. have also settled and they are mostly engaged in business and government service. Because of development and construction activities in the state various people work and the working class consists of a small part of the population of migrant labourers from the plains and from Nepal plumbers, masons and carpenters from Orissa, Bihar and West Bengal and Sherpas who are hired by the army to maintain the roads at high altitudes. A few thousand Tibetan Refugees are there who settled well in Sikkim.

Cultural and economic forces are reshaping the way of life of the Sikkimese. The young boys and girls sporting the latest fashions probably picked up from a new Hindi movie or BBC's Clothes Show gaily tromp up and down. The cable TV is definitely attempting to remold the cultural landscape of Sikkim. But in spite of such powerful external influences, Sikkimese have proved to be resilient accepting the benefits of progress while retaining their ethnic identity.

In Sikkim, women are not confined to home and the hearth. In the vegetable market a lady puffing away at her bidi, i.e. local made cigarette can be seen. In the small local restaurant, women sales girl can be seen. At a busy traffic intersection a smartly turned out woman police constable is busy regulating the traffic while another is issuing a ticket to an errant woman driver. On construction sites, women work side by side with men, carrying material in wicker baskets and pulverising stones. Women, even those belonging to the conservative Marwari community run many of the shops in town. In the Government Sector, more than fifteen per cent of the employees are women.

Lepchas

The Lepcha population is concentrated in the central part of Sikkim. This is the area that encompasses the confluence of Lachen and Lachung rivers and Dickchu. The terrain here is rugged and Lepcha dwellings are perched precariously on the steep hillsides. No wonder the word Lepcha means the Ravine folk. They mostly live on agriculture of paddy, cardamom and oranges.

The Lepchas are predominantly Buddhists but many of them are also Christians having been converted to this faith by the missionaries.

Before adopting Buddhism or Christianity as their religion, the earliest Lepcha settlers were believers in the Bon faith or Mune faith. This faith was basically based on spirits, good and bad. Witchcraft and exorcism were very common. They worshipped spirits of mountains, rivers and forests which was but natural for a tribe that co-existed so harmoniously with the rich natural surroundings. The well-known deities of the Lepchas are Itbumoo, Rom, Itbu Debu Rom, Kongchen Konglo and Tamsang Thing, who is also said to have invented the Lepcha script. One major festival of the Lepchas is the Namsoong which marks the beginning of the New Year. A highlight of this festival is the week long mela or fair held at Namprikdam at the confluence of Tista and Tolung-chu near Mangan in North Sikkim. The Lepcha priests are known as Bomthing and they perform intricate ceremonies to invoke the blessings of the spirits.

The Lepcha or Dzongu folklore is rich with stories. One of the very popular story has a parallel with the legend of the Tower of Babel. It describes that the Rongs or Lepchas once attempted to ascend to Rum or Heaven by building a tower of earthen pots. When Rum was about to be reached, God thought he must put an end to this venture. He made them speak in different tongues with the intention of creating confusion. The man at the top of the tower shouted "Kok vim yang tale", i.e. Pass the pole with the hook but the men at the bottom heard the words "Chek tala", i.e. cut it down. The tower was hacked down and its remains are still found in Daramdin near Sombaria in Western Sikkim.

The Government feels protective towards the Lepchas, believing that they represent a conservative force. They are a balance wheel which helps save a way of life from being overwhelmed by Western culture.

Nepalis

At the present time the Nepalis constitute more than 80 per cent of the total population of Sikkim. A major subcultural stock of the Nepalis are the Kiratis. The Kiratis include Limbus, Rais, Magars, Gurungs, Tamangs and some others as well. Originally most of them were hunters and shepherds and semi-nomadic. The Limbus who are also called *Yakthambas*, i.e. yak-herders or traders are divided into three sects. The names can be mentioned as Kashigotra, Bhuiphuta and the Lhasagotra or Tsongs. Each Kirati sect has a dialect of its own. Some of the tribes of the Kiratis are animists attributing the soul to non-living things like mountains, whereas the others are either Hindus or Buddhists. The deities of the Limbu community are Shri Janga, Tagyera Ningwa Poma and Yuma Shamma. Similarly the Rais also have many subsects. The other important communities of the Nepalis are the Pradhan Newars, Bahuns or Sharmas, Chettris and the service class such as the miners or Mangars, blacksmiths or Kamis, tailors or Damais and cobblers or Karkis.

The language spoken by Nepalis is understood all over by the state. This language is similar to Hindi and uses the Devanagri script. The great Hindu epic Ramayana has been translated to Nepali by a Nepali poet named Bhanu Bhakta who lived in the last century. The birthday of Bhanu Bhakta holds a special significance for the Nepalis specially to those belonging to the intellectual class. During this day special functions, debates and essay competitions are held in memory of the great poet and writer.

Bhutias

The Bhutias are evenly distributed throughout the state of Sikkim. In Northern Sikkim, where they are the major inhabitants, known as the Lachenpas and Lachungpas. The Lachenpas and the Lachungpas who mainly inhabit the areas around Lachen and Lachung respectively have their own traditional legal system known as Zamsa to settle disputes. Zamsa means public meeting place and the village headman, who is also known as the Pipon metes out justice and is chosen once in a year by the villagers voting by the show of hands. The Pipon takes all decisions regarding the village life like when the crops should be harvested. The Bhutia aristocrats are known as the Kazis. The language spoken by the Bhutias is Sikkimese and as a matter of fact this is a dialect of Tibetan language. The script is the same. Bhutias constitute about ten per cent of the total population of Sikkim. Bhutia villages are large as those compared to those of Lepchas.

Demographics

Sikkim demographics implies the population of the state which is 406,457. The demographics of Sikkim is an account of the total number of people residing in Sikkim.

Sikkim is among the least populated states of the Indian Union. The demographics in Sikkim boasts of having about 214,723 males and about 188,889 females. The density of population in Sikkim is about 76 persons per square kilometre. Moreover, statistics prove that the urban population in Sikkim is about 11 per cent of the total population in Sikkim.

In Sikkim, demographics is mostly composed of the people from different races and ethnic groups. Among the important ethnic groups of Sikkim that deserve a special mention in the demographics of Sikkim are:

- Chettris,
- Limbu,
- Rai,
- Gurang,
- Tamangs,
- Thakurs,
- Lepchas,
- Nepali,
- Bhutias, etc.

These ethnic groups of Sikkim have a distinct culture and socio-economic pattern; in fact, it is the socio-economic background that largely determines the plight of these ethnic groups in Sikkim.

It is interesting to note that the demographics at Sikkim owes largely to the Indo-Aryan, Tibeto-Burmese and Tibeto-Mongoloid races. Moreover, people belonging to Hinduism and Buddhism are predominant in Sikkim. We also come across a small Christian population within Sikkim: these Christians are mostly Lepchas who have converted into Christianity during the British period in India.

Religion

Buddhism is the predominant religion in Sikkim. Among the other religions of Sikkim are Hinduism, Christianity, Sikhism and Islam.

Talking about the religion of Sikkim, it can be said that in Sikkim, religion seems to lie at the root of all sociocultural activities. Every aspect of the society in Sikkim has a strong bearing upon religion.

Moreover, Buddhism is the most predominant religion at Sikkim. The Bhutia and the Tibetans at Sikkim generally follow the Buddhist cult. The Sikkimese follow the Tibetan Buddhism, which is divided into Red and Yellow Sects. The Red Sect Buddhism in Sikkim includes the Nyingma, Sakya and Kargya lineages; whereas the Yellow Sect in Sikkim implies Gelugpa lineage. These sects comprise an integral part of religion in Sikkim and are marked by different religious practices and the rituals performed by them.

Hinduism is another predominating religion at Sikkim. In Sikkim, we find the Nepali Hindu cult, which calls for a lot of festivities and rituals. The Nepali Hinduism is an orthodox cult of Hinduism. As a result, the society in Sikkim shows a strong Hindu flavour: the predominance of caste system is one of the chief attributes of Hinduism.

Beside Buddhism and Hinduism, we also come across a number of other religions in Sikkim. Among the other religion in Sikkim are:

- Islam,
- Sikhism, and
- Christianity.

All the religion clubbed together constitute the society of Sikkim.

The enigmatic land of Sikkim is home to numerous equally mysterious tribes that have transformed the state into a heavenly delectable locale. These tribes have also evolved an unique language of Sikkim which is spoken by most of the people residing in this state. Amongst all the languages in Sikkim, the most revered and propitious lingo is Nepalese. It is absolutely needless to mention that the dialect of Nepalese have been formulated by the illustrious Nepalese residing in the thumb-shaped state of Sikkim. There is, however, a reason behind this dominance of Nepalese language of Sikkim over other languages. It is due to the fact that the Nepalese people are way too advanced and sophisticated as compared to that of the other tribes that still believe in age-old traditions like educating their young ones in monasteries and following religious cults.

The other languages includes touches of English and Hindi as there are plenty of Marwaris and Bengalis who are quite proficient in these lingoes. These two languages are regarded as the most aristocratic dialects in the state after Nepalese. Amongst the other recurrently spoken languages across Sikkim are Bhutia, Lepcha, Sherpa, Tamang, Rai, Gurung, Groma, Yakha and many more.

One similitude that lies in all these languages within Sikkim is the fact that they are all spoken by the tribes. As the tribes comprise of a major portion of the population of Sikkim, these languages at Sikkim are quite frequently heard.

Other languages include Majhwar, Nepal Bhasa, Thulung, Tibetan and many more.

Economic Aspects

This is a chart of trend of gross state domestic product of Sikkim at market prices estimated by the *Ministry of Statistics and Programme Implementation* with figures in millions of Indian Rupees.

Year	Gross State Domestic Product
1980	520
1985	1,220
1990	2,340
1995	5,200
2000	9,710
2003	23,786

Sikkim's gross state domestic product for 2004 is estimated at $478 million in current prices. Sikkim's economy is largely agrarian. The British introduced terraced farming of rice, in addition to crops such as maize, millet, wheat, barley, oranges, tea and cardamom. Sikkim has the highest production and largest cultivated area of cardamom in India. Because of the hilly terrain, and lack of reliable transportation infrastructure, there are no large-scale industries. Breweries, distilleries, tanning and watchmaking are the main industries. These are located in the southern reaches of the state, primarily in the towns of Melli and Jorethang. The state has a high growth rate of 8.3 per cent, which is the second highest in the country after Delhi.

In recent years, the Government of Sikkim has extensively promoted tourism. As a result, the state revenue has increased 14 times since the mid-1990s. A fledgling industry the state has recently invested in is gambling, including online gambling. A casino was opened in March 2009, the Casino Sikkim, and seven further casino licences are being considered by the State Government. The Playwin lottery has been a commercial success and operates all over the country. In October 2009 the Government of Sikkim announced plans to offer three online sports betting licences. Among the minerals mined in Sikkim are copper, dolomite, talc, graphite, quartzite, coal, zinc and lead.

The opening of the Nathula Pass on July 6, 2006 connecting Lhasa, Tibet to India is expected to give a boost to the local economy, though the financial benefits will be slow to arrive. The pass, closed since the 1962 Sino-Indian War, was an offshoot of the ancient Silk Road, which was essential to the wool, fur and spice trade.

Economic Plans

During the economic plans special efforts were made to develop agriculture on scientific lines. With the initiation of economic plans an agriculture department was established to look after the progress and development of this vital organ of the economy. Improved varieties of seeds and fertilizers were distributed in all parts of the country and trained personnel were posted at various places to assist the cultivator in day-to-day matters relating to increased agricultural production. Pesticides were also distributed in areas where crops suffered from insects and pests.

Many personnel from Sikkim were trained in different agricultural research institutes of India. During the second plan a 200 acres (about 80 hectares) seed multiplication farm for paddy, maize and vegetables was developed at Gyalshing. Another 150 acres (about 60 hectares) potato seed farm was set up at Ribdi in western Sikkim. Farmer orientation schemes were accelerated in the third plan. To save the valuable crops of paddy, maize, cardamom and oranges from insects and pests an extensive Plant Protection Scheme was successfully introduced.

The Government of Sikkim passed two acts, one preventing landowners from terminating the cultivating rights of the tillers and receiving more than half of farm produce as share or rent and the other restraining the land lords from selling or other wise interfering with land. This gives the tiller of the land a real sense of security against the menace of the feudal land lords. The Sikkim Government has initiated a plan of land survey and have also succeeded in procuring SFDA (Small Farmers Development Authority) project for the entire state.

Industry

The growth of industries is a recent phenomenon in Sikkim. The situation where there was no industry is now changing and giving place to a number of industrial units. They produce such items as fruit jams and juices, biscuits, other bakery products, beer, matches, washing soap, plastics, electric cables, barbed wires, watches, leather goods and industrial jewels. The tax free status of the state in term of income tax and other inducements offered by Sikkim have become good attractions for entrepreneurs from within the state and other parts of the country to set up industrial units. Hundreds of licenses have been issued to the small scale units on a permanent or temporary basis. Tiny cottage units have been received incentives and other benefits from the department of industries.

Trade

The main exports from Sikkim are cardamom, oranges, tea, potatoes, apples, liquors, wines, handicrafts, canned fruit and timber. The trade in the past has mainly been with Tibet through the passes of Nathu La and Jelep La. When Chinese invaded these parts and sealed the borders the pattern of trade has turned to India.

Sikkim imports many consumer goods and manufactured goods from other parts of India. Food grains, Beverages, cloth, cosmetics, electrical equipment, engineering goods, synthetic goods, chemical fertilizers, insecticides, pesticides, medicines and drugs, surgical equipments, sanitary goods, hardware, paints,Varnishes, machine tools, etc. are the important articles imported by Sikkim.

Agriculture

Sikkim is a land of villages. Agriculture is the main occupation of the people. Agriculture has an history of its own in Sikkim. By and large, Sikkim's wealth is derived from agriculture and forests. The original inhabitants were not agriculturists. They led a very primitive life. Gathering of wild roots, fruits, hunting and fishing were their means of livelihood. When Bhutia people migrated to Sikkim they started a semi pastoral economy and sedentary farming. They ploughed only the flat pieces of land available here and there. Settled agriculture stepped into Sikkim only with the arrival of Nepali immigrants. These sturdy, hardy, energetic and innovative people cleared large tracts of woodlands and made the land fit for cultivation.

The nature of the terrain and varied micro climatic conditions influence agriculture in Sikkim. Maize, paddy, wheat, barley and buck wheat are the main cereals grown in

Sikkim. Sikkim has the largest area and the highest production of large cardamom in India. Cardamom and potatoes are two important cash crops. A special kind of tea much valued by the connoisseur for its taste and quality is also produced in the state. A government Tea Estate is being developed in Kewzing in the western part of Sikkim. There is one more tea estate at Temi. Both these estates extends over an area of 400 acres. Under horticulture, large quantities of oranges and apple are raised. Vegetables, pineapple and banana are other cash crops of Sikkim.

The humid tropical zone foothills of Southern Sikkim constitute the maize cultivation belt. Needing high temperatures and good amount of rainfall, maize is sown in early summer and harvested in September-October. Maize is an exacting crop and required a good amount of human labour for thinning and weeding process. To save the land from soil erosion longitudinal ditches have to be prepared in Maize fields. Maize is a staple food of this belt. Maize is also used for preparation of poultry feed and beer.

Paddy is another important crop of Sikkim. Paddy is a crop mainly of river valleys. Along river beds the crop is raised with the help of irrigation. Small channels taken out of the rivers irrigate the surrounding land. On higher areas where temperature and rainfall conditions permit the cultivation of paddy, the crop is grown on terraced fields. In the river bottoms transplantation method has been employed but on the higher terraced fields broadcasting method is employed. Now with the assistance of Agriculture Department new high yielding varieties of paddy are grown on the terraced farms with Japanese method. Paddy is a summer crop and it is grown every where in the state except very higher areas and most of the paddy is raised on unirrigated fields. Because of copious rainfall during its growth period it is possible to raise paddy on unirrigated fields.

Wheat and barley are winter crops. Wheat is raised in Southern and Central Sikkim where temperature and growing period during winter permit the cultivation of this crop. In areas with short growing period and insufficient moisture during winter barley and buck wheat are raised. On the soils which are not fit for paddy or wheat cultivation or where short growing period does not permit the cultivation of superior cereals, millets are raised. Cardamom, oranges and apples constitute an important part of Sikkim's trade with other parts of the country. Luscious oranges are grown in the southern warmer area of the state whereas apple are grown in elevated areas of Central and Northern Sikkim. Cardamom is a foreign exchange earner crop also. Therefore special steps are being taken to augment the production of cardamom.

Agriculture, horticulture and animal husbandry constitute a mainstay of the largest segment of Sikkim's population.

Animal Husbandry

Cattle, buffaloes, yak, sheep, goats, pigs, mules and ponies are the important domestic animals of Sikkim. Poultry birds are also domesticated in different parts of the state.

Buffaloes and cattle are mainly limited to the tropical humid belt and temperate zone. In the higher cold areas, Yak is the important animal. Government of Sikkim has established a separate department of animal husbandry. During the first three plans the animal husbandry department formulated a scheme to meet the increasing demand for meat and dairy products, poultry birds and eggs. Veterinary health services were made available in villages and like farmers, those interested in animal breeding and poultry farming were trained at different stations in India. Exotic breeds of sheep that thrive well under the vagaries of climatic conditions prevailing in Sikkim were introduced in the state.

Capital of the State: Gangtok

Gangtok is the capital and largest town of the Indian state of Sikkim. Gangtok is located in the Shivalik Hills of the eastern Himalayan range, at an altitude of 1,437 metres (4,715 ft). The town, with a population of thirty thousand belonging to different ethnicities such as Nepalis, Lepchas and Bhutia, is administered by various departments of the Government of Sikkim. Nestled within higher peaks of the Himalaya and enjoying a year-round mild temperate climate, Gangtok is at the centre of Sikkim's tourism industry.

Gangtok rose to prominence as a popular Buddhist pilgrimage site after the construction of the Enchey Monastery in 1840. In 1894, the ruling Sikkimese Chogyal, Thutob Namgyal, transferred the capital to Gangtok. In the early 20th century, Gangtok became a major stopover on the trade route between Lhasa in Tibet and cities such as Kolkata (then Calcutta) in British India. After India won its independence from Britain in 1947, Sikkim chose to remain an independent monarchy, with Gangtok as its capital. In 1975, after the integration with the union of India, Gangtok was made India's state capital.

The precise meaning of the name *Gangtok* is unclear, though the most popular meaning is "hill top". Today, Gangtok is a centre of Tibetan Buddhist culture and learning, with the presence of several monasteries, religious educational institutions, and centres for Tibetology.

History

Like the rest of Sikkim, not much is known about the early history of Gangtok. The earliest records date from the construction of the hermetic Gangtok monastery in 1716. Gangtok remained a small hamlet until the construction of the Enchey Monastery in 1840 made it a pilgrimage centre. After the defeat of the Tibetans by the British, Gangtok became a major stopover in the trade between Tibet and British India at the end of the 19th century. Most of the roads and the telegraph in the area were built during this time.

In 1894, Thutob Namgyal, the Sikkimese monarch under British rule, shifted the capital from Tumlong to Gangtok, increasing the city's importance. A new grand palace along with other state buildings was built in the new capital. Following India's independence in 1947, Sikkim became a nation-state with Gangtok as its capital. Sikkim became a suzerain of India, with the condition that it would retain its independence, by the treaty signed between the Chogyal and the then Indian Prime Minister Jawaharlal Nehru. Trade between India and Tibet continued to flourish through the Nathula and Jelepla passes, offshoots of the ancient Silk Road near Gangtok. These border passes were sealed after the Sino-Indian War in 1962, which deprived Gangtok of its trading business. The Nathula pass was finally opened for limited trade in 2006.

In 1975, the monarchy was abrogated and Sikkim became India's twenty-second state, with Gangtok as its capital. Gangtok has witnessed annual landslides, resulting in loss of life and damage to property. The largest disaster occurred in June 1997, when 38 were killed and hundreds of buildings were destroyed.

Geography

Gangtok is situated in the lower Himalayas at an altitude of 5,500 ft (1,676 m). In addition to being the state capital, it is the headquarters of the East Sikkim district. The town lies on one side of a hill, with "The Ridge", a promenade housing the governor's residence, at one end and the palace, situated at an altitude of about 6,000 ft (1,829 m), at the other. The city is flanked on east and west by two streams, namely Roro Chu and Ranikhola, respectively. These two rivers divide the natural drainage into two parts, the eastern and western parts. Both the streams meet the Ranipul and flow south as the main Ranikhola before it joins the Teesta at Singtam. Most of the roads are steep, with the buildings built on compacted ground alongside them.

Most of Sikkim, including Gangtok, is underlain by Precambrian rock which contains foliated phyllites and schists; slopes are therefore prone to frequent landslides. Surface run-off of water by natural streams (*jhora*) and man-made drains has contributed to the risk of landslides. According to the Bureau of Indian Standards, the town falls under seismic zone-IV (on a scale of I to V, in order of increasing seismic activity), near the convergent boundary of the Indian and the Eurasian tectonic plates and is subject to frequent earthquakes. The hills are nestled within higher peaks and the snow-clad Himalayan ranges tower over the town from the distance. Mount Kanchenjunga (8,598 m or 28,208 ft)—the world's third-highest peak — is visible to the east of the city. The existence of steep slopes, vulnerability to landslides, large forest cover and inadequate access to most areas has been a major impediment to the natural and balanced growth of the city.

There are densely forested regions around Gangtok, consisting of temperate, deciduous forests of poplar, birch, oak, and elm, as well as evergreen, coniferous trees of the wet alpine zone. Orchids are common, and rare varieties of orchids are featured in flower shows in the city. Bamboos are also abundant. In the lower reaches of the town, the vegetation gradually changes from alpine to temperate deciduous and subtropical. Flowers such as sunflower, marigold, poinsettia, and others bloom, especially in November and December.

Area, Population and Headquarters of Districts

S .No.	District	Area (sq km)	Population	Headquarters
			(1991 Census)	
1.	East Sikkim	954	1,78,452	Gangtok
2.	North Sikkim	4,226	31,240	Mangan
3.	South Sikkim	750	98,604	Namchi
4.	West Sikkim	1,166	98,161	Gyalshing

Climate

Gangtok features a monsoon-influenced subtropical highland climate. Because of its elevation and sheltered environment, Gangtok enjoys a mild, temperate climate all year round. Like most Himalayan towns, Gangtok has five seasons: summer, monsoons, autumn, winter and spring. Temperatures range from an average maximum of 22°C (72°F) in summer to an average minimum of 4°C (39°F) in winter. Summers (lasting from late April to June) are mild, with maximum temperatures rarely crossing 25°C (77°F).

The monsoon season from June to September is characterised by intense torrential rains often causing landslides that block Gangtok's land access to the rest of the country. Rainfall starts to rise from pre-monsoon in May, and peaks during the monsoon, with July recording the highest monthly average of 649.6 mm (25.6 in). In winter temperature averages between 4°C (39°F) and 7°C (45°F). Snowfall is rare, and in recent times Gangtok has received snow only in 1990, 2004 and 2005. Temperatures below freezing are also rare. During this season the weather can be sporadic, and change abruptly from bright sunshine and clear skies to heavy rain within a couple of hours. During spring and autumn the weather is generally sunny and mild. Owing to its elevation, Gangtok is often enveloped in fog during the monsoon and winter months.

Economy

The hospitality industry is the largest industry in Gangtok as the city is the main base for Sikkim tourism. Summer and spring seasons are the most popular tourist seasons. Many of Gangtok's residents are employed directly and indirectly in the tourism industry, with many residents owning and working in hotels and restaurants. Ecotourism has emerged as an important economic activity in the region which includes trekking, mountaineering, river rafting and other nature oriented activities. An estimated 351,000 tourists visited Sikkim in 2007, generating revenue of about Rs. 50 crores (Rs. 500 millions).

The Nathula Pass, located about 50 km (31 mi) from Gangtok, used to be the primary route of the wool, fur and spice trade with Tibet and spurred economic growth for Gangtok till the mid-20th century. In 1962, after the border was closed during the Sino-Indian War, Gangtok fell into recession. The pass was reopened in 2006 and trade through the pass is expected to boost the economy of Gangtok. The Sikkim government is keen to open a Lhasa-Gangtok bus service via Nathula pass. Sikkim's mountainous terrain results in the lack of train or air links, limiting the area's potential for rapid industrial development. The government is the largest employer in the city, both directly and as contractors.

Gangtok's economy does not have a large manufacturing base, but has a thriving Cottage industry in watch-making, country-made alcohol and handicrafts. Among the handicrafts are the handmade paper industry made from various vegetable fibres or cotton rags. The main market in Gangtok provides many of the state's rural residents a place to offer their produce during the harvest seasons.

The majority of the private business community is made up of Marwaris and Biharis. As part of Sikkim, Gangtok enjoys the status of being an income-tax free region as per the state's 1948 Income tax law. As Sikkim is a frontier state, the Indian army maintains a large presence in the vicinity of Gangtok. This leads to a population of semi-permanent residents who bring money into the local economy. The Sikkim government started India's first online lottery *Playwin* to boost government income, but this was later closed by a ruling from the Sikkim High Court.

2

Salient Features

- -

Sikkim state is situated between 27° 04' to 28° 07' North latitudes and 88° 01' to 88° 55' East longitudes. The state is almost rectangular in shape and covers an area of 7,096 sq km Nepal bound the state in the west by the vast stretches of the Tibetan plateau, in the north, in the east by Bhutan and Chumbi valley of Tibet and Darjeeling district of West Bengal stretches along its southern boundary.

The mountainous terrain of Sikkim consists of a tangled series of interlacing ridges, rising one above the other, from south to the foot of the high peaks that mark the abode of snow in the north. The entire state is covered with steep hills and deep valleys. The trend of the mountain system viewed as a whole is in a general east west direction.

The general run of the main ridges is north-south with subsidiary interlacing spurs from each ridge in a roughly east-west direction. Main ridges in Sikkim run in more or less north-south direction. Sikkim is primarily the catchment of Teesta drainage system. Teesta River while flowing north to south divides the state into two parts.

The river rises from north district fed by snows from Kanchenjunga: its other tributaries join it from Lhonak, Zemu, Talung glacier of Kanchenjunga group in the west. The chief tributaries of Teesta — the Great Rangit fed from the snow of Narsing and Kabru peaks, south of Kanchenjunga. There are two predominant zones, viz. Gnessic and Daling group and also with some intermediaries.

Daling group consists of predominantly phyllites. At the boundary between this and gneissic rocks they pass into silvery mica schist. Dark clay slates with thick quartzite bands prevail in certain areas: silt stones and siliceous limestone is also found in certain areas.

The climate of the state varies generally from sub-tropical to alpine depending upon the elevation of the place. Within the same catchment watershed of a stream, sub-tropical or even tropical climate is often observed at the lower end of the watershed in the valley, while temperate climate prevails at the upper reaches of the stream. Sikkim is richly endowed with natural flora and fauna. The natural vegetation consisting of evergreen trees, grasses and bushes extends up to 5,000 m MSL only. At elevation above 5,000 m MSL, hardly any vegetation is found. Distribution pattern of natural vegetation in the state may be divided into 5 mixed forest zones — Lower Hill Forest (<900 m), Middle Hill Forest (900-1,800 m), Upper Hill Forest (1,800-2,450 m), Rhododendron and Oak Forest (2,450-3,350 m) and Conifer and Alpine pastures (>3,350 m).

Administratively Sikkim has been divided in four districts namely North District, South District, East District and West District. Each District has further been divided into two subdivisions. Gangtok, Pakyong and Rongli in East district, Namchi and Ravangla in South, Magan and Chungthang in North and Gyalshing and Soreng in West. There are 12 major towns namely Gangtok, Namchi, Jorethang Soreng, Ravangla, Singtam, Pakyong, Mangan and Chungthang. There are 447 villages out which 440 are inhabited. A total of 4,05,505 population was recorded in 1991 with an average density of 57 persons per square kilometres. Lepcha, Bhutias and Nepalis are three major ethnic communities here. Lepcha and Bhutias are Buddhists while majority of Nepalis are Hindus. Major population resided in East district followed by South district. Sex ratio in the state is 875 females per 1,000 males. Amongst districts the highest sex ratio rate had been seen in West District with 919 females per 1,000 males followed by South, East, North. STs are the major population spread in almost 98 per cent of the revenue blocks.

State literacy percentage is 54.39 per cent. Male literacy is 63.44 per cent and female literacy is 44.06 per cent. East district occupies first rank in literacy. It also boasts on two-degree college, one in Gangtok and another in Namchi. In the urban areas, Jorethang has highest literacy rate of 83.50 per cent followed by Gangtok (80.18%). Industrially, Sikkim is a backward state. However, the government has adopted the philosophy of industrial development and as a result some cheese plant, dairy farms, bottling plants have come to existence. Besides this, tourism is the biggest industry.

Small but beautiful, Sikkim is situated in the Eastern Himalayas. Spread below the Mount Kanchenjunga, (8,603 m), the third highest Mountain in the world and revered by the Sikkimese as their protective Deity. Sikkim shares her borders with Tibet in the North, Bhutan in the East, Nepal in the West and State of West Bengal in the South.

With an area of 7,096 sq km and measuring approximately 100 km from North to South and 60 km from East to West, the elevation ranges from 244 m to over 8,540 m above sea-level. Amidst the grandeur of the mountain peaks, lush valleys, fast flowing rivers, terraced hills, Sikkim offers her visitors a rare and singular experience. Within a matter of hours one can move from the sub-tropical heat of the lower valleys to the cold of the rugged mountain slopes that reach up to the areas of perpetual snow.

Nature has been generous. Sikkim is noted for her floral wealth and an estimated 4,000 varieties of flowering plants and shrubs are found. There are over 600 varieties of orchids. From an altitude of 2,400 m Rhododendrons can be found. The gentle slopes of the high altitudes are covered by a variety of beautiful flowers like the primula, meconopsis, gentians, etc.

The rivers have trout, salmon and carp. Naturalists have catalogued over 550 species and sub-species of birds, among them many flamboyant pheasants and over 600 species of butterflies. Animals abound in the dense forest of Sikkim: The dreaded Himalayan bear, musk and barking deer, marbled cats, red panda, the blue sheep, etc.

Three main groups of people make up the population of Sikkim — The Lepchas, Bhutias and the Nepalese. Sikkimese by nature are simple, polite and non-aggressive a people with a nature.

Sikkim's West District is probably the most enchanting, certainly the most sacred place in the Eastern Himalayas. It was here that in 1641 AD the first Chogyal (King) of Sikkim was consecrated by the three great Lamas at Yoksum. The oldest monastery of Sikkim is also in this District.

Besides heritage sites and monasteries, west Sikkim is extremely rich in biodiversity. It has a mind-boggling array of flora ad fauna. The hills and valleys abound with numerous orchid, primula, rhododendrons, marigolds, magnolia and cherry, to name a few. The exotic aroma of the large cardamom waft along mist-laden hillsides, home of the musk deer and the red panda. Innumerable butterflies flit among the verdant woods lending colour to the rich green hue. Sikkim has more that 500 species of butterflies. Perhaps the pride of the flora of West Sikkim are its dense rhododendron forests varying from the towering giants of the lower regions to the dwarf varieties found above the snow-line. The delicate flowers too are as variegated, from the blood-red thomsonii to pale lilac to brilliant white.

West Sikkim is indeed a favourite of the Gods, blessed with the rich and natural heritage of Sikkim, truly a jewel of the Gods.

The laid back, scenic, but rapidly swelling hamlet of Pelling, situated 2,085 m above sea level only 2 km beyond Pemayangtse, looks north towards the glaciers and peaks of Kanchenjunga. High above the forest-covered hills, in an amphitheatre of cloud, snow and rock, the entire route from Yoksum over Dzongri La to the Rathong Glacier can be seen. Sikkim is the 22nd state of India came into existence with effect from 26th April, 1975. Sikkim has been divided into four districts and each district has further been bifurcated into two subdivisions for administrative purpose. Sikkim state, being a part of inner mountain ranges of Himalayas, is hilly having varied elevation ranging from 300 to 8,540 m But the habitable areas are only up to the altitude of 2,100 m, constituting only 20 per cent of the total area of the state.

The highest portion of sikkim lies in its northwest direction. A large number of mountains having altitudes of about seven thousand metres stands here with Kanchenjunga (8,598 m), the third highest peak in the world. The high serrated, snow capped spurs and peaks of Kanchenjunga look attractive consisting of Kumbha Karna (7,711 m), Pendem (6,706 m), Narsingh (5,825 m), Kabru Dome (6,545 m), etc. A number of glaciers descends from eastern slopes of Kanchenjunga into Sikkim where snow clad line is found above 5,300 m. The biggest of them is Zemu, from whose snout above Lachen monastery rises the river Teesta. Teesta is the main river and its main tributaries are Zemu, Lachung, Rangyong, Dikchu, Rongli, Rangpo and Rangit which form the main channel of drainage from the north to the south.

It boasts of the great mount Kanchenjunga as its crown. Ethically Sikkim has mainly three groups of people, viz. *Nepalis, Bhutias, Lepchas*. The local language is Nepali. English is the official language. This jewel-like mountain state of ethereal beauty with an area of 7,096 sq km, nestles in the heart of Himalayas. Cradled in the manifold splendours of nature, deep within the snow clad Himalayas, is Sikkim's capital *Gangtok*. Wrapped in mists and clouds, a garden state with an incredible variety of rhododendrons and a host of other flowers.

The Northeastern Indian Himalayan enclave of the state of Sikkim and the district of Darjeeling lies tucked between eastern Nepal and western Bhutan.

Sikkim is unique as being a rare stronghold of the Nyingmapa sect of Tibetan Buddhism for this is where they took shelter and propagated their faith, following persecution in Tibet hundreds of years before. Until its official merger with India in 1975, Sikkim was a Buddhist Kingdom under a Nyingmapa ruler for over three hundred years. In witness to the fact, more than two hundred monasteries can be found around this tiny Himalayan state. Darjeeling and its district, the Autonomous Darjeeling Gorkha Hill Council of West Bengal, India, has seen its historical development in another unique fashion. Vied by the British conquistadors in the early nineteenth century, it was snatched away from Sikkim and developed as a summer resort for the British rulers of East India. Here one will find relics of the British Raj in quaint English country cottages and bungalows, steepled churches and buildings amidst wafts of cool mountain breeze.

Adding to the grandeur of this region is the mighty Kanchenjunga range. Standing aloft on the northwestern horizon one is able to gaze into probably the most alluring set of mountains in all of the Himalayas; as viewed from the hilltops of Darjeeling district and Sikkim.

Sikkim is picturesque and verdant with clean crisp air, deep blue mountain lakes, gorgeous Buddhist monasteries and hillsides ablaze with rhododendrons against a backdrop of snow-clad mountains. If you are looking for exciting trekking routes in unspoilt terrain, or a quiet communion with the mountains, there are few places in India that would match the Himalayan state of Sikkim. This tiny state, bigger only than Goa and Delhi and India's least populated, lies tucked in between Nepal and Bhutan in India's eastern region.

Just 110 km from north to south and 60 km across, Sikkim is entirely mountainous with altitudes varying from 800 ft. in the south to the 28,199 ft. Mt. Kanchenjunga, in the northwest (India's highest peak, and the third highest in the world). The awesome mountain is revered by the Sikkimese as their protecting deity. The capital of the state, Gangtok is an attractive and interesting town in eastern Sikkim, well developed and with absolutely amazing views of the snow-clad Himalayan peaks including the Kanchenjunga.

Sikkim, a mountainous region in the eastern Himalayas, has 600 species of birds, or about half of the over 1,200 species to be found in India.

Perched between Nepal in the west, Bhutan in the east, and Tibet(China) in the north, Sikkim is 7,300 square miles in area and contains Mount Kanchenjunga, the third-highest peak in the world. Formerly a kingdom, since 1975 it has been a tiny land-locked province to India.

Sikkim, with its rich biodiversity, has 150 lakes ranging in altitude from 200 metres to almost 8,000 metres. Besides birds, Sikkim has 4,000 species of flowering plants, making it a botanist's paradise. It has 600 species of orchids and 40 species of rhododendrons.

With the introduction of eco-tourism, including serious birding, Sikkim has begun to focus on enterprise-based conservation.

Sikkim offers the magical feel of a Himalayan fairy-tale land. It is an amazing place of hidden valleys, mystical monasteries, snow-fed lakes and a mountain setting covered with flowers and forests. This former kingdom is home to three major population groups — the Lepchas, Bhutias and Nepalese — providing a colourful composite of cultures. Mt. Kanchenjunga, the third highest peak in the world at 8,586 m, dominates the landscape and is revered as Sikkim's guardian deity. Sikkim is a state of India, tucked in the Himalaya across Nepal's eastern frontier. It is crammed in between Tibet (China) to the north, Bhutan to the east and Darjeeling to the south.

Small but beautiful is Sikkim, the pearl of the eastern Himalayas, with its majestical 8,534 m high Kanchenjunga in the West, the Tibetan high plateau in the North and the Kingdom of Bhutan in the East. Kanchenjunga is not only a mountain but also protector deity of Sikkim.

Surrounded by snow-covered mountain peaks, fertile valleys, wild mountain streams and paddy rice fields live a variety of people: The Lepchas and Bhutias, originally from Mongolia and Tibet, live together in harmony with people belonging to different tribes of Nepal. Rice, corn, potato and millet is grown in the paddy fields. Mandarins, apples, papaya and even bananas are amongst Sikkims wealth in fruits. Cardamom and ginger are grown commercially and make up Sikkims main export goods.

Within few hours one can move from the subtropical heat of the lower valleys all the way to the alpine zones of the mighty mountain world. This variety of climates on a small area of land is responsible for Sikkims unbelievable variety in plants and animals. Over 600 different types of Orchids grow in the forests of Sikkim and the beauty of the colourfully blooming rhododendron forests in spring is breathtaking and unforgettable. For bird and butterfly lovers Sikkim is the place to be. In no other place of the world of comparative size, (more types of birds call it their home) than in Sikkim where between 500 and 600 species are living.

For a long time Sikkim was known, as one of the worlds most remote and secret places. Even today Sikkim is connected with the mainland of India with only one road. Up until 1975 Sikkim was an independent Buddhist Kingdom. India annexed Sikkim however and made it its 22nd state. It was only in 1990 when one of the most beautiful trekking area was opened up for foreigners. Even today one requires a special permit in order to be able and visit this fascinating and secluded mountain land.

The Lepchas are Sikkims original inhabitants. They are said to have moved into Sikkim from Mongolia. The Lepchas call their land Nye-Mal-Ale which simply means heaven. In Lepcha language they call themselves Mutanchi, the dearest human beings on mother earth. Literature describes them as kindhearted and shy people. With the arrival of the Tibetan immigrants the Lepchas began to give up their animistic religion in favour of Buddhism. Today most Lepchas are farmers and herdsmen and they live mostly in the North and West as well as in Darjeeling and Kalimpong. Hunting and gathering as well as fishing still play an important role in the live of the Lepchas.

The Bhutias are the second oldest people of Sikkim. From the 9th century onwards they began migrating into Sikkim from Tibet. The fraternisation of the Lepchas and the Bhutias was sealed by a contract and in 1642 the first King of Sikkim was coronated in Yoksum, West-Sikkim. The boundary of Sikkim extended at that time up to the Tibetan Chumbi valley and including Darjeeling to the south. The holy teacher and monk Padmasambhava, also called Guru Rinpoche who brought Buddhism to Tibet and Sikkim whom he called Bay-Yol-Dre-Ma-Jong, the hidden land of treasures, fruits and flowers. Padmasambava prophesied that Buddhism would once again flourish in this country after it will be destroyed through dark forces in Tibet.

Today, Mahayana Buddhism is the state religion. Gompas (monasteries) and Lamas (monks) play an important role in the daily live of the Bhutias. Most monasteries exist through donations of the indigenous population. Even today it is a custom amongst traditional Bhutia families to send the second oldest son to a monastery.

From the 19th century onwards, encouraged by the British, the immigration of people from Nepal began. The Nepalese brought paddy-rice-cultivation to Sikkim and also the commercial cultivation of cardamom. Though this improved Sikkims agriculture enormously, its side effects were erosion and the destruction of forests. Today, name for Sikkim originates from the Nepalese word Sukhim which means new homeland. Amongst the Nepalese people, the Limbus are considered the third-oldest ethical groups of people in Sikkim.

They have their own language and writing and their religion is a mixture between Buddhism and Shaivism. The rest of the Nepalese, with the exception of the Sherpas, Tamang and Gurung, are Hindus. Today three thirds of Sikkims population consist of Nepalese. The Lepchas and Bhutias have become a minority in their own homeland. Besides the mentioned people, Tibetan refugees as well as Indians mostly traders in the cities, live in Sikkim.

Under the Namgyal-Chogyal Dynasty from 1642 up until 1975 Sikkim was a Buddhist Kingdom. In 1835, the King of Sikkim was force to gift Darjeeling to the British. At the same time Sikkim was made Britains protectorate. In Darjeeling the British actively encouraged Nepalese immigration. They were used as workforce to plant the first tea garden and made Darjeeling a resort for the India-stationed British.

In 1918, Sikkim regained independence. However, the King lost his absolute power. When India became independent in 1947, it took over the protectorate. The foreign policy representation and the national defence of Sikkim were transferred to India. When the Constitution came into effect in 1955, the political influence of the Sikkimese King was reduced. In 1973, bureaucrats mostly belonging to the Nepalese settlers in Sikkim planned to overthrow the monarchy and bring it to an end. India increased its influence and in 1975 India annexed Sikkim as its 22nd state.

On April 8, 1975 Indian tanks and soldiers surrounded the palace and placed the King under Indian observance. In the process of this annexation one member of the Sikkim guard was shot dead. The next day the Chogyal wrote the following to Mrs. Indira Gandhi who had ordered the attack: I have no words when the Indian army was sent today in a surprise attack on Sikkim Guards who are less than 300, strong and were trained, equipped and officered by the Indian army who looked upon each other as comrades. This is a most treacherous and black day in the history of democratic India in solving the survival of our little country by use of arms.

The overthrown King spent the rest of his live under Indian surveillance. The Sikkimese national flag was banned and so were books containing documentation about the annexation. Lal Bahadur Basnet wrote in an article published in the Times of India on October 15, 1979, we have always said and still say that the manner of Sikkims merger with India was not legal and constitutional. The 12th Chogyal Palden Thodup Namgyal who became known due to his marriage to the American Hope Cooke, died in 1982 with a broken heart. His son Wangchuk Namgyal from first marriage, was coronated as Sikkims 13th King. His responsibility includes, however only religious matters.

Sikkim is a destination that inspires wealth of superlatives, landscape unsurpassed terrains of almost every elevation strata, mountains, fast flowing rivers that originate in the mountains, defining the states boundaries. Abundant in nature are animals like the Red Panda, snow leopard and Blue Sheep among others. Some 600 to 1,000 species of orchids and flowers add to this wonderful collection of natures bounty. Sikkim imbued with qualities of generous hospitality, smiling people of unforgettable friendliness. A unique blend of ethnic groups, culture, religion and customs presenting a kaleidoscopic picture.

Foreigners must obtain Inner Line Permit (ILP) to visit Sikkim. The permits can be obtained from all Indian missions/Embassies/Consulates, Tourism Office — New Delhi, Sikkim Tourism Office, Kolkata and Sikkim Tourism Office — Siliguri, Rangpo Tourist Lodge on the strength of an Indian visa. The 15 days duration permit is issued on the spot without any delay, provided photocopies of passport and visa details along with two passport photos of the applicants are made available then and there. The permissible duration of stay by foreign tourists would be 15 days initially with the State Government authorised to extend the same by a further period of 60 days of 15 days each.

The extension of permits can be obtained from FRO at Gangtok, Superintendent of Police of the North, West and South districts. For those interested in going for trekking in the interior regions of the state, the Department of Tourism issues protected area Permit (PAP) at Gangtok which is available for certain specified areas for groups consisting of two or more foreigners subject to the conditions that the trekking programme can be arranged through us.

Sikkim is a trekker's paradise. It has been blessed with an unspoiled nature, geographical conditions and variety of flora and fauna that offers a lot for lovers of adventure tourism, *i.e.* trekking, tours, mountaineering and mountain biking, etc.

Mt. Kanchenjunga, Guardian deity of Sikkim and the third highest mountain in the world revered and worshipped by the local people provides one of the most beautiful and spellbounding background. The mountains seem formidable and unapproachable at first. But as you approach nearer, it's welcoming and the beauty of them unfolds before you.

Dzongri in West Sikkim is a proper and well-beaten track. At Yuksam, the motorable road stops and the trek starts. The trek ranges from an altitude of 1,700 metres to 4,950 metres, the trek trails through forests of Rhododendrons, Magnolia, Silvers firs and Alpine vegetation, meandering rivers with views of Mt. Kanchenjunga and surrounding peaks like Mt. Pandim, Jupono, Frey peak, Kabru North/South, Kothang, Thinkchenkhang, Thalung and a lot more.

The Singilila trek route which has been recently opened lies on the ridge, defining the boundary between Sikkim and Nepal. One can see the different peaks of Mt. Kanchenjunga range, Chola Range and also villages of Nepal on the other side. On the trail there are lot of blue pristine lakes to be seen and sometimes it is also known as the lake trek.

North Sikkim is relatively less explored by trekkers and has its own adventure to offer. It is harder and the altitude goes up to 5,250 metres high. The scenic view is a lot similar to the Tibetan plateau with Mt. Kanchenjunga, Tent peak, Chorten Nyima Range and one of the world's most beautiful peaks Mt. Sinolchu, the vegetation here is mostly alpine.

The treks can range from 5 days to 30 days or more. There are also shorter treks and day hikes options like Tendong, Maenam, Varshey treks offering views of mountains and variety of flora and fauna.

Sikkim's original inhabitants are the Rongtub (literally "the dearest people of Mother Earth"), who named their home Ley Mayal Lyang, or "heaven." Crammed in between Tibet, Nepal, Bhutan, and West Bengal, this tiny, mountainous state is as pristine a pocket of India as you are likely to encounter, with some 4,000 varieties of wildflowers (including 600 varieties of orchids), snow-fed lakes, high-altitude mountain forests, and hidden Buddhist monasteries.

Some travellers come simply to enjoy the refreshing views and clean air, but most are here to tackle the fantastic treks through western Sikkim, exploring remote valleys and villages of yak-herding Tibetans. Ideally, you should spend a day or two in the state capital, Gangtok, to organise permits and transport/trekking arrangements, then head to Pelling before undertaking a demanding high-altitude trek for several days. Or you can skip Gangtok, either hiring a jeep that goes directly from Siliguri (near the railway station at New Jalpaiguri) to Pelling, or travel from Bagdogra, the nearest airport; both are about 6 hours away by road.

Sikkim is a small, extremely mountainous state in the Indian Himalayas with sharply defined and extremely steep watersheds. Although Sikkim is only about forty miles in width and seventy miles in length, its altitude escalates rapidly from about 2,500 feet above sea level in the South to about 27,000 feet along the Himalayan Kanchenjunga range. Most agriculture is concentrated in the lower mountain reaches, primarily in the East and South Districts. Nomadic high-altitude livestock herding (primarily goats, sheep and yaks) is found along the borders with Nepal and Bhutan, and in the North District approaching the Tibetan Plateau.

Sikkim has very diverse ecological conditions, from subtropical to alpine, and is endowed with great biological diversity of plants and animals. A wide range of crops are cultivated in a range of agro-ecological zones, including upland rice, vegetables, pulses, potato, and ginger. Its extreme topography and altitude mean that most agriculture is done on narrow-terraced benches on very steep slopes. The country is subject to torrential monsoonal rains, which contribute to rapid run-off on the slopes, resulting in landslides and flooding in river bottoms.

Most arable land has already been put under cultivation. Sikkim's growing rural population is slowly expanding upwards, bringing steeper forested slopes under cultivation. In addition, demand for cardamom, an export crop, has also contributed to conversion of forests to agriculture. Each village has different endowments of various types of lands, and very different patterns of access to public and common lands. Average holding size for poorer households is under three acres. Most agriculture is rainfed.

The most recent census data for Sikkim (1991) gives a population of 4,06,457 persons. Population has been expanding very rapidly, from 3 16,385 in 1981 and 2,09,843 in 1971. This represents an approximate doubling of the population in twenty years. Overall population density was 57 persons per square kilometre in 1991. According to the 1981 census, the literacy rates were 22.2 per cent for females and 43.95 per cent for males; by 1991 this number had risen significantly to 46.7 per cent for females and 65.7 per cent for males. In spite of GOS efforts, educational facilities, especially in rural areas, are still inadequate. The low level of female literacy also indicates the lack of motivation for social change and inadequate facilities for women to avail of education, in comparison to males.

The population is diverse in its ethnicity, religions, and languages. At least fifteen languages are spoken, but Nepali is spoken by the majority of the population. Nepalis now represent the majority population at 70 per cent of total, with Lepchas, Tibetans and Bhutias also comprising major ethno-linguistic groups. There are numerous other groups drawn primarily from minority or scheduled castes. The ownership of cultivable land, as well as cardamom production, was historically been under the control of Bhutia kazis (landlords and aristocrats), which continues to influence the distribution of land and natural resources even today. Nepali immigrants leased lands from the kazis, and gradually acquired land from the Bhutias and Lepchas. The result is a scarcity of arable land, with fragmentation of holdings and greatly expanded cultivation on very marginal steep slopes. The distribution of income, and patterns of poverty, are closely linked to land ownership, with Bhutia families tending to be better off than other groups.

Sikkim is one of the primeval lands unlike other Himalayan lands, and remains pristine and well-preserved. The land offers the magical feel of a Himalayan fairy-tale. Where one dreamy day blends into next. It is an amazing place of hidden valleys, mystical monasteries, snow-clad lakes and landscape covered with flowers and forests and snow-capped mountains. Kanchenjunga (8,586 m), the jewel in Sikkim's crown is the word's third highest Peak, which overlooks the state from the western side. This majestic five summited mountain forms the spectacular backdrop.

Sikkim was previously an independent kingdom, ruled by a dynasty, which descended from the Tibetan Royal family. Until the end of nineteenth century, when Sikkim came under the protection of Britain, very little was known about the country, which was completely closed to outsiders. India took over as the protector of the independent state of Sikkim in 1950 and in 1975 Sikkim became the 22nd state of India. Bordered by Tibet, Bhutan, Nepal and West Bengal, Sikkim's jagged and spectacular terrains has elevation variations ranging from 284 m to 8 540 m. A great variety of landscapes, ranging from intensively farmed lowland valleys in the south, to a higher alpine environment in the centre of the country and unto the Himalayan peaks on the northern and western margin. This mystic land casts an enthralling spell that captivates a visitor in utmost thrill.

Sikkim is one of the most enthralling regions in Himalayas. This hidden valley of rice or "Bayul Demojong" as called by the local people and is a tiny State of the Union territory of India. It is inhabited by Nepalese, Lepchas, Bhutias, Tibetans and surrounded by the Tibetan Plateau in the North, Nepal in the West, Bhutan in the East and West Bengal along its Southern border.

The awe-inspiring Kanchenjunga peaks guards its valley, turquoise lakes, steams and gorges. Its Capital is Gangtok with its mysterious mist, fluttering prayer flags, painted pagoda roofed houses, rich culture heritage and its friendly smiling people. Sikkim offers to her visitors a rare and singular experience of a lifetime.

Since the major portion of Sikkim has opened to both the domestic and foreign visitors in recent time, one can experience the most fascinating scenic beauty, breathtaking experience and chilling white river water for River Rafting bonanza.

Sikkim has population of about three lakhs, made up of Lepchas, Nepalese and Bhutias. The Lepchas are the oldest inhabitants of Sikkim. There is an old Lepcha legend that long ago, the laughter of the Lepchas wafted into the sky and it scattered and froze into shimmering stars. In the 15th and 16th centuries, the Tibetans arrived bringing with them the Red Hat Lamist tradition-Nying-ma-pa, which became the dominant culture and official state religion.

This tiny Himalayan state is a wonderland by all accounts. Overlooked by Mt. Kanchenjunga, the world's third highest peak, Sikkim is attractive equally for the sightseer, the adventure sports enthusiast and those interested in Buddhism and Tibetology.

A hospitable population that's predominantly Buddhist, many fine old monasteries rich with frescoes, religious paintings on silk and statues of the Buddha's various incarnations make it a soothing place to be in. Gangtok, the capital, abounds with pagoda like roofs of many buildings and the presence of crimson-robed monks in the bazaars. The Institute of Tibetology, the only one of its kind in the world, was set up by the erstwhile ruler to promote research on Mahayana Buddhism, and on the language and traditions of Tibet.

Lower down the hill is the famed orchid sanctuary where 500 species of orchids, indigenous to Sikkim, are cultivated. Sikkim offers several treks that lead through pine forests, through picturesque valleys, monasteries and to mountain lakes. It is also the base for mountaineering expeditions and the rivers Teesta and Rangeet offer excellent river rafting. A number of good hotels and lodging houses exist in Gangtok.

The hill farmers of Sikkim are composed of different ethnic groups — Lepcha, Bhutia, Limbu and Nepalis. They grow varieties of rice, rice beans, peas, beans, turmeric, and cardamom. The major cropping systems are maize-pulse and ginger, maize-potato, paddy, and large cardamom under tree cover. The main cash crops are large cardamom, mandarin oranges, ginger, and potatoes. The first three are indigenous, whereas potato is an introduced crop. This diversity in crops and varieties is associated with specific ethnicity.

The large cardamom (*Amomum subulatum*) is a good example. It is native to Sikkim where its five wild relatives, *A. linguiforme, A. kingii, A. aromaticum, A. corynostachym*, and *A. dealbatum*, are still found. The many species of cardamom now grown in Sikkim are all derived and propagated from these wild types. Farmers can recognise different varieties and their special characteristics. The common varieties maintained by farmers are Ramsey, Golsey, Sawney, Madhusy, and Ramla. The Lepcha tribe in the Sikkim mountains was the original custodian of this crop.

This tribe identified the large cardamom in forests and domesticated it. Cardamom farming practises developed through innovative experimentation by Lepcha farmers. Knowledge about cultivation was gradually passed to the Bhutia and Nepali people living in Sikkim. Now cultivation of large cardamom has spread to the adjoining hills of Darjeeling, Bhutan, and eastern Nepal. Improving this technology was initiated through a farmer-to-farmer network. This crop has been doing well in terms of both varietal development and crop management without research or extension support from formal institutions.

Cardamom farming is a perennial, low-volume, high-value, non-perishable, cash crop and it demands less nutrients and other inputs in comparison to other crops. By cultivating large cardamom, farmers have harnessed the mountain niche to its greatest advantage. Farmers in Sikkim have provided an example of how indigenous agro-biodiversity can be harnessed for cash cropping and have identified beneficial species, varieties, and farming practises for this crop. The crop domestication process was performed by the farming community, thus ensuring that farmers conserve and manage a large number of cardamom varieties on each farm.

There seems little danger of genetic erosion of the large cardamom as more and more farmers plant cardamom under Alnus forest in marginal lands. Since large cardamom is propagated by splitting the rhizomes, there is less concern for varietal loss.

The cases of turmeric and ginger are similar. Nevertheless, genetic erosion of ginger land races is becoming a possibility. The seed requirement for ginger is substantial, and much space is needed for storage. To avoid the problem of space and loss due to soft rot during storage, farmers do not keep seed rhizomes but buy them from the weekly market at planting time. Ginger cultivation requires high fertility and mulching with forest litter. In recent years, forest degradation has forced farmers to discontinue ginger farming, thus the gradual disappearance of ginger land races is a matter of concern.

Sikkim is rich in local germplasms of arable crops. Crops such as large cardamom and buckwheat are still grown using land races only, whereas hybrids are now used for ginger, turmeric, finger millet and barley. The land area under ginger increased by 191 per cent, and the area under potatoes by 311 per cent, between 1981 and 1992. The trend of switching over from traditional agriculture to cash crop agriculture has become obvious in the last decade.

The cultivation of cash crops is leading to a decline in local crops and varieties. At present, minor crops are maintained by farming households on a small scale to meet the needs of their traditional religious and food cultures. There is no longer sufficient land available for the cultivation of all crops, and farmers' preference is for expansion of cash crops. The threat to traditional crops will increase as the amount of cropland available per household is reduced.

In marginal and low-input farming systems, women have been the traditional managers of germplasm. The agricultural biodiversity that has been maintained by women, through traditional systems, has diminished with the promotion of hybrid seeds, monocropping, and changes in traditional agricultural practises.

Sikkim is the mystic land of legends, Kings and bravery of knights. It is also the land of flowers and smiles of village children. Mount Kanchenjunga, the third highest peak of in the world. Here the air is bathed with the scent of flowers with fleeting butterflies and birds while rivers carry crystal clear waters from snow-capped mountains.

Sikkim was an independent country till 1897 ruled by the Chogyal. The royal palace at Gangtok — the capital, and other hamlets bear testimony to the splendours of the past. Tucked away into a niche in the mighty Himalayas, Sikkim lies cocooned between Nepal, Tibet and Bhutan. The city of Gangtok "meaning hilltop" is perched high on the hills overlooking the monastery of Rumtek — the second largest Tibetan monastery in the world. Coloured Buddhist prayer flags flap all over this tiny state — spreading messages of peace in the winds. Sikkim has endless variations of natural beauty. Flowers, verdant glades, lofty forests are criss-crossed by numerous streams.

Tibetan Buddhism is divided into the red and yellow sects. The red sect comprises of the nyingma, kargyu and sakya lineages and the yellow sect consists of the gelugpa lineage. The sects and the lineages are differentiated from each other by the rituals performed, monastic discipline and the founder. However, the differences tend to blur with rituals of one lineage overlapping the other.

The land of mountain crests lies between the Kingdom of Bhutan, Nepal and the plateau of Tibet. This small stretch of rugged land may just be a speck on the world map but its size belies its richness and diversity of culture, customs, heritage, flora and fauna. Sikkim, one of the most beautiful nooks in the Himalayas, offers the visitors, nature in all its grandeur. The third highest mountain of the world, Kanchenjunga (8,598 m) and attendant peaks present a surreal vista unmatched.

Crowning hilltops are fabled centres of Buddhist worship and learning, such as the monasteries at Rumtek, Enchey and Pemayangtse, to mention only a few. Awe-inspiring Stupas and Chortens are set amidst fluttering prayer flags, and numerous prayer wheels spun by clear mountain streams, tinkle melodiously to remind you that you are in the abode of the Gods. Come and explore the wonder that Sikkim is.

The capital Gangtok, which is situated in the east district, is the principle urban centre; in this district more than one-third of population resides now. The capital of the state can be said to constitute the focal point of all socio-political and cultural activities. It is connected by well-developed road links with all four districts. Gangtok, is the principal commercial centre of the state. Being the seat of the government, it has become the most important centre of administrative and political activities. The population of Gangtok is composed of all ethnic groups — the Bhutia-Lepcha, the Nepali and the plainsmen.

Sikkim is a land of rich and varied scenic beauty, magnificent mountains, eternal snows, dark forests, green fertile valleys, raging torrents and calm, placid lakes. Her magnificent variety of flora and fauna are the naturalist's dream; the steep variations in elevation and rainfall give rise to a glorious multitude of species within a comparatively limited area. The scenic grandeur of mighty snow-capped peaks, the highest of which is the 28,162 feet Kanchenjunga on the Nepal-Sikkim border, has been a symbol of romantic awe and wonder for the people. It is the world's third highest peak. Kanchenjunga has five satellite peaks: Jano, Kabru, Pandim, Narsim, Simiolchu.

Two principle mountain ranges are the Singilela and Chola which start in the north and continue, following a more or less southernly direction. Between these ranges are the principle rivers, the Rangit and the Teesta, forming the main channels of drainage. These rivers are fed by the monsoon rains as well as by melting glaciers.

Sikkim is a landlocked Indian state nestled in the Himalayas. It is the least populous state in India, and the second smallest in area after Goa. Sikkim was an independent state ruled by the Chogyal monarchy until 1975, when a referendum to make it India's twenty-second state succeeded. The thumb-shaped state borders Nepal in the west, the People's Republic of China to the north and east, and Bhutan in the southeast. The Indian state of West Bengal borders Sikkim to its south. The official language is Nepali, and the predominant religions are Hinduism and Vajrayana Buddhism. Gangtok is the capital and largest town.

Despite its small size, Sikkim is geographically diverse, owing to its location at the Himalayan foothills. Terrain ranges from tropical in the south to tundra in the north. Kanchenjunga, the world's third highest peak, is located in Sikkim, straddling its northern border with Nepal. Sikkim has become one of India's most visited states owing to its reputation for untouched scenic beauty and political stability.

Sikkim's climate is sub-tropical in the lower valleys, but changing fast to temperate and alpine with increase in elevation. For most of the year, it is cold and humid as rainfall occurs right through the year. The area experiences heavy rainfall due to its proximity to the Bay of Bengal. The rainfall in the north district is comparatively less than the other districts. The general trend of decrease in temperature with increase in altitude holds good everywhere. Pre-monsoon rain occurs in April-May and the southwest monsoon operates normally from the month of May and continues up to early October.

Places with a moderate altitude (4,000 ft to 10,000 ft) have a more or less pleasant climate from March to June and September to November. Needless to say, the winter months of December-February are very cold. Some of the better known places situated at a moderate altitude are Gangtok, Pelling, Yuksom and Lachung.

In the higher altitudes of 10,000 ft plus, the temperature rarely rises above 15 degree centigrade. Some of those places are Yakshey Lodge above Lachung; Yumthang valley, Tsango Lake and Dzongri where heavy snowfall occurs during the winter months. Tsango and Yakshey sometimes receive snowfall even during April or mid-November.

The mean temperature in the lower altitudinal zone varies from 1.5 to 9.5 degree centigrade. Temperature varies with altitude and slope. The maximum temperature is recorded usually during July and August, and minimum during December and January.

Sikkim, in India's eastern Himalayan region is a land of deep gorges amid some of the highest mountains on earth. In olden days it was called *Basyul*, meaning "Hidden Land".

To the southwest, along the main range, is the pride of the Sikkim Himalaya "Kanchenjunga". A Dzong is a fortress, and even a look from afar at Kanchenjunga's butresses and icy pinnacles, confirms it as an apt name for this redoubtable mountain, standing tall at a lofty 8585 metres. Kanchenjunga's lower slopes are girdled by glaciers, whereas it's north-south orientation creates an east-west watershed.

Sikkim occupies a unique position in the Himalaya due to it's incredible biodiversity, and this is itself the result of what has to be one of the terrestrial world's steepest altitude gradients. From the plains of north Bengal to the top of Kanchenjunga, a leap of some 8,000 metres, is a distance of a mere 80 km as the crow flies. In between we find flora and fauna ranging from the tropical to the palearctic. Sikkim is like a green house. Over 4,000 species of everyday and exotic plants including 454 known species of Orchid alone. A large number of these were identified by one of the greatest explorers that Sikkim saw — Sir Joseph Hooker who later collaborated with Charles Darwin on the Origin of Species.

Hooker identified a large number of Sikkim's bountiful flora and these are chronicled in his Himalayan Journals published in the middle of the last century. The story of course doesn't stop at Orchids. Sikkim's Rhododendrons are a class apart. 30 species including the gigantic R. grande, a tree 30-40 feet in height and with girths up to 5 feet. Actually, for the botanist, the story goes on and on. Sikkimese Primulas are enough to send anybody into raptures.

The steep altitude gradient also makes Sikkim's main river, the Teesta, one of the wildest and most turbulent of all Himalayan rivers.

Flowing on a north-south axis through Sikkim, at Manang the Teesta meets up with a major tributary from Mt. Siniolchu, Sikkim's other great mountain, immediately due east of Kanchenjunga. From here, the Teesta cuts south, through the southern foothills, to the old bazaar town of Kalimpong.

The Teesta valley receives intense rainfall, even for the eastern Himalaya, which in any case averages far more rain than the western Himalaya. This is due to Sikkim's positioning, *viz.* the plains of Bengal. There is a height differential of 2 800 metres between Siliguri and Darjeeling, in a short distance of just 30 km. Consequently, the southeast monsoon hits the lesser Himalaya around Darjeeling with the same intensity as at Cherrapunjee on the Shillong plateau, one of the world's rainiest places.

Landslides are thus common all over the Teesta valley. The Teesta and it's major tributaries like the Rangit bring down what is probably the highest sediment yield of all the Himalayan rivers and in turn impart to Sikkim what is probably the highest denudation rate in the entire Himalayas.

Over the last 200 years Sikkim suffered extensive deforestation, thus exacerbating the destabilising effect of heavy rainfall. In addition the rocks in the region are comparatively fragile, the strata consisting of sandstone, shales and quartzite.

What remains of the forests is home to some of the most rampant biodiversity observable anywhere on earth.

The source of the Teesta is to be found, like all major Himalayan rivers, on the north side of the great range, in the Trans-Himalayan barrenness of the Chorten Nyima range. Here lies the magnificent Gurudogmar lake at a breathtaking altitude of 17,200 feet above sea level. Gurudogmar is the largest lake in Sikkim and certainly the highest lake of any consequence in the entire Himalayas. While the lake itself is always covered over with ice, one corner never freezes, (foreground of picture) probably due to the presence of a subterranean aquifer carrying heated water.

After it's plunge through Sikkim, the Teesta meets up with the Rangit. Also originating in the south eastern glaciers of Kanchenjunga, the Rangit has carved out the valley overlooked by the colonial hill station of Darjeeling.

The Teesta has always been a wild and unpredictable river. Till 1787, the Teesta flowed into the Ganga, when, after extremely destructive flooding, it switched course and joined up with the Brahmaputra.

The original inhabitants were the Lepchas. The Lepchas call themselves Rong-pa meaning 'ravine folk' and are thought to have migrated from the hills of Assam in the 13th century. They were followed by the Bhutias from Tibet, in the 17th century. The last three decades have seen a population boom in the state mainly due to large scale migrations from eastern Nepal. The Lepchas now constitute a mere 10 per cent of the population and the majority community today are the Nepalese.

In today's world of increasing environmental concerns, the Lepchas make model citizens. A culture and lifestyle traditionally close to nature, originally animists and now, Mahayana Buddhists, an extraordinarily rich zoological and botanical vocabulary, make the Lepcha a natural 'naturalist'.

A Lepcha legend is very revealing .... "long ago, the laughter of the Lepchas wafted into the sky, where it froze into the shimmering stars."

Buddhism came to Sikkim as a result of factional strife amongst the Tibetan Buddhists in the 15th and 16th centuries.

The great schism in the Tibetan church, between the red hats and the yellow hats, was naturally, a result of far more, than a dispute over the colours of the hat. At the root was the reformation in Tibetan Buddhism introduced by Dipankar Srijana or "Atisha", an Indian Buddhist monk who visited Tibet in the 10th century. Atisha preached celibacy and moral abstinence and weighed against the tantric arts.

The Gelugpa, or the reformed order, headed by the Dalai Lamas, dates back to this period. The unreformed residue, the Nying-ma-pa or the old order, continued to draw inspiration from the great mystic yogis of the time. Resisting the influence of the 'reformed' Gelugpa school, the Nyingmapa continued to adhere to older tantric practises frowned upon by the Gelugpa. In fact, the Nyingmapa trace their roots to the great yogi Milarepa.

The divide between the followers of the two sects deepened over the centuries and as the Gelugpa sect headed by the Dalai Lama gained ascendency in Tibet, the Nyingmapa sect sought refuge in Sikkim. Consequently Sikkim is the site of some of Himalayan Buddhism's most important monasteries.

From the rarest of the rare Red Panda, to the equally rare Clouded leopard and the Snow leopard, the diversity in the floral realm is more than matched by a similar variety in the animal kingdom. Of the 1,400 butterfly species recorded from the Indian subcontinent, nearly 50 per cent are from Sikkim. Birds, fish, reptiles are equally prolific, and remember, all this in the tiny area of just 7,096 sq km.

Unfortunately very little is known of the current status of the large mammals, though over a hundred species were recorded by the early naturalists. The Red Panda for example, a rather small member of the bear family, is arboreal, living mostly on tree tops between 6 and 12 thousand feet. Little information is available as far as it's current status in the wilds of Sikkim goes.

Origin of the Name

The Kingdom of Sikkim was established in the vicinity of Nepal as a "new kingdom" by a very brave, courageous, dexterous and dauntless adventure. It is believed by some scholars that the word Sikkim involve Nepalese dialect refers to a "new place." In all probability it points towards a "new place" or "new kingdom" set tip by Phuntsong Namgyal somewhere during the 17th century AD. On the other hand, the people of neighbourly Tibet have been calling it by the name Densong which means "a land of rice" in one of the dialects spoken in parts of Tibet. Even at present the valley of the Teesta is referred to as Be Yul Densong, *i.e.*, a hidden valley producing rice, in soiree of the Tibetan dialects. The Lepchas who are taken as the original inhabitants of this religion by the social scientists had been calling their habitat by the name of Nyemael or Mayal Nyank, i.e., heaven or paradise.

The homeland appears to be paradise to everybody and more so to the simple and unsophisticated folks living in a pollution-free region situated at the breath taking altitude surrounded by awe inspiring snow clad peaks and inaccessible mountain ranges. The linguists are nevertheless of an opinion that the nomenclature has in all probability, been derived from a Sanskrit word Sikkim which means "a mountain crest." The entire geographical area of the state consists of numerous mountain crests running in different directions. In the Gazetteer of Sikkim H. H. Risley has given yet another explanation. In his opinion Limbu is one of the dialects spoken in some parts of Sikkim. In this dialect, one finds two syllables, Su and Khim, which respectively mean "new" and "place or house." He further says that when a Tibetan ruler (who probably was the first ruler of this region) Panche Namgye built a palace at Radbentse it was obviously called Sukhim and may be the territory surroundings the new palace also came to be referred as such and ultimately as Sikkim.

In a map of the area prepared by Hamilton, the spot where the Redbentse palace stands is marked with the word Sikkim. According to the Gazetteer itself it is of interest to note that "Kirk Patrick writing in 1793, speaks of the town and district of 'Sookhim', and of a place Sikkim in the itinerary from Bizapur to Daling and this place would fall somewhere near the Runjeet. It is clear, therefore, that the name was originally given to a place and not a country."

Historical and Geographical Features

The early history of Sikkim starts in the 13th century with the signing of a blood-brotherhood treaty between the Lepcha Chief Thekong Tek and Tibetan Prince Khye-

Bumsa at Kabi Lungtsok in North Sikkim. This follows the historical visit of three revered saints to Yuksam in 1641 in west Sikkim where they met Phutsog Namgyal, a sixth generation descendant of Khye Bumsa, and formally consecrated him as the first Chogyal of Sikkim at Yuksam in 1642, thus heralding the beginning of the Namgyal dynasty in Sikkim. With the march of history, events in Sikkim saw the state pass democracy and become an integral part of the Indian Union in 1975.

Bounded by Bhutan in the east, Tibet in the north, Nepal in the west and the state of West Bengal in the south, Sikkim lies in the heart of the towering eastern Himalayas. Personally consecrated by Guru Padmasambhava during his sojourn to Tibet, Sikkim is a blessed land where people from all communities live in harmony. The world's third highest mountain, Khang-hen-dzo-nga, regarded as the guardian deity of Sikkim, dominates the tiny Himalayan State with its awe-inspiring beauty and majesty. Over 4,000 species of different plants and shrubs, around 700 species of rare orchids and rhododendrons and flowers of myriad hues and shapes have transformed Sikkim into a nature lover's paradise. Most of the 7,096 sq km of Sikkim consists of mountainous terrain, interpersed with ravines and green valleys. The two main rivers are Teesta and Rangit.

Cultural Features

The Sikkimese celebrate all major Hindu festivals such as Diwali and Dushhera. Nepali festivals like Tihar and Bhimsen Puja are common. Losar, Loosong, Saga Dawa, Lhabab Duechen, Drupka Teshi and Bhumchu are Buddhist festivals. During the Losar (Tibetan New Year) most offices and educational institutions are closed for a week. Muslims celebrate Id-ul-Fitr and Muharram. Christmas has also been promoted in Gangtok to attract tourists during the off-season.

Western rock music and Hindi songs have gained wide acceptance among the Sikkimese. Indigenous Nepali rock and Lepcha music are also popular. Common sports in Sikkim are Football and cricket. Hang gliding and river rafting have also been introduced in order to promote tourism.

Noodle-based dishes such as the thukpa, chowmein, thanthuk, fakthu, gyathuk and wonton are common in Sikkim. Momos, steamed dumplings filled with vegetable, buff (buffalo meat) or pork and served with a soup, are a popular snack. Beer, whiskey, rum and brandy are widely consumed. Sikkim has the third highest per capita alcoholism rate amongst all Indian states, behind Punjab and Haryana.

Dance

Khang-chen-dzod-nga Dance: The two day festival of dance performed during the worship of snowy range of Kanchanjunga (Khang-chen-dzod-nga) is a dance peculiar to Sikkim alone. Kanchendzonga is portrayed as a fiery red — countenanced deity with a crown of five skulls, riding the mythical snow lion and holding aloft the banner of victory.

Esoteric masks, flashing silks, opulent brocades and embroidered boots are the costumes of the dancers. The dancers are all male. This mask dance is termed as Singhi Dance, i.e. Lion Dance by Nepalese. They visualise the ferocious god of Kanchanjunga riding over a lion and hence call this dance as Singhi Dance.

Black Hat (Kali topi) Dance: On Lossoong, the Sikkimese New Year Day, Black Hat (kali topi) Dance demonstrating the triumph of good over evil is demonstrated. This masked dance is also performed by male dancers mostly the Lamas. The dance revives the old story which narrates that about twelve centuries ago King Land-Darma was slain for suppressing Buddhism in Tibet.

Other Dances

These include 'Bara Singha Dance (the Stag dance) and Kankal Dance (the Skeleton Dance) and folk dances like, the Limbus celebrating a good harvest. There are some soft rhythm dances too in which women can participate. The Tamang (Dampu Dance) and Maruni dances (Nepali Dance) are such in which a couple wavering lighted tapers on their open palms participate. The Limbus perform the Dhol Dance after harvesting their paddy crop. Lepcha people also perform a group dance after harvests. The Lepcha folk dances are quite bristle and Gay. The Sikkim dances find their roots in the traditional culture seasonal cycles of this fabled Himalayan state.

Crafts

Woollen Carpets: They are hand woven with traditional Sikkimese motifs and unique designs and combinations of rich colours. They are in great demand in Sikkim and abroad. The handsome woollen texture is durable, plush and is dyed not with synthetic dyes but traditional vegetable Sikkimese dyes. The designs vary from sophisticated harmonising tones to the brilliant rioting of vermilions against intense blues.

Choktse or Sikkimese Table: It is another exclusive product of the state. These foldable Choktse are prepared in varying designs and dimensions.

Sikkimese Hand Made Paper: It is another product which has a great demand both in and out of the state.

Miscellaneous Crafts: The traditional Sikkimese weaves and woollen blankets which can be designed into bags, shawls, jackets, opulent Sikkimese thankas (traditional tapestry), leather works, dolls, variegated applique work, batiks, an exquisite selection of dolls and a variety of fashionable garments for modern people are the other specialties of the state.

Festivals

The two day festival of dance performed during the worship of snowy range of Kanchanjunga (Khang-chen-dzod-nga) is a dance peculiar to Sikkim alone. It is celebrated in September. The third Chogyal of Sikkim, Chador Namgyal (1686-1716) introduced this dance about two and a half centuries ago as a result of a vision. Kanchanjunga is about 40 km from Gangtok and is the most unifying force in the myth and identity of the state. Khang-chen-dzod-nga means the five treasures represented by five summits of this gigantic mountain. According to tradition the five treasures are salt, precious stones, religious scripts, medicines and grains and invincible armour.

Sikkimese believe that their prosperity and even their lives depend on the good humour of the deity, for he has the power to destroy human habitations with devastating floods and avalanches, wash away their bridges and ruin their crops by sending terrible hail storms down the valleys. Kanchendzonga is portrayed as a fiery red — countenanced deity with a crown of five skulls, riding the mythical snow lion and holding aloft the banner of victory.

Esoteric masks, flashing silks, opulent brocades and embroidered boots are the costumes of the dancers. This mask dance is termed as Singhi Dance, i.e., Lion Dance by Nepalese. They visualise the ferocious god of Kanchanjunga riding over a lion and hence call this dance as Singhi Dance.

Lossoong

On Lossoong, the Sikkimese New Year Day, Black Hat (kali topi) Dance demonstrating the triumph of good over evil is demonstrated. This masked dance is also performed by male dancers mostly the Lamas. The dance revives the old story which narrates that about twelve centuries ago King Land-Darma was slain for suppressing Buddhism in Tibet. The King was slain by a Lama wearing a fantastic black robe lined with white and riding a white horse blackened with soot.

Saga Dawa

Celebrated on full moon day of the 4th month in the Tibetan Lunar Calendar, around end of May and early June, Saga Dawa is a very important festival for the Buddhists. This day is considered to be the holiest of the holy Buddhist Festival. On this day Lord Buddha took birth, achieved Enlightenment and passed away attaining Nirvana.

Phang Lhabsol

This festival is held on the 15th day of the 7th month around the end of August. This festival is unique to Sikkim. Popularised by the 3rd Chogyal (king) of Sikkim, Chakdor Namgyal, this festival marks the signing of the treaty of brotherhood between the Lepchas and the Bhutias by Khye Bumsa and Tetong Tek when the local deities and the snowy ranges of Khanchendzonga are worshipped. The lamas portraying the guardian deity perform colourful masked dances. Jesters called 'Atchars', lighten the mood of the spectators, who come in hordes to witness this festival.

Losar

It is the Tibetan New year and is marked with a lot of gaiety and festivity. It falls normally in the month of February.

Dasain

Also known as Durga Puja, this fortnight long Hindu festival usually falls in the month of October. The festival symbolises the victory of the Hindu Goddess Durga over evil. Barley seeds are sown in the soil on the first day of this festival and their growth foretells good harvest. A week later is "Phulpati" meaning the day of flowers, followed by Maha Ashtami and Kala Ratri and Navami. The 10th day of the festival is known as Vijay Dashmi and also marks the victory of Lord Rama over Ravana. During this day people smear their foreheads with coloured rice and the barley sprouts, which was sown on the first day of Dasain, are picked and placed over the ears.

Tihar

Tihar is the "Festival of Light" and symbolises the return of Lord Ram to his hometown from exile after victory over Ravana and covers a period of five days. The festival honours certain animals on successive days. The first day, known as a "Kak Tihar is dedicated to crows which are offered rice. On the second day, which is known as "Kukkur Tihar", dogs are garlanded. On the third day, the cows are honoured with garland and their horns are painted in bright colours. It is the turn of bullocks on the fourth day. Deepali, which falls on the third day is considered to be the most important day when goddess Lakshmi comes visiting every home which is lit bright with candles and electric lights. The fifth day is also known as Bhai Tika in which brothers visit the home of sisters and they apply tikas vermilion to each other's forehead. It is also an occasion for exchanging gifts. During Tihar, traditional carols called *Bailo* or *Deusi* are sung.

Magh Sakranti

This festival falls in the month of January and marks the lengthening of days. Fetes are held on banks of the confluence of rivers. This is one festival were people from all walks of life attend.

Gutor Cham

Gutor Cham is performed two days prior to Losar or the Tibetan New Year, this Cham or dance depicts the battle between good and the evil and the ritualised destruction of evil.

Bhumchu at Tashiding

The Bhumchu which takes place on the 14th and 15th day of the first month of the Tibetan lunar calander, around February-March, is one of Sikkim's most intriguing festivals.

The water contained in the sacred Phumba or vase is measured into 21 cups of equal measure. The level of water is studied to divine the fortunes of Sikkim for the next year. Devotees from Nepal, Bhutan and the neighbouring hills all come for blessings.

Drukpa Tseshi

This festival celebrates Lord Buddha's first preaching of the Four Noble Truths to his first five disciples at Saranath. The festival is held on the 4th day of the 6th month of the Tibetan lunar calendar. Prayers are conducted in the main monastery.

Tendong Lho Rum Faat

On the 8th of August, the Lepachas worship Mount Tendong which they believe saved their race from destruction by a great flood. While the Lepcha 'Bongthings' or priests worship Mt. Tendong in South Sikkim, the Lepchas in Gangtok take part in day long cultural and literary programmes in their traditional costumes.

Educational Features

Literacy in Sikkim is 69.68 per cent, which breaks down into 76.73 per cent for males and 61.46 per cent for females. There are a total of 1,478 government-run schools and 471 private schools. Twelve colleges and other institutions in Sikkim offer higher education. The largest institution is the Sikkim Manipal University of Technological Sciences, which offers higher education in engineering, medicine and management. It also runs a host of distance education programmes in diverse fields. There are two state-run polytechnical schools, Advanced Technical Training Centre (ATTC) and Centre for Computers and Communication Technology (CCCT) in Sikkim which offer diploma courses in various branches of engineering. ATTC is situated at Bardang, Singtam and CCCT at Chisopani, Namchi. Sikkim University a central university, began operating in 2008 at Yangang, which is situated about 28 km from Singtam. Many students, however, migrate to Siliguri, Kolkata, Bangalore and other Indian cities for their higher education.

Schools

With the advent of the 21st century, the Sikkim schools have undergone a major transition, as a result of which the pupils are bestowed with many different sorts of facilities that one dreams of. As a matter of fact, Sikkim schools have beyond a shadow of a doubt lifted up the standards of education in this state and continues to get even better. The major schools across Sikkim which have taken it to their responsibility to nurture the youth of the state and procure them with a platform so that they can excel in any field of their choice, are mentioned below:

Tashi Namgyal Academy (TNA): Previously dowered with the designation of 'Nepali-Bhutia School', this school is so spacious that it can accommodate a maximum of 1747 students without any major hindrance. The ICSE board from Delhi has granted affiliation to this esteemed school.

Sa-Valle-Row Academy: Ever since its erection in the year 1995, this school can house a total of 300 students at a time. This school has obtained its affiliation from the CBSE Board and includes 4 non-teaching staff.

Children's Preparatory School (CPS): Regarded as one of the most cost-effective schools, the Children's Preparatory School has however made no compromise with the quality of education that it imparts to its students.

Holi Cross School: Amongst all the missionary schools at Sikkim, the Holi Cross School is regarded as the most reputed and has a capacity to accommodate 1,300 students.

Army School: This is one of those few schools of Sikkim, that aims towards procuring education to the heirs of the army personnels.

Colleges and Institutes

Among all other Northeastern States of India, Sikkim has the best educational infrastructure. In last few years, there has been a phenomenal growth of education in Sikkim. The state has quite a few pre-primary schools and CBSC affiliated Senior Secondary Schools. Unsurprisingly, Sikkim has won the title of 'Best performing small state in Education' in 2004 and 2005 and also the 'Skoch challenger award for best use of Information Technology'. Higher education in Sikkim has been smoothened by the rapid growth of various colleges and institutions in Sikkim. Some of the important Sikkim colleges and Institutions are:

- *Sikkim Government Law College:* Established in 1977, this college offers honours courses in English, Nepali, Political Science, Accountancy, History, Geography, Zoology and Botany and also Law course.

- *Namchi Degree College:* Here honours courses in English, Economics, Education and Nepali are taught along with pass courses in English, Geography, Nepali, Sociology, Economics, Political Science and Education.

- *Damber Singh Degree College:* Set up in 1944, this college teaches only pass courses in English, Political Science, Sociology and Education.

- *Loyala College of Education:* This college is specifically for B.Ed. Course.

Apart from these colleges in Sikkim, Sikkim colleges and institutions also include Government College at Rhenock, Harkamaya College of Education at Deorali, Pakim Paletine College at Pakyong, Himalayan Pharmacy Institute at Mazitar. There are management Institutes in Sikkim like Sikkim Manipal Institute of Technology, Polytechnic institutes like Advanced Technical Training Centre, research centre like the National Research Centre for Orchids. There is scope for hotel management studies in Sikkim, at Institute of Hotel Management, Tadong. Famous colleges and institutions are:

- Management Institutes.
- Engineering Colleges.
- Medical Colleges.
- Pharmacy Colleges.
- Polytechnic Institutes.
- Computer Institutes.
- Research Institutes
- Hotel Management
- Sikkim Dental College.
- Ayurvedic Colleges.
- Homeopathy Colleges.
- Nursing Colleges.
- Veterinary Colleges.
- Research Institutes.
- Law Colleges.
- Mass Communication.
- Computer Centres.
- Libraries in Sikkim.

Universities

Sikkim universities allow the students to opt for higher studies within the territory. The universities of Sikkim provides a peaceful academic atmosphere for the students, so that the students of Sikkim can be keep abreast with the latest technologies.

Sikkim universities helps the students within the territory of Sikkim to pursue a higher degree at the tertiary level. Moreover, it is noteworthy that in Sikkim, universities witness a large variety in the population of the students, who enrol in the universities at Sikkim to pursue their higher studies. Apart from students from within the territory, Sikkim also witnesses a large number of students from the neighbouring countries who come to Sikkim to harness their future. The Sikkim Manipal University is one of the renowned universities of Sikkim that is helping the students to strengthen their prospects in life.

Moreover, the Sikkim University Bill, 2006 also seems to be instrumental in the development of the universities in Sikkim. According to this Bill, there should be a university in Sikkim under the name of Sikkim University. The Bill further states that the Sikkim University must be given certain powers which are as follows:

- To provide instructions to the institutions under the Sikkim University.
- To grant diplomas and degrees to the students on the basis of examinations.
- To undertake and extend extramural studies and trainings.
- To provide the facilities such as distance education and correspondence education.
- To provide Principalships, Professorships, etc.

Thus, we can see that the universities of Sikkim largely help the students of Sikkim to strengthen their prospects in future.

Libraries

The libraries in Sikkim bespeak the long tradition of learning that the state has upheld for a very long time. The State Government is committed towards maintaining and enhancing the facilities of the libraries in Sikkim. The Sikkim libraries can be divided into two halves. There are state libraries, which are spread over the various district towns. Then there are the monastery libraries, which provide a great infrastructure to facilitate Buddhist learning in the state. These monastic libraries are great repositories of Buddhist manuscripts and ancient documents to be accessed only by the initiated and the residents of the monasteries. They form an integral part of the libraries in Sikkim. The various educational institutes also maintain some extremely rich libraries, which provide the students and the interested scholars with all the necessary knowledge of modern science and humanistic learning. The community library is one such library. Then there is the Science and Technology library in Gangtok. Both these libraries in Sikkim are extremely well equipped and sought after by the interested scholars.

The district libraries of Sikkim are extremely well equipped. There have been great efforts taken by the state authorities to update the books and the stacks of the libraries. Recently, the state libraries received a shot in the arm and ministry of culture, government of India along with the Raja Ram Mohan Roy library foundation of Kolkata, has supplied grants to improve the library facilities. Similar amount of funds have also gone into the up-gradation of the basic facilities and infrastructure of the various district libraries.

Several other library based projects have also been initiated by the government to improve the infrastructure of the various community centres and community based libraries at Sikkim. The Nepali Literature and Cultural Research Centre at Gyalshing and the Limboo literature and culture study centre at Hee-Bermoik in West Sikkim are two such efforts taken by the Government of Sikkim.

Economic Features

Industry

Sikkim has been declared industrially backward state. The Department of Industries lays emphasis on the promotion and development of various small scale industries. The

Directorate of Handloom and Handicrafts at Gangtok provides training to youth in traditional arts and crafts.

There are three public sector undertakings in Sikkim. Sikkim Time Corporation (SITCO) is owned by the State Government. In collaboration with IIMT it assembles watches, manufactures digital watches and M.I.C. chips. Sikkim Jewels Limited is one of the sophisticated and precision oriented industries for the manufacture of jewel bearings for electric metres, water metres and other measuring instruments like watches and clocks. Ten ancillary units have been set up to manufacture watch jewels. Sikkim Industrial Corporation was established in March 1977 with twin functions of State Financial Corporation and Small Industries Development Corporation. It provides long-term loans for cottage, tiny, small and medium-scale industrial units, hotels, hospitals/nursing homes and taxis.

Agriculture

The State's economy is basically agrarian. Maize, rice, wheat, potato, large cardamom, ginger and orange are the principal crops. Sikkim has the largest area and highest production of cardamom in India. Ginger, potato, orange and off-season vegetables are other cash crops. The area available for cultivation constitutes only 11 to 12 per cent of total land utilisation in the state, the scope of increasing production through area expansion is limited. The main thrust is in agricultural development, which has maximised productivity and net income per unit area. Emphasis is being laid on the development of commercial and horticulture crops and floriculture.

Irrigation and Power

During the Seventh Plan period many new irrigation schemes for providing assured water both for *kharif* and *rabi* cropping were taken up and to avoid damages to open channels due to landslide, concrete hume pipes and IIDPE pipes in sinking areas, were used extensively within this period. An additional irrigation potential of 6,359 hectares was created and a corresponding 5,530 hectares of potential was utilised. The State has initiated steps to prepare a master plan for irrigation in the entire State in collaboration with the Agriculture Finance Corporation. A 200 KW micro hydel scheme at Lachung in North Sikkim has been commissioned. Similar schemes were taken up during the Eighth Plan period. The total power potential of the state is about 8,000 MW.

Transport

Roads: Gangtok is connected by road with Darjeeling, Kalimpong, Siliguri and also with all the district headquarters within Sikkim. Road length in the state is 2,383 km.

Railways: The two closest railway stations are Siliguri (114 km) and New Jalpaiguri (125 km) connecting Kolkata, Delhi, Guwahati, Lucknow and other important cities.

Aviation: There is no airport in Sikkim. Bagdogra airport in West Bengal which caters to the state is 124 km from Gangtok. Bagdogra has regular Indian Airlines and Jet Airways services from Kolkata and Delhi and also the North-East.

Tourist Centres

Some important tourist centres are Gangtok, Bakhim, Yumthang, Dubdi, Dzongri, Varsey, Tashiding, Rumtek monastery, Pemayantse monastery, Tsomgo and Phodong monastery.

3

History

Historical Sources

Once a "fabulous kingdom" for the travellers and adventurers, Sikkim, one of the Himalayan States, has an unparalleled ethereal charm and appears to be godlike in its grandeur. As soon as one crosses into Sikkim from the northern part of West Bengal, he faces prayer flags, stupas, nunneries and monasteries. The blowing of long trumpets by the saffron-robed lamas (monks), the respect to the extent of reverence shown by the simple country folk to any outsider amidst the thick layer of fog extends and environment resounding with mysticism.

Nevertheless, very few scholars have studied the sociocultural mosaic or economic spectrum of either the land or the people of Sikkim. Hence, there are almost no resources which can trace the ancient historical profile of the region.

However, there are mythological and legendary accounts available with monasteries. Though not directly yet indirectly some of the Buddhist scriptures and other writings of Tibet and Bhutan throw a beam of light on some of the historical events that occurred in Sikkim. Similarly for deciphering some historical events, the chronicle of Nepal comes to rescue since for centuries this region had interaction. However, by and large, these accounts are found written in local languages and Tibetan dialects which for obvious reasons are not academically accessible to every one.

Nonetheless, some of the British and Indian historians who were entrusted the task of writing the First Volume of the Imperial Gazetteer of India have rendered a yeoman's service in this regard. They not only widely travelled, braving hostile relief and inhospitable climate in Sikkim, to collect accounts and authenticate some of the available facts but also got translated some of the relevant writings available in Buddhist shrines. Small wonder, today we have to rely upon this volume for obtaining the authenticated historical account of Sikkim.

But lot of work, in this context, still remains to be done. It shall be in the fitness of things that the State Government sets up an Academy of History, Culture and Language of Sikkim which pursues the research in a methodical manner in the desired direction.

Ancient Times

The ancient period of the Sikkimese history continues to be shrouded with obscurity and its fruitful deciphering and inferences await the dedicated academic pursuits of devoted scholars, particularly the historians. Until the forties of the seventeenth century AD Sikkim did not constitute a part of the complex popularly termed as Himalayan border states, which had otherwise attracted the attention of academicians, researchers and administrators because of strategic considerations.

Hence, for having a peep into the ancient past of the state we have to take recourse to the prevalent myths and legends. The Lepchas and Limbus are two important tribes living in Sikkim. One Lepcha legend narrates the Rongpa (literally meaning the inhabitants of river valley tracts), now known as Lepchas, who ethnically form a Mongolian group, were the indigenous natives of Sikkim. These simple and shy folk who have always preferred green wooded valley pockets, believe their ancestors to have sprung up from a sacred stone or a bamboo thicket.

The Lepchas, like many tribal people in different parts of the world lived a life harmoniously woven within the Nature. That is why till more them two decodes ago they led a subsistence living through primitive modes. Hunting of wildlife, gathering of fruits, collection of tubers and edible roots provided them need based sustenance.

Some of them also practised slash and burn based shifting cultivation (popularly called Jhuming in Northeastern India) to raise coarse grains like maize, millet as foodgrains besides pumpkin, gourd and cucumber as vegetables. For all their socio-economic and cultural activities they meticulously followed the dictates of their tribal chief. The Village was the important territorial as well as administrative a real unit in the tribal hierarchy. The Lepchas during the ancient period followed polyandrous (sharing of common wife by a set of males, particularly the real brothers) matrimony.

Apart from negotiating inter-tribal marriages they also intermarried among the Bhutias, Dupkas, Sherpas, Magars and Limbus living in the adjacent mountainous sections. The polyandrous matrimony had its origin in economic base but with passage of time it obtained social sanction and thus became a cultural tradition. In mountainous areas where cultivable land is very limited and can not be appreciably expanded without causing serious ecological dislocations, people intended to save their tiny landholdings from being subdivided and fragmented. They found a pliable solution to their enigma in the custom of polyandry which follows the principle of primogeniture for inheritance.

Moreover, when there is only one women-folk in a family, the joint family shall be saved from dissensions and divisions. The inter-tribal matrimonial alliances, on the other hand, helped in maintaining good neighbourly relations amongst different tribes. Thus the inter-tribal and inter-clan feuds and warfares were avoided by at least the interlinked tribes. These people at that time were completely animistic and believed in all superstitions, sacrifices and related rituals.

There is another legendary account of Nepalese which narrates the ancient history of Sikkim in a different way. It narrates the life, activities, faith, customs and traditions of the ancient Sikkimese people in the similar fashion as done by the Lepcha legend. The only difference is that as per this legend the ancient Sikkimese were the Kirats, who also lived in the adjoining Kingdom of Nepal. Padamsambhava, the great Tibetan Buddhist tantric master (also called *Rimpoche*) is supposed to have come amidst these Kirats at some stage of the ancient history.

He started preaching Buddhism among these people who till then were animistic in their faith. The teachings of Rimpoche (the Tibetan name of Padamsambhava) made the Kirats enlightened and awakened who showed great enthusiasm to come out of the archaic practices slowly and gradually and started marching towards civilized way of living. With the passage of time, they not only became Buddhists by faith but also banished primitive ways of living.

Still one more legend rooted in the Sikkimese soil explains the ancient history in another way. According to this religion. The God Almighty created a human couple beneath the slopes of the sacred mountain peak of Kanchenjunga. It further says that the Sikkimese people are the Chronological descendants of this couple. These earliest people came to be known as Lepchas later on while the territory inhabited by them was named as Meyel Nyang. These earliest Lepchas were very simple, shy and unassuming people who obtained their succour through the activities of hunting, gathering and collection. They were the inhabitants of cold land and thus could not go naked like the tribals of hot and tropical lands. Besides using the skins of the hunted animals they also wove coarse fibre from the fibrous plants growing in forests.

Now some scholars who have made in-depth studies in the chronicles of the Himalayan region are of the opinion that the ancient history of Sikkim started with the heirs of the King named Indrobodhi who is said to have ruled some region of the present Himachal Pradesh. It is further surmised that at a time when Buddhism started waning in India, the tribes then inhabiting parts of the Western Himalayas started migrating to suitable packets of the Eastern Himalaya under the leadership of some adventurous zealot princes. Under the such move some of the subjects of King Indrabodhi, led by King's heirs arrived

the distant mountainous pocket of the Kham in Tibet. A Prince from amongst these heirs
of King Indrabodhi is believed to have founded the Minyak Kingdom in Tibet somewhere
during the ninth century AD. It was from this kingdom that the ruling houses of Sikkim
emerged.

Medieval Times

The Minyak dynasty in Tibet ruled for centuries together. The twenty-fifth Prince in
the Minyak lineage is said to have moved out of the palace for a sojourn-cum-pilgrimage
towards the west somewhere during the first half of the 15th century of the Christian era.
He was accompanied by his wives, five sons, male and maid servants as well as provisions
loaded on mules. The Sakya monastery at that time was under construction but the royal
encourage visited it to pay their homage.

At the construction site they found some of the lamas struggling in vain to lift and
erect a monolithic pillar in the main Chapel of the monastery. To their utter pleasant
surprise a son of the Minyak Prince single handedly lifted the pillar and erected it in the
proper manner at its required place. The pleased lamas endowed the title of Khye Bamsa,
i.e. one who possesses the strength of hundred thousand elephants, on the Prince.

The Sakya Chief who was getting the monastery constructed offered the hand of his
daughter to the Minyak hero in marriage and also offered him some land for permanent
settlement. Both the offers of the Sakya Chief were accepted and the Minyak heir settled
down in a village named Phari in the Chumbi valley after his marriage.

During the first decade of the following century Phari emerged as a nucleus of the
region. Other sons of the Minyak Prince has moved further south to some place now
falling in Bhutan. The Lepchas of the region at that time were ruled by their tribal Chief
Thekong Tek. His seat of governance then lay in Be Yul Deunzang, a place south of Phari.

For many years after their marriage the Minyak couple did not beget any heir. The
learned lamas of the monastery advised the couple to seek the blessings of the Lepcha
Chief Thekong Tek who was said to have possessed some prophetic powers Khye Bamsa
and his spouse went to the Lepcha Chief prostrated in front of him, offered him the gift
of valuables and explained the purpose of their visit.

Thekong Tak after meditating for some time spoke that the couple will be blessed
with three sons and also predicted that their descendants shall in times to come rule over
the entire Sikkim.

In times to come Lepcha Chief's prophecy came true. Turn by turn the Minyak couple
were blessed with three sons. The couple also moved from Phari in Tibet to Gangtok for
settlement Khye Bamsa and his wife felt undoubtedly obliged to the Lepcha Chief. A very
deep and reciprocal friendship grew between the Lepchas and the new-comers. Thekong

Tek and Khye Bamsa swore by a blood brotherhood and singed the friendship treaty with their own blood at a place named Khabe Longstsok.

After the death of Khye Bamsa his third son Mipon Rab stepped into the shoes of his father as Chief Mipon rab himself had four sons and it is believed that the four principal clans of Sikkim have sprung up from them. The fourth and the youngest son of Mipon Rab named Guru Tashi succeeded his eldest brother as Chief after the sad and untimely demise of the former, since at that time none of the sons of deceased had come of age. Guru Tashi after assuming Chiefship shifted to Gangtok.

On the other hand after the death of Thekong Tek none could contain the Lepchas as a united tribe. The Lepcha tribe consequently fell into divisions and all divisions felt leaderless and rudderless. Finding Guru Tashi as an effective, kind and capable leader the different Lepcha clans also started looking towards him for guidance and leadership.

Finding that the subject of his later friend could unite under his banner Guru Tashi agreed to be the Chief of Lepchas also. To run the Lepcha affairs Guru Tashi appointed Sambar, a promising gem among men, as his Chief Advisor and Lieutenant. Guru Tashi who belonged to a ruling house that had been established by non-natives look all the steps to effectively integrate the members of the ruling house into the native soil. This step besides effecting emotional integration also paved the way for the establishment of a regular monarchy.

Thus, it was Guru Tashi who became the first regular ruler of Sikkim and he was crowned as such. He was a medieval ruler who was in no way different in his behaviour from the medieval rulers of the near-by hill states.

He was followed by Jowo Nagpo, Jowo Apha and Guru Tenzing as Sikkim rulers, who followed the policy of Guru Tashi towards the Lepchas, i.e. of creating progressively amicable relations with the Lepchas.

The next ruler was Penchu who renamed himself as Phuntsog Namgyal. He was Guru Tanzing's son and successor and was born in 1604 AD. It is also gathered that it was Phuntsog Namgyal's coronation which attracted all the royal pomp and show amidst week long celebrations and merry snaking. Till then the coronation ceremony in Sikkim had been a simple affair bereft of any feast or festivities.

There is a story behind the coronation of Phutsog in a particular manner. It is said that three highly learned and esteemed Lamas entered Sikkim from three different directions and met together at Yokshom (meaning a meeting place of wise man) to deliberate upon the possibility of having a temporal and religious head as the ruler of Sikkim on the lines of the Lhasa (Tibet) ruler. In their opinion the region was till then inhabited by pageants who needed a head who besides ruling them could also guide them to seek salvation. Two of the Lamas, who thought themselves to be learned and well-versed in the theology furthered their own claim.

However, the third Lama reminded them the prophecy of Guru Padamsambhava who had predicted that a man coming from east and Phuntsog by name would be the new ruler of Sikkim. He further told them that since none of the three had come from east and none was named Phuntsog, the real man had yet to be sought. Resultantly messengers were sent to search for Phuntsog. Near Gangtok a young man coming from east giving the appearance for a majestic personality was found to be marching towards Yokshom. On enquiry he revealed his name as Phuntsog. He was detained by the messengers and the Lamas were summoned to the place.

After making relevant enquiries the Lamas made him sit on the rock slab and proclaimed him as the first religious and temporal head of Sikkim amidst the chantings of hymns and sprinklings of water from the sacred urn. The Lama who had reminded the other two lamas about the prophecy of Padamsambhava was named as Lhatsun Chenpo Nalugyal. Hence, Phuntsog was also given the name of Chenpo Namgyal and the title of Chogyal (a religious King) was conferred on him.

The coronating lamas learnt to their surprise that Phuntsog was already a Prince who had to inherit the rule from his father. He was, therefore, allowed to retain his first name, *i.e.*, Phuntsog but it was made obligatory for him to add the suffi of Namgyal. Phuntsog Namgyal was thereafter in his father's palace with all pomp and show. It was also made obligatory that thence after every chogyal of Sikkim would be coronated with royal festivities. Phuntsog Namgyal was coronated in 1642 AD.

Modern Times

The modern period of Sikkimese history initiated with the coronation of Phuntsog Namgyal who even during his short rules of only two years introduced far-reaching changes in the polity and theology of the state. The first consecrated ruler at that time ruled over a vast territory, the frontiers of which lay far beyond the borders of the Sikkim of today. His kingdom extended up to Tibtalia on the borders of Bihar and Bengal in the south, Thang La in Tibet in the north and Tagong La (near Paro) in Bhutan on the south.

The settlement of Timar Chorten located on the bank of the Timar stream in Nepal made the western border of the Kingdom. Phuntsog genealogically was a distant descendant of Raja Indrabodhi, but by his domicile he hand now become a Bhutia. He was also advised by the coronating Lamas to seek the recognition of his Chogyalship (a heavenly ruler or a ruler who ruled with righteousness) from the Dalai Lama, the temporal and religious head of Tibet who commanded supremacy among all the Buddhist kingdoms. The then Dalai Lama of Tibet accorded recognition to Phungtsog Namgyal as Chogyal and entrusted him the rule of the southern slopes (Sikkim) of the Himalaya.

As a token of recognition the Dalai Lama sent ceremonial gifts such as the silken scarf bearing the seat-emblem of the Dalai Lama, the devil dagger (phmrpa), the hat (mitre) of the Guru Rimpoche, i.e. Padamsambhava and the most precious sand image of the Guru. This act led to the linking of the newly set up Bhutia principality of the Namgyal dynasty to the Tibetan theocracy.

Thus right from the mid-fifteenth century to the 19th century the Bhotia principality of Sikkim always looked towards Tibet for obtaining protection from the foes and their aggressions.

Phuntsog Namgyal paid equal attention towards the welfare of his subjects. He found it difficult to attend to the problems, hopes and aspiration of his people himself. Resultantly he divided the kingdom into a dozen districts called *dzorigs* in the local language. Each dzong was placed under the administrative charge of a Dzongpona, *i.e.*, Governor. Since at that time the Lepchas enjoyed an overwhelming majority, he prudently appointed Governors from among the Lepchas.

Yatung, the greatest commercial centre of Tibet being closer to Gangtok, posed some problems to Chogyal and his administration. So as to avoid any embarrassment to the Dalai Lama, he took a wise step of shifting the seat of his government from Gangtok to Yoksham, with which he had emotional association. He declared Mahayana sect of Buddhism to be the state religion and it continued to be so under all the Namgyal Chogyals.

Phuntsog Namgyal through his tactful and diplomatic ways kept the Bhotias, Lepchas and Limbus in harmonious relationships. He also appointed a Council of Ministers for him consisting of twelve member. The Lama who had helped him become the religious and temporal head of Sikkim was also paid his due. The Chogyal got constructed the first monastery, *i.e.*, Sangla Choling in Sikkim under the direct supervision and guidance of the Lama Lhatsun Chenpo Namgyal. According to Doig and Persin, "An image of this famed Lama is enshrined in the monastery of Enchey above Gangtok and seated on a leopard skin and crowned with a diadem of skulls. In his left hand he holds a human skull filled with blood and in his right hand a trident on which human heads are impaled."

The Namgyal dynasty ruled over Sikkim with hereditary Kings, enjoying divine rights, for about 332 years. However, some scholars challenge this assertion and advance arguments to prove that Gyurmed Namgyal died issueless at the age of 26 in 1733 and this way the Namgyal dynasty came to an end. The situation, it is believed, was saved by a crafty lama who declared that the deceased King had illicit relations with a nun who was pregnant at that time and carried a child of Gyurmed Namgyal in her womb.

The nun was delivered of a male child, who was accepted as heir to the deceased King and this way the Namgyal dynasty was saved from extinction. The child was named as Phuntsog Namgyal II after the founder of the dynasty. Some other scholars narrate this story is a different manner and this fact shall be explained at the relevant reference.

After the demise of Phuntsog Namgyal, he was succeeded by his son Tensung Namgyal in the year 1644. He moved his administration headquarters to Radbentse from Yoksham.

He got married thrice and each time he brought the princesses of Tibet, Bhutan and Nepal as each his Queens. The offspring from these Queens, having associations with their parental territories, started picking up quarrels among themselves for vested interest.

Such intra-family feuds and greedy activities led to restlessness inside and outside the palace. The palace intrigues and conspiracies not only involved the royal employees but had their impact on the overall administration of the state. The Chogyal who was a weak man could not rise to the occasion although the otherwise was ruler for more than five decades. He thought that the multiplicity of the clans of his subjects was the root cause of the disorder and disturbances. With a view to appease all the people, he, from all the eight clans, appointed as Councillors. Notwithstanding such steps he was an utter failure and could not curb the divisive tendencies prevailing inside and outside the state. He breathed his last in the year 1900 AD.

When Tensung Namgyal expired, there ensued a war of succession among his offspring form different Queens. Chador Namgyal who was a minor son at that time from the second wife of Tensung succeeded to the throne with the help of some Tensung loyalists. The Queen who originally hailed from the Bhutanese royal family had a daughter named Pedi, who in turn raised revolt against he minor King. She did not simply challenge the succession but sought the Bhutanese intervention in her favour.

Yugthing Yeshe who had been a very loyal minister to Tensung apprehended some physical danger to the minor King at the hands of the Bhutanese. In a swift but sneaking move he eloped with the minor King in the darkness of a night and reached Lhasa safely with the young Prince. The minister as well as the minor King were extended asylum in Lhasa in a monastery.

During his asylum the minor Prince distinguished himself in Buddhist theology and Tibetan learning. He devoted his time for learning astrology and also started predicting events. In no time by dint of sobriety, learning correct astrological predictions and capabilities he rose to the position of the State Astrologer to the Sixth Dalai Lama, who himself originally belonged to a place near Twang in Arunachal Pradesh. The Dalai Lama was so much pleased and impressed by the work, conduct and scholarship of the young scholar that he bestowed high honours and titles on the young King in exile. He was also awarded an estate in Central Tibet with sovereign rights over it.

On the other hand, the Bhutanese forces in sudden attack and captured the palace at Rabdentse and overpowered a son of the Minister Yugthing Yeshe as hostage. However, on the intervention of the Dalai Lama, who was religious head for all the Tibetan kingdoms including Bhutan, the Bhutanese ruler King Deb withdrew from Sikkim

Such a development paved a way for the comeback of Chador Namgyal, who on reaching Rabdentse cleared Sikkim of the remaining Bhutanese. The south eastern part of the region was however lost to Sikkim for ever since this part had been heavily colonised by the Bhutanese. This section also became a ground for further attacks on Sikkim. After sometime Bhutanese forced again Sikkim to capture some of its territory though Chador Namgyal offered a very tough resistance yet the areas of Kalimpong and Rhenock, which were the parts of Sikkim also lost for all times to come.

Chador Namgyal was a deeply religious man who took quite effective steps for the propagation of Mahayana Buddhism in the territory held by him. The Sixth Dalai Lama who hailed from Twang had ordained the Twang tradition of sending every second son of a three-son family to the monastery. Chador Namgyal too commanded such a tradition and desired that every Sikkimese three son family would send its second son to be ordained as a monk of the Pemingehi monastery which was also open to others. He built the Guru Lhakhong Tashiding monastery in 1715 and patronised all the sacred places.

He also adapted the religious dances (mystery plays) to keep alive the martial and native traditions. He also invented an alphabet for the Lepchas with an intention that his subjects could create interest in learning and religion. In spite of all such welfare steps, his half-sister Pedi had not reconciled to the new situation. She was always looking for an opportunity when she could eliminate Chador and grab the rule.

In her bid to do so she conspired with a Tibetan man of medicine who caused the untimely demise of Chador Namgyal by way of blood letting from a main artery when the King was a sleep during his holidays at Raland hot water springs near Namchi in the year 1716. A force was sent to Namchi. The Tibetan medicine-man was slaughtered while Pedi was strangulated to death with the help of a silken scarf. Thus ended a very promising man of religion and administration.

Chador Namgyal was succeeded by his son Gyurmeed Namgyal when the Dzungar, *i.e.,* Mongol hordes invaded Tibet with the intention of capturing territory and punishing the people who propagated or followed the Nyigma sect. Afraid of imminent persecution the Mindoling Abbot family fled to Sikkim and obtained refuge there. Gyurmeld Namgyal till then was a wandering mendicant. Mindiling Abbot with a view to strengthening his relations with the Sikkimese ruling family got his sister married to the Namgyal ruler. During this period the fear of a Gurkha invasion was looming large over Sikkim. The Namgyal ruler intended to fortify his position and garrison at Rabdentse.

Thus the people were forced to work on the fortification project without any reward. The Tsongs who did not wish to be unpaid bounded labourers fled to Limbuana. In no time Limbuna became a rebel territory which started challenging the Namgyal ruler. Ultimately Limbuana broke way from Sikkim even before the Gurkhas invaded Sikkim. Bhutan also raised a dispute over boundary.

Tashi Bidur, the then Chieftain of the Magar clan also revolted against the King but his revolt was suppressed with an iron hand. But Limbuana was lost to Nepal for ever. Gyurmeld had no child but while at his death bed in 1733 at the young age of 26, he told his confidants that a nun in Sangana Choling nursery was carrying his child in her womb.

Nevertheless, some people do not believe it. In their opinion the Namgyal ruler was impotent physically and he always kept his wife at bay. Therefore, the story goes, that in order to save the Namgyal dynasty from extinction the crafty lamas of Sikkim concocted a story. Whatsoever it may be, the nun was pregnant at that time and she was delivered of a male child. The lamas and loyalists convinced the people that the newly-born child was the progeny of the King.

The nun also stated in affirmative. Thus the child was accepted as heir to the deceased King and given the name of Phuntasog Namgyal II.

Phuntasog Namgyal II was opposed by some influential persons and even the Bhutanese ruling house opposed to it on grounds of illegitimacy. Tamdang who had been a treasurer with the later ruler, as also one of his closest confidants and lieutenants opposed the coronation of Namgyal II tooth and nail. When he found that his voice went into wilderness, he arranged a coup and assumed all power of the ruler. He got hold over a sizeable section of the forces also. No wonder he continued to rule for three years and succeeded in braving all hostility from the pro-king faction.

Ultimately the pro-king faction succeeded in obtaining the help of the Lepchas who came forward with all their might to back the baby King. Under the leadership of Chandzok Karwang, the Lepchas fought battle after battle to dislodge Tamdang. After persistent thrusts by the Lepchas, Tamdang left the ground and fled to Tibet to seek help and guidance.

Nevertheless the Dalai Lama who intended to keep Sikkim under the Tibetan tutelage thought it wise to side with the baby King instead of with the hawk. The Tibetan authorities not only turned a deaf ear to Tamdang but instead sent Robden Sherpa as Resident to the baby King with clear-cut instruction that the interests of the baby ruler be protected at all costs.

The Regent got convened a convention of the representatives of all tribes, all clans and all districts. The convention defined the duties, powers, functions and responsibilities of the government as well as the resident. So as to augment the fast-depleting resources, the convention also decided to introduce the annual system of taxation. At about the same time the Chieftain of the Magar tribe died all of a sudden. Other well-to-do persons of the tribe wished the son of the deceased to be nominated as next chief. For this purpose they approached the Regent who in turn expressed his inability to interfere in the affairs of the clan.

The flat refusal of the Regent enraged the Magars, who instead sought the help from Bhutan ruler and the Bhutan ruler by endorsing their demand won them to his side. This way Sikkim lost the allegiance of a martial tribe. The Tsongs also rose in arm against the Regent but their revolt was curbed by Chandzok Karwang, the loyal Lepcha Chief to the minor ruler. The rise of Gurkhas in Nepal also posed threat to the political stability of

Sikkim. The Gurkhas of Nepal under the banner of Raja Prithvi Narayan Shah of Nepal started making secret inroads in the Sikkimese territory and fomented rebellious elements. Bhutan also wished to cash in on the situation. In a sudden attack Bhutan captured all the Sikkimese territory lying east of the Teesta river. However, agreed to withdraw to the present boundary after an agreement arrived at Rhenock. The Gurkhas invaded the Sikkimese territory seventeen times but were beaten back every time.

Nevertheless, the Sikkimese ruler thought it prudent to purchase peace with the Gurkhas. A peace treaty was thus signed with Nepal in 1775 vide which Gurkhas, pledged to abstain from any further attack and also agreed not to abet the Bhutanese move. But the Gurkhas, at a later stage, violated the Peace Treaty and occupied some territory of western Sikkim.

Phuntsog Namgyal II had three wives, but he got his only son in 1769 froth his second wife. The King died in 1780 and his son Tenzing Namgyal succeeded as new ruler. The new ruler after some years got married to the daughter of the Lepcha Chief Chandzok Karwang. He accorded top priority in reorganising the Sikkimese with the objective of exterminating the Nepalese influence. In a strategic move, two strong columns of the Sikkimese were despatched to oust the Nepalese and regain the lost territory. One of the columns reached right up to the bank of the Artin river but at the eleventh hour failed to achieve its aim primarily because of the exhaustion of ammunition and secondarily due to the chance killing of its general.

The second group defeated the Gurkhas at Morang but the victory could not be decided because soon after the Gurkhas strengthened their position and retaliated. In the year 1788 the Gurkhas not only occupied some areas of southern Sikkim but they also took Rabdentse by surprise. Tenzing Namgyal had to retreat to Khybe and ultimately to Lhasa. In 1790 some of the Nepalese influence was exterminated but it relaxed completely only when Nepal got involved with Tibet. The three combined forces of the Lepchas, the Bhutias and the Tsongs succeeded in vacating the Nepalese aggression to a large extent. But their enthusiasm was sapped by Namgyal's death at Lhasa in 1793.

After the death of Tenzing Namgyal, Tsugphud Namgyal succeeded who ruled over Sikkim for the longest span of period among all the Namgyal Chogyals. From 1793 he ruled till 1863 a period of seven decades. He was a very brilliant person and some priests believed him to be the incarnation of Manjushri, i.e. Buddhist deity (Bodhisattva) of wisdom. It was during his regime that the British, who had established themselves firmly in India, penetrated even to this Himalayan Kingdoms. The British merchandise reached even across the Himalaya into Tibet.

The Sikkimese ruling house fell prey to the British diplomacy and after some time the ruler Tsugphud Namgyal found himself sandwiched between the British authorities on the one side and the Sino-Tibetan powers on the other. It was an impossible task for the Sikkimese ruler to retrace his steps and in due course of time Sikkim became involved in the Anglo-Nepalese War and Sikkim had to accept the position of a British ally. Nonetheless, in this bargain ultimately Sikkim was also a gainer when with the help of the British the Nepalese were ousted from southwestern Sikkim was close to Nepalese territory and thus on the advice of the British the Sikkimese ruler moved his administrative headquarters to a safer place Tumlong.

To settle the border dispute with Nepal, Sikkim signed the Treaty of Titalia in 1817 vide which the Nepalese-Sikkimese boundary was demarcated along the Singalila range and the courses of the Mahanadi and Michi streams. This demarcation was not acceptable to the Sikkim ruler since he wanted that the area around Titalia be also included in Sikkim. But the British so as to safeguard their vested interest made Sikkim to sign the treaty and acquired the disputed territory from the Gurkhas and gave a secret unwritten assurance to the Sikkim ruler that after sometime the territory would be handed over to him. However, it never happened so.

One of the wives of the Sikkim ruler Tsugphud Namgyal hailed from the Panchan Lama (equivalent to Prime Minister, second in hierarchy after the Dalai Lama) family of Tibet. Consequent upon the strained relations between the Panchan Lama and the then Regent of Tibet, Tsomoiling, the relations between the Sikkim and Tibet became cold and stagnant. Chandzok Bolek, a descendant of Chandzok Karwang, was made the Prime Minister in Sikkim. His unexpected elevation raised many an eyebrow and many jealousies and rivalries came to plague the palace scenario. The sad result of this tug of war led to the assassination of the entire family of Bolek. The other relations of the family fled to Elam and obtained Nepalese protection.

Obviously, the territory of Elam was lost to Nepal by Sikkim. These relations hailed from the Kotpa clan, who were known for their avenging nature. The Kotpas kept on having skirmishes with the Sikkimese forces every now and then. All diplomatic moves, tads and threats by the Sikkimese to win back the Kotpas proved futile and Kotpas continued to be a perpetual source of headache for the Sikkim rulers.

The Sikkim-Nepal boundary dispute has also been a perpetual affair. The British who had by then become the overlords of the Indian subcontinent thought it to be their duty to resolve all such disputes, since in the bargain the British always gained.

In the year 1828, a British officer came to the region to resolve one such dispute. The Officer Captain Lloyd was taken aback by the bewitching panorama and charm of the Darjeeling Hills and he was bitten by a desire of turning the hill sport into a health resort for the British who could spend a couple of months away from the sweltering heat of the plains in these cool and beautiful as well as quiet hills. He forced the Sikkim ruler to handover the place to the British.

The Chogyal once again succumbed to the British pressure. He handed over Darjeeling for the development of a sanatorium by the British East India Company out of friendship to the Governor General. However, as per one condition, it was expected that the border dispute would be resolved favouring Sikkim and an equivalent tract of land shall be given to Sikkim.

The Company, on the other hand, forced rent on the ruler which the ruler had always been refusing. At a later stage the British Deputy Commissioner of Darjeeling Champbell desired the Sikkim ruler to extricate the criminals and slaves from the Terai area of Morang and also wished the ruler to collect taxes in a manner suggested by him. Such a move, however, led to the gradual deterioration of relations between the British and Sikkim.

The worsening relationship reached the climax when Champbell and Hooker were detained in Sikkim in 1859, obtaining any permission from the Sikkim authorities. The British got enraged by this act and they lost no time in dispatching a punitive expedition to Sikkim to obtain the release of the British officers. This also led to the complete annexation of Darjeeling and Morang tracts by the British in 1860.

The following year, a treaty was forced upon the Sikkim ruler and the annexation of Darjeeling was confirmed for all times to come. The treaty, in fact, was got forcefully signed from the heir apparent Prince Sidkeong Namgyal while Tsugphud Namgyal was away to the Chumbi valley on the other hand Tibet had never liked the Ghogyal's act of giving away the Darjeeling territory to the British.

Obviously the Tibet-Sikkimese relations also went from bad to worst. Tibet banned the entry of Sikkim rulers to Lllasa, except once in eight years. When Sikkim was in such hot waters, its ruler Tsugphud Namgyal breathed his last in 1863.

Sidkeong Namgyal succeeded his father as ruler at a mature age of 44 years. Some priests had already declared him as the incarnation of Karmapa Lama of Khania and he had been treated with veneration by the Sikkimese. When his father had become very old and infirm, he used to look after the administration of the state. That is why he had signed the treaty with the British. He was a very far-sighted man who loved peace.

Through mutual give and take, he amicably resolved two long-standing disputes, with Bhutan over grazing rights in certain hill meadows and alpine pastures in 1973 he went down to Darjeeling himself to pay a courtesy visit to the Governor of Bengal who was holidaying there. In this meeting he impressed upon the necessity of improving the British Sikkimese relations. In a way he succeeded through persuasive techniques to resolve the strained relations with the British. He was still negotiating with the British on the issue of modernising the Sikkimese army when the cruel hands of death lifted a very capable, just, tactful and progressive ruler of Sikkim in 1874.

Thutob Namgyal, a son of the deceased ruler, became the ninth consecrated ruler of Chogyal of Sikkim in 1874. He was married twice. His first wife belonged to the Tashi Lhumpo family of Tibet. She died in birth pangs in the year 1880. The second spouse of

Chogyal hailed from the Lhading House of Lhasa. She became Queen in the year 1888. She was an uncommon female who was a very capable and wise person who bravely shared her husbands ordeals, ups and downs through all thick and thin.

When Thutob ascended to the throne, the British paramountcy had extended its wings almost over whole of Asia and Sikkim had completely fallen in the British clutches. Thutob was a young man of a tender age and had no experience of worldly affairs. He had to deal with the British, the men of age and experience, who would spare no efforts in instigating the vested interest in Sikkim, to work on unpatriotic and treasonable lines. On the other hand, the Nepalese Chauvinism had been glowing fast right from the days of the Nepali ruler Raja Prithvi Narayan Shah.

The first thrust of this Chauvinism was territorial aggrandisement through which the Nepalese got hold over the chunk of their neighbour's territory while the second thrust was to send the Nepalese outmigrants to the neighbouring countries for setting up Nepalese Colonies. The Sikkim ruler Tsugphud Namgyal had read in between the lines of the writings on the wall and had prohibited the settlement of Nepalese in Sikkim.

During the initial years of the rule of Thutob Namgyal some influential local persons including brothers Khangsa Dewan and Phedong Lama violated the ban with impunity and got some Nepalese immigrated to Sikkim for permanent settlement to achieve some personal gains. The common man in Sikkim, however, strongly resented the "unlawful settlement of Nepalese within the Sikkimese territory." The Nepalese who had got settled along the banks of the Teesta were forcefully ejected by the Sikkimese. However, they again came back after sometime to face ejection thereafter. This way they were ejected thrice. The Khangsa brothers through their cunning ways and shrewder manners worked their way to the young ruler and ultimately reduced the ruler to a mere figure virtual rulers.

Nevertheless, some of the honest Sikkimese royal servants apprised the King of the impending dangers and persuaded the ruler to have a dialogue with some British authority to find a solution to the problem. Sensing the highly partial and mischievous attitude of the then Deputy Commissioner, the Chogyal approached Ashley Eden the Governor of Bengal. A meeting between Eden and Chogyal was held at kalimpong. Eden agreed to the policy of prohibiting the settlement of non-Sikkimese on the Sikkimese soil. He further made it clear that even if some non-Sikkimese had to be brought for the settlement of some barren lands, such settlers shall not be given the right of holding any office or village headship.

The Sikkim government drafted the document of prohibiting the settlement of the Nepalese in Sikkim but the document had to be ratified by the Deputy Commissioner of Darjeeling. The Khangsa brothers played a trick. After the document had been signed by the Chogyal and impression of his seal put on it, they very cleverly added in Tibetan language on the document, "according to the desire of the Governor I promise to abide by the policy of allowing the Gurkhas to settle on uninhabited and wastelands of Sikkim." The Khangsa brothers had entered into connivance with the White Deputy Commissioner of Darjeeling.

Consequently after some time the Khangsa brothers with a tacit support of the Deputy Commissioner started settling the Nepalese immigrants on the uninhabited lands around Rhenock. The Sikkimese on the other side started ejecting such settlers. A clash between the pro and anti-settlers was imminent. The Khangsa brothers took the dispute to the Deputy Commissioner of Darjeeling for adjudication. The Deputy Commissioner gave the verdict in favour of the settlers. Such a verdict led to the increased tempo of Nepalese settlement in Sikkim.

The highly partial attitude of the British and their continued unwanted interference in the affairs of Sikkim turned the Chogyal highly frustrated who retreated to the Chumbi valley during summer. The British were unhappy with the ruler who did not seek British advice for his affairs. They thus wanted the Chogyal to come back from the Chumbi valley and hand over the reins of administration to the Khangsa brothers and Sheo Dewan. In the year 1885-86 the relations of the British became highly streamed with Tibet battle was feared. The Chogyal visualised that in case of invasion by any party up and this valley became a part of Tibet. The treaty arrived at was forced upon the Chogyal.

Resultantly Claude White was appointed as the first Political Officer in Sikkim. In this the Chogyal of Sikkim was reduced the position of a *de juro* ruler while British became the *de facto* ruler of Sikkim. The Chogyal or any of his officer was prohibited to enter into any type of dialogue with foreign country without the prior permission of the British authority.

On the arrival of Claude White Chogyal retreated to the Chumbi valley in silent protest. The Political Officer constituted an administrative council consisting of himself and the Khangsa brothers Chogyal's income was frozen and he was directed to come back from the Chumbi valley. On their return the Chogyal and his wife were taken into custody and sent to Kalimpong, pending the arrival of Chogyal's sons back from the Chumbi valley. The Chogyal agreed to bring his sons back but the maternal grandparents of the Children refused to send them to Gangtok in view of the maltreatment meted out to the royal couple. The British banned the Sikkim-Tibet trade and instead wanted to enter into trade relations with Tibet themselves. White also, in a planned way, started destroying the traditional economy of Sikkim. After several months of ordeal the Chogyal and his wife were freed.

Since at that time the capital town of Gangtok had been ravaged by an epidemic the royal couple chose to stay at Nabey. On hearing that her elder son had fallen ill, the Queen rushed to the Chumbi Valley without obtaining prior permission of the British. The British got annoyed and lost no time in interning the Chogyal. During this internment the King was harassed and tortured in many ways. He was kept in solitary confinement for 13 days. Even food and water was not supplied to the King after repeated entreaties and humiliations. Even after being freed the Chogyal was forced into some odd jobs. Meanwhile the Queen came back from the Chumbi Valley along with her elder son.

Because of the usurpation of authority by the British and humiliations at every step, the royal couple got so frustrated that the Chogyal and his wife preferred to move in Sikkim on a pilgrimage. The royal couple was so much upset by the domineering and unwarranted behaviour of the Deputy Commissioner that it sought the intervention of the Governor and also expressed desire to retire to Dobtah, a Sikkimese enclave near Khampzong in Tibet.

But as ill luck would have it, the ruler marched towards Dobtah without seeking permission to do so could reach him. On the way in Walong valley he was intercepted by the Nepalese and handed over to the British. The Chogyal and his Queen were interned at Ging and later on at Kurseong. In 1894 the higher British authorities realised that the excesses committed by White on the royal couple were contrary to the Policy of the British and even expressed displeasure and resentment on the usurpation of the powers of Chogyal.

Resultantly in 1895 the Chogyal and Maharani were released, When they reached Gangtok they were ostensibly received by White with open arms. He offered them presents, apologised and asked them to bury the past and also assured them of his full support and assistance. But Claude White was a very shrewd man, who kept the entire administrative machinery in his control leaving only judiciary to the Chogyal.

The higher British authorities, on the other hand, were very eager to establish deep and strong trade relations with Tibet and they desired the Maharani to mediate for this purpose. While the Maharani was still in the pipeline, the British got impatient and dispatched an expedition to Tibet via Sikkim under Francis Young Husband in 1904. So as to repair old roads and construct new ones for the expedition a large number of Sikkimese were requisitioned for road building activity just as bonded labourers.

In the year 1905 when Prince of Wales was in India, Panchen Lama of Tibet and King Deb of Bhutan met him at Kokata and pleaded for the restoration of their administrative powers. By this time the Khangse brothers had fallen out with Claude White. The Political Officer handed over the administrative powers to Chogyal retaining the power of reviewing any transaction. The Chogyal, whom the vicissitudes had made more wise, distributed his powers among the Council of Ministers and also set up a Civil Secretariat.

In the year 1908, the Chogyal visited Nepal for a pilgrimage and there signed a blood brotherhood treaty with Chandra Shamsher, the Prime Minister of Nepal. The heir apparent Prince Sidkeong Tiulku had also returned from Oxford after completing his education and starting extending a helping hand to his father in day-to-day administration. The Maharani expired in 1910 while Chogyal himself breathed his last in the year 1914.

Sidkeong Tulku, the foreign educated young man, much against his formal education, was made to believe that he was the incarnation of one of his illustrious predecessors, the eight ruler Sidkeong Namgyal, who in turn was thought to be the incarnation of a Kham based Lama Karmapa. He came to the throne in 1914. He undoubtedly was a man of high acumen and extraordinary qualities. At a very young age he had exhibited the signs of a developing forceful personality with a high degree of intelligence. That is why he was sent to Oxford so that his potentialities could be fully developed.

During his father's time, after coming from the United Kingdom he used to manage the affairs of schools, monasteries and forests. He was a kind-hearted man who had been equally enlightened by Western education and thus never hesitated to take bold steps in the interest of public welfares. He abolished imprisonment as a punitive measure for non-payment of debts since he knew that the tricks played by moneylenders were such complex and intricate that any borrower who once borrowed money could never hope to be out of the web the moneylender weaves through complex interplay of compound interest and other underhand as well as questionable practices. He also took steps to remove all vested interests from the shrines and worked for the unity of all Buddhists.

He brought out reforms in monasteries and made them to come up to their social obligations. He proposed to liquidate landlords and intended to distributed land among actual tillers. This step made him very unpopular with the landed aristocracy. Being independent, assertive, bold and progressive he was bound to have strained relations with the British Political Officer. Charler Bell was then the Political Officer who wanted to get rid of "such a stubborn ruler."

When the Chogyal was somewhat indisposed in December, 1914, a British physician from Bengal was summoned for his treatment. It is shocking by bewildering but true that the physician gave him a heavy dose of brandy and wrapped him in number of blankets while keeping fire lit under his bed. Small wonder the ruler died within an hour. Thus suddenly and prematurely ended the highly progressive and promising ruler, who was otherwise sure to bring far- reaching reforms in the polity and economy of Sikkim.

For his death the connivance of the landlords and the British political officer was suspected. The ruler died a bachelor on December 5, 1914. Tashi Namgyal his younger brother succeeded him. Tashi was born in 1893 at Kurseong while his parents were in British captivity. Though he was 21 years old, Charles Bell kept him under his tutelage for some time. Only after about three years he was restored all the administrative powers.

Tashi Namgyal was coronated Chogyal suppressing the claim of another elder Prince Tchoda Namgyal. It was done on the behest of the British who wanted to prove that in Sikkim they were the real King-makers. However, Tashi Namgyal who ruled over Sikkim for about fifty years proved to be an enlightened and capable Chogyal who introduced many socio-economic reforms in Sikkim.

He took concrete steps to eradicate social evils and socio-economic inequities. He banned public gambling in 1921 while in 1944 the bonded labour and non-paid forced labour. In those days the Sikkim government also practiced beggar, popularly named as Jharlarigi but the British extended to this practice with very serious dimensions when simple folks were even whipped to construct roads for British expeditions. Tashi- Namgyal, knowing it fully well that this reform shall invite British wretch on him, did not hesitate to wipe off this stigma from the forehead of Sikkim.

The hired persons of landlords were also prohibited to act as policemen. So as to introduce land reforms in the real sense, the Chogyal got his territory surveyed trigonometrically for the first time. The landlords were not prepared to part with even an inch of their large holdings but the Chogyal clipped their wings by steeply curtailing their powers and limiting their functions. The courts managed by the landlords were abolished. The lease system was done away with and the peasants were required to pay their taxes and revenues directly to the State Treasury.

During the Second World War, The Chogyal became a British ally and placed his men and six thousand Sikkimese youngman joined the British forces and fought at different points. Even the heir apparent Prince Paljor Namgyal was commissioned in the Air Force and he was killed while in active service in the year 1941. The Chogyal had also drawn up a detailed plan for the social uplift and economic resurgence of his subject to be launched after the end of the War. However, the shattered economy as a result of war and acute shortages of financial resources stood in the way. Only when Pandit Jawaharlal Nehru, the First Prime Minister of Independent India assured Sikkim of all help and support during his visit in 1952, that the Government of Sikkim started slowly and gradually moving towards economic planning.

After Pandit Nehru's visit, Sikkim though as Indian Protectorate started showing inclination towards Indian plans, projects and reforms finding that this country had started achieving some very concretely fruitful results. In the year 1953-54 Sikkim adopted the Indian Penal Code and the Civil Code. Even the Indian Marriages Act with adaptations suiting local conditions was adopted by Sikkim. Prior to it in the year 1950, the treaty signed with the British in 1861 was reviewed and a new treaty based on peace, economic cooperation and mutual friendship was singed with India.

Thus with the signing of this Treaty Sikkim instead of being a British Protectorate had become an Indian Protectorate. The loan advanced by the Indian Government in the earlier years of its existence was later converted into an economic aid to the Himalayan State. This economic aid helped in bringing about certain well-desired socioeconomic reforms in Sikkim. However, it was too late, since the people had already started agitating against the apathy of the authorities towards their genuine grievances. The under-surface restlessness among the masses afforded an opportunity to some people with political ambitions and thus some political organisations started emerging in Sikkim. The Sikkim

State Congress was one such political party that raised the banner for a full responsible, government and also demanded the abolition of zamindari system (landlordism).

Above all this party favoured the merger of Sikkim with India. To counter the demand for States accession to India the Sikkim National Party came into being which opposed the demand for State's merger with India but desired a Treaty relationship.

Tashi Namgyal, the Sikkim Chogyal enlarged his council by introducing representatives of the people of all shades and views. He also broadbased his administrative set-up and took some steps to give the impression that his government meant business which solely aimed at public welfare. The Sikkim State Congress formed a new Cabinet much to the discomfiture of the Chogyal.

Tashi Namgyal, however, shortly dismissed the Cabinet on the charges of inefficiency and anti-constitutional activities. He asked the Government of India to send a trained and efficient administrator as Dewan (almost equivalent to Prime Minister) to Sikkim. In the transitional period, till the Dewan, arrive the state administration was entrused to the Political Officer. In fact the freedom attained by India had its echoes in the state of Sikkim also.

And the political activity had stepped up in the state right in 1948 when all the aforesaid developments had taken place. The Dewan arrived in Gangtok in 1949 who had instructions to work for the welfare of the Sikkimese people in close collaboration with the Political Officer. A campaign for regular tax collection was started to augment the public revenue because for want of funds many welfare projects could not be launched there. The house tax charged per house was reduced in quantum. Zamindari system was completely abolished.

The Dewan and the Political Officer worked assiduously to bring about a reapproachment between the political parties so as to pave the path for setting up the State Council. On March 23, 1953 the first general elections were held in Sikkim, an event unheard in the history of Sikkim. The State Council consisted of 6 members two each representing the Bhutia, Lepcha and Nepalese communities. Five members were nominated by the Chogyal through his discretion provided to him under the constitution. An Executive Council was also set up to run the administration.

Tashi Namgyal as Chogyal had a chequered career and very busy schedule because of fast dawning of political awareness among the Sikkimese masses. Nonetheless, he was man of fine testes and used to snatch time for art and literature out of his hectic schedule. He had inherited these tastes from his mother. He extended patronage, finances, help, subsidies and moral support to scholars engaged in Buddhist studies as well as the scholars engaged in the exploration of Nature's bounty in Sikkim.

Though Chogyal himself was a follower of Mahayana sect of Buddhism, yet he was least bigot and intolerant to other sects and faiths. He himself was a painter who sometimes was seen painting landscape. He passed away on December 2, 1963. The reforms introduced by other agencies during his time had no moral sanction by him. In fact the reforms were introduced not as public welfare measure but as baits to quell uprisings and disturbances.

Palden Thondup Namgyal succeeded his father Tashi Namgyal as Chogyal and became incidentally the last Chogyal of Sikkim. As already stated his elder brother Prince Paljore Namgyal, the heir apparent had been killed during the Second World War. Palden Thondup Namgyal was sent to the Indian Public Administration Academy Mussoorie to receive training in administrative skills.

In the year 1944, he was elevated as President of the Sikkim State Council and he enjoyed this coveted office for a full term of five years. He also acted as the Principal Advisor to his father in all judicial and executive matters. He advised the late Chogyal on External Affairs and it was he led the delegation to New Delhi for negotiating the terms of the Indo-Sikkim Treaty arrived at in 1949-50.

Treaty with Indian Federation

In 1950, a treaty defining India-Sikkim relations was signed following a serious law and order situation in the state. India had to rush police contingents from the neighbouring Darjeeling district. Under the treaty, the Himalayan State became protectorate of India which was responsible for defence, external relations, communications and territorial integrity of Sikkim.

The Government of India had the right to take such measures as it considered necessary for the defence of Sikkim or the security of India whether preparatory or otherwise and whether within or outside Sikkim. In particular, the Government of India announced that Sikkim would enjoy autonomy, subject to the ultimate responsibility of the Government of India for the maintenance of good administration and law and order.

Suffering as it did from all the defects of a half-way house, the arrangement was subjected to severe strains by Chogyal's proclivity to be difficult. His American-born wife, Gyalmo Hope Cook's vision of a fully independent Sikkim further exacerbated the atmosphere of intrigue.

Since the late fifties, and particularly after his marriage with her, the Chogyal had been trying for an independent status. He became active particularly after Bhutan became a member of the United Nations. After the thaw in the Sino-US relations and change in the US attitude towards India, the Chogyal and his American wife wanted the treaty revised. An element of instability was added to this as the political parties aroused the people to demand an end to the Chogyal's authoritarian misrule and installation of a Representative Government.

It was in pursuance of this treaty and at the request of the then Chogyal Tashi Namgyal that the Government of India intervened when political parties launched a movement for full democratic rights, land reforms and electoral reforms in 1973. The Chogyal's Palace was besieged and the Indian forces had to rescue him. Soon after, the Chogyal set up a popular Ministry but dismissed it within a month.

From the beginning the administration was run by an Indian official, nominated by the Government of India and appointed by the Chogyal, but soon the Chogyal took over this office himself. The Indian nominee, Mr. I. S. Chopra, however, continued as the President of the Sikkim State Council (State Assembly).

The Indian Government could ill-afford the turbulence in an area which is of tremendous geo-strategic importance for India's defence. Amidst the icy-heights of Nathula barely 30 miles from Gangtok, Indian and Chinese troops face each other, eyeball to eyeball, a point of confrontation, as it were between democracy and Communism. Therefore, New Delhi acted to restore order in the area, its natural inclination to support the forces of democracy.

State under Protection

On May 8, 1973, an agreement was signed providing for a democratic set-up for Sikkim, administrative reforms and closer links with India. The agreement, tabled in the Lok Sabha the next day, envisaged a constitutional monarchy under the Chogyal but with India having a final say in matters which would remain its responsibility. Apart from defence and foreign affairs, political and economic relations, India would ensure that all sections of Sikkimese population enjoyed their basic rights and fundamental freedom. It was also laid down that the Chief Executive of the kingdom would be a nominee of the Government of India to be formally appointed by the Chogyal. In case of a difference of opinion between the Chogyal and the Chief Executive, the matter would be referred to New Delhi for advice, "which will be binding".

It also laid down that the Chogyal would retain exclusive control over ecclesiastical matters, palace affairs and the small Sikkim Guard attached to the palace. Questioning the Chogyal or members of the royal family are matters outside the preview of the Assembly as the matters falling within India's sole jurisdiction.

The agreement incorporated an assurance from the Government of India that it would keep the interests of the Sikkimese people in mind while discharging its responsibilities as well as those derived from the old treaty arrangements.

On June 20, 1974, the Sikkim Assembly passed the new Constitution Bill prepared by a constitutional adviser deputed by India providing for more powers to the legislature and the Cabinet. It paved the way for responsible Government and close links with India.

Earlier, Palace Guards had surrounded the Assembly building and prevented members from entering it and police had to resort to a lathicharge to enable the members to attend the crucial session. Of the 32 members, 26 were present and they voted for the resolution endorsing the 34-clause Constitution. The Sikkim Congress Legislature Party boycotted an emergency meeting of Assembly convened by its President, Mr. D. S. Das, at the request of the Chogyal. The party told Mr. Das that the Sikkim Bill had been passed by the Assembly twice on June 20 and June 28 and that it saw no reason for summoning an emergency session of the Assembly.

Third Time: However, the next day the Assembly passed the Bill a third time without any amendment and the Chogyal gave his assent on July 4. Kazi Lendhup Dorji formed new Ministry under the new Constitution, assumed office in Gangtok on July 23, 1974. It had four members besides the Chief Minister.

The Lok Sabha voted on September 4, 1974, the Constitution (35th Amendment) Bill, to associate Sikkim with the Indian Union paving the way to put an end to its protectorate status.

The then Congress President, Mr. D. K. Baruah, announced on March 10, 1975, the Constitution of an *ad hoc* Sikkim Pradesh Congress Committee consisting of 106 members. The Chief Minister, Kazi Lendhup Dorji was made the President. Mr. S. K. Rai and Mr. B. B. Gurung the General Secretaries and Mr. B. P. Dahal the treasurer. Earlier, the Sikkim Congress had unanimously decided to fully integrate with the Indian National Congress.

Formation of State

On April 10, 1975, the Sikkim Assembly unanimously adopted a resolution abolishing the institution of Chogyal and declaring Sikkim as a constituent State of the Indian Union. The resolution which came within 24 hours of disarming the Palace Guards, said that the Assembly "solemnly declares and resolves" that "the institution of Chogyal is hereby abolished and Sikkim shall, henceforth become a constituent unit of India". At a referendum on the resolution on April 14, 59,637 Sikkimese voted in favour while 1,496 voted against it. Thus on April 26,1975, Sikkim became the 22nd State of India. The same day the Rajya Sabha passed the Constitution (36th Amendment) Bill with the support of 157 members.

When the Janata Party came to power at the Centre in March 1977, three 'Janata' units emerged in Sikkim, but the Central Janata Party was reluctant to recognise any of them. In the meantime Mr. Nar Bahadur Bhandari formed his Sikkim Janata Party on March 22. The Central Leadership rejected his application for affiliation with the Janata Party. However, when Kazi Lendhup Dorji's Sikkim Congress decided on May 8, 1977, to merge with the Janata Party, it was accorded recognition. At that time there were 16 Nepalese MLAs and 16 Lepcha-Bhutias on the House of 32. The Lapcha and Bhutias had eight MLAs each.

Merger with Federation

During his tenure as the Prime Minister, Mr. Morarji Desai, in March 1978, said the government of his predecessor, Mrs. Gandhi, should not have annexed the tiny Himalayan

Kingdom of Sikkim in 1975. "But", he said as he denounced the move, "I cannot undo it now". According to him, it was not a desirable step, but it has been accomplished and most of the people wanted it. The reason for this was that the Chogyal of Sikkim, 53 years old Palden Thondup Namgyal, was not popular with the majority of his people. Nevertheless, Mr. Desai argued, "It is wrong for a big country to do that. Many of the neighbouring States were bothered about it because they are smaller and they thought that if it could be done to Sikkim it could be done to others. But I cannot undo it."

Such a statement by the Prime Minister created quite an uproar, in all the political circles which the Prime Minister explained as his own personal opinion and not as that of the Prime Minister of India. The Chief Minister of Sikkim, Mr. Dorji felt let down and betrayed by the Prime Minister, Mr. Morarji Desai.

On July 5, 1979 an Indian Front had been formed and was being supported by Ramchandra Poudyal, Mr. Nar Bahadur Khatiwada and Mr. Nar Bahadur Bhandari. Before the dissolution of the Assembly on August 13, 1979, there were reports that some wanted to table a motion to countermand the state's merger. Mr. Dorji, who was asked to continue as the Chief Minister, resigned on August 17 paving the way for President's rule. Earlier 17 legislators had crossed over to Mr. I. C. Poudyal reducing Mr. Dorji's strength to a mere 10. Subsequently, in August 1979, the people of Indian origin in Sikkim also organised themselves under the banner of the Nagrik Sangharsha Samiti.

Under Federation

This process of Integration with the Indian Union has been unique, mainly because Sikkim had for long earlier remained a protectorate. The experience has shown no trace of sociocultural alienation, political resistance and concomitant problems of adaptability and assimilation, despite the fact that Sikkim had its own sociocultural and politico-economic systems a traditional paradigm of development and powerful neighbour in China which is yet to recognise it as a part of India. Historically also it represented a very different political culture from the mainstream India's.

The post-merger Sikkim has consistently followed a policy of indigenous cultural plurality while placing an abiding faith in the explicitly secular Constitution of India. Despite its distinct ethnic character, with the indigenous Nepalese constituting an overwhelming majority of 78 per cent of the population of 4.05 lakh and the rest shared by the tribals Bhutias and Lepchas, Sikkim always managed to portray itself as a single cultural entity. But it can no longer do so.

The Challenge

Signs of mass mobilisation on the lines of caste, religion and language can now be seen in the once socially highly progressive State. Equally disturbing is the fact that these divisive activities are being witnessed after the advent of political democracy and with urbanites as a strong support base. One wonders how the modernising agents in a State with strong semi-feudal recent past would be able to stop this new process of social stratification based on caste cleavages. This is a formidable challenge to the local political elite.

The history of the quest for ethnic parity in Sikkim is much older than the saga of merger. All the successive Chogyals had increasingly realised the degree of disparity that historically existed among various ethnic groups in Sikkim. This disparity transcended economic frontiers and touched the spheres of society, culture and polity. In an attempt to minimise the magnitude of the disparity, the Maharaja abolished charges like 'bethis' and equalised 'dhuri khajanas' as paid by the Nepalese subjects in 1949. This was soon followed by the abolition of another discriminatory practice of 'jharlangis'.

The Proclamation of August 30, 1956 of the Maharaja of Sikkim declared that, 'notwithstanding the continuance of measures for the protection of the interests of the indigenous people, all duly recognised subjects of Sikkim should be accorded equal treatment" in terms of the rate of land revenue.

The Disparity

However, the disparity suffered mainly by the Nepalese Sikkimese was so deep-rooted that it was virtually impossible to bring them at par at least socio-economically with their native ruling counterparts. This was one crucial factor which was said to have influenced the Sikkimese to opt for the merger. Simmering discontent over the disparity continues to find expression like the ouster of Nar Bahadur Bhandari's 15-year-old Government.

Therefore, the question of providing equal opportunities to all the three ethnic groups will continue to dominate the political agenda of the state. The only likely difference will be the degree of assertiveness of various groups, the interplay of extra-regional forces and the changes in the responses of the Centre.

Sikkim's political development has in it all the ingredients for the creation of a progressive democratic society except for the fact that its political institutions have not reached a level of maturity. The virtual absence of both pressure and interest groups has seriously hampered this process over the years. In the last 15 years, however, the democratic leadership has been able to achieve greater popular involvement in the tasks of economic development. It is because of this that the instability and disorder usually found in a transitional society could hardly be noticed in case of Sikkim. An eminent fallout of the advent of democratic politics in Sikkim was expected to be the threat of popular frustration at an excessive gap between aspirations and reality.

This threat should have been the graver in Sikkim's case because of the historical nature of its nation-state and its political socialisation and culture. Amazingly all these fears have been belied by the inconceivable manner in which the Sikkimese have accepted the Indian acculturation. They have achieved the essence of political stability by their ability to absorb perpetual change amidst a strict adherence to continuity.

After Sikkim emerged as a constituent State of India, all the basic instruments of development were geared into action. This needed to be done to give an Indian identity to the Sikkimese economy which primarily had been a feudal State with aristocracy usurping the cream of development.

Since the mid-70s the entire fulcrum of development in Sikkim has undergone a metamorphosis in social, economic and ecological spheres. Socially, people have become more outward-looking, economically, the quality of living has improved, and, ecologically, the state continues to remain a much-protected region.

But the real potential of Sikkim continues to remain unharnessed. For instance, it is estimated to have hydro-power potential of 3,000 MW as against today's total installed capacity of 20 MW. It is rather sad, a State with this potential has to import power from Chukha in Bhutan and Farakka in West Bengal.

New Era in State

During twentieth century, in a number of colonial countries struggles for freedom were marching ahead without any abatement. India was in the forefront where a very novel and unprecedented weapon ahimsa had been employed by the people for winning freedom. Although at times on the smooth surface of "non violence" and "self suffering" did emerge hateful ripples of violence yet by and large the weapon of ahimsa worked well. The application of such a unique weapon not only inspired other colonial countries to fight for freedom but even the people revolted against the feudal and autocratic systems of governance. With the attainment of freedom by India, the sleeping giant of Asia awoke from its slumber and hectic movements for the restoration of liberties of thought, expression, faith as well as for the setting up of democratic governance.

After the lapse of British paramountcy in India and signing of the Indo-Sikkimese Treaty in 1950 Sikkim ceased to be a British protectorate and instead it became a protectorate of Free India. However, the people of Sikkim, particularly the awakened and enlightened elite, desired a completely democratic set-up. This group persuaded even the have-nots of the society to wage a battle against the acrotic monarchy of Sikkim and asked for self rule. But such a gigantic goal could not be achieved by a handful of people. It needed a mass movement, wherein particularly its torch-bearers were ready for countless humiliations, imprisonment, confiscation of their property and were ready to face tortures, repressions, harassment and the like. Although a simmering discontentment had already started seeping in Sikkim, yet the people became more restless when feudal order in 565 native states of India came to an end and their people fully started sharing the fruits of democracy and liberty.

On the pattern of the Indian National Congress, the Sikkim State Congress had come into existence and this political party had become quite active. In its historic convention held on December 7, 1947 among other demands it had asked for the establishment of a popular democratic government and the merger of Sikkim in India.

Such a charter of demand was highly unpalatable to Tashi Namgyal, the then Chogyal of Sikkim. Counselled by his close lieutenants, the Chogyal had helped in the emergence of another political party, i.e. the Sikkim National Party in April, 1948. The political manifest to this party was just the anti-thesis of the Sikkim State Congress manifest. Just around the same time another political party under the banner of Rajya Praja Sammelan appeared on the political horizon of Sikkim.

This party desired a complete merger in India and closer interaction with the Gurkha population of Darjeeling and North Bengal. Obviously this party was dominated by the Nepalese section of State's population. In sum, by the end of 1948 Gangtok had become a full-fledged theatre of political activity with the autocratic theocratic monarchy fully supporting the Sikkim National Party.

The Sikkim State Congress was branded as anti-national consisting of Indian agents bent upon selling the motherland. Notwithstanding this sort of propaganda and mudslinging, the Sikkim State congress stepped up its political activities. The Chogyal Government became panicky and ruffled as a result of increasing popularity of the Sikkim State Congress and bewildered as it stood, it took into custody the stalwart leader of the party. This led to agitations and protests but the government instead of boldly and tactfully facing the situation imposed curfew on the Capital town of Gangtok. Despite these steps, procession condemning the hasty and unwise government actions were taken out in the city violating the prohibitory orders.

However, on the advice of the political officer all the detained leaders were released on February 12, 1949 expecting that such an action shall ease out the tension. The people on the other hand took it as their first victory of their movement and particularly that of the Sikkim State Congress. On May Day, 1949 thousands of Sikkim State Congress members demonstrated in front of the palace at Gangtok shouting slogans like Inkilab Zindabad, i.e. long live Democracy.

The day-long shouting and protesting made the Chogyal very panicky who felt quite unsafe and thus fled to the complex of the Indian political Officer seeking refuge. Finding that the Chogyal had left the palace, they picketed the palace continuously to bar the entry of any member of their royal family. Under such circumstances the political officer advised the Chogyal to form a popular government in the state. The Maharaja agreed to do so and when he extended this assurance to people they withdrew the agitation.

On May 9, 1949 the first popular government was sworn in the state with Tashi Tshering leader of the Sikkim State Congress as Chief Minister. The Cabinet had only three members. This was another feather in the Cap of the Sikkim State Congress. The Maharaja had acted on the advice of the political officer but his palace advisers did not lose any time to convince the Chogyal that he had committed a blunder and that he had been misguided by the political officer who in fact was the brain behind the Sikkim State Congress.

Thus the reluctant Chogyal started creating stumbling blocks in the functioning of the popular government. The bureaucracy was still on the side of the Maharaja and did not comply with the orders of the Cabinet. The administration came to a halt within no time. This led to feuds, clashes and highly strained relations between the Chief Minister and the Chogyal. The latter without giving any serious thought to the problem dismissed the popular government on the charge of inefficiency on June 2,1949. Under these conditions the Political Officer had to take the administration into his hands.

The followers of the Sikkim State Congress had feeling that the Chogyal had taken this step also on the advice of the political officer. No wonder the political officer. Harishwar Dayal became very unpopular with the Sikkim State Congress and there was a demand for his withdrawal. J. C. Lall a senior Indian Civil Services Officer soon replaced Dayal as Dewan instead of Political Officer because the Chogyal had asked for a Dewan instead of a political officer.

Lall after having apprised himself of the development in Sikkim and discussing the current situation with the Chogyal as well as the leaders of different political parties found it that the Sikkim State Congress had a hold over the masses and had also succeeded selling its idea to the people. After considering all the demands put forth by this party he came to a conclusion that two of the demands could be acceded to without any delay. The quantum of House Tax was reduced and beggar, i.e. forced labour was abolished. He also constituted an Advisory Committee consisting of representatives of different shades of people to advise the Dewan on administrative matters.

However, in view of the diverse and opposing interests of the members, the Committee could not serve any useful purpose. Soon the Indo-Sikkimese Treaty was singed on December 5, 1950, which unfortunately fell far short of the expectations of the Sikkim State Congress. The pro-palace elements, on the other hand, started following the policy "divide and rule". They managed to created a gulf even between the Bhutia an Lepcha sections of the Sikkim State Congress through their wilful whispering campaigns.

The Chogyal and his supporters, through their shrewdly cunning moves, created such confusing environment that the State Congress was entrapped in the cobweb trying to clear misunderstanding and thus finding no time for meeting its goals, ideals an principle.

In the year 1963, the socio-political milieu of Sikkim took a turn when the Prince Palden Thondup, a widower for half a dozen of years, got marries to an American Buddhist Scholar Hope Cook who had come to Sikkim for her field study. As Shukla states, "In certain quarters it was openly suggested that Cook was a CIA plan and was sent here to fish out information for logistic and diplomatic importance and send the same to her masters.

Her duties perhaps also included to win the Maharaj Kumar who was shortly to be new Maharaja, away from Indian and help as far as possible the establishment of an Independent State, where USA might build up some sort of defence structures against China." Seven months after getting married to Hope Cook, Maharaj Kumar Palden ascended to the throne as Chogyal Palden Namgyal.

His formal coronation, however, took place on April 4, 1965 when Hope Namgyal was also crowned as Gyalmo (the consort of the deity) of Sikkim. As usual an official delegation from India also graced the occasion. Nonetheless, the delegation besides feeling relatively neglected also noted some other changes. One this occasion quite unusually the Indian National Anthem was not played upon.

The strength of the palace guard had also been enhanced from 60 to two companies of troops. Soon after a Study Forum came into existence in Gangtok whose basic objective was to spearhead anti-India propaganda. The Gyalmo Hope Namgyal also challenged the 1950 Indo-Sikkimese Treaty as "unjust" and emended the territorial integration of Darjeeling with Sikkim.

During this time another political party under the banner of Sikkim National Congress had been established. The polls due at that time were swept by the Sikkim National Congress led by Kazi Lhendup Dorji but the Gyalmo saw to it that this party was not associated in any way with the political affairs of the state. The pro-palace group under the direct guidance of the Gyalmo continued unabatedly its activities of sowing the seeds of discontentment and divisive tendencies among the rank and file of the different political parties. The Chogyal spared no efforts to throttle any group that mustered courage to act as Opposition in the Executive Council.

If he could not succeed through his autocratic moves then he used to throw bait. As observed again by Shukla. "It was a very peculiar feature of Sikkim politics that all parties were keen to be in the Executive Council and there remained no party to function as the opposition party to pinpoint the mistakes of administrations. Just by throwing crumbs of office the Chogyal was in a position to buy off their loyalties."

The Sikkim National Congress was represented on the Executive Council but soon the favouritism, nepotism, corruption, misrule, high-handiness and the like perpetuated by the Chogyal and pro-palace group brought frustrations for this party. The people who had whole-heartedly voted and supported this party also got disappointed.

Thus to save their image the party started criticising the functioning of the Chogyal administration. Kazi Lhendup Dorji issued a strongly-worded memorandum scathingly attacking the acts of omission and commission of the Chogyal administration and demanded redressal. However, the Chogyal lobby was still powerful and the matter was raised in the meeting of the Executive Council.

Since the Chogyal tycoons held a majority there, censure motions were passed against Kazi and his lieutenants. The administration also issued arrest warrants against Kazi and his strong supporters but by this time Kazi along with his European spouse Elisa Maria had left for Europe. In fact he had secretly come to know about the move to arrest home and he finding no other recourse, managed to reach Europe. D. B. Gurang was another person against whom also arrest warrants had been issued. He appeared in the court and saved his skin (in all probability he had been won over) throwing the entire blame on Kazini (Elisa Maria) and another stormy petal of the party, Nar Bahadur Khaliwada, who had gone underground.

The general elections in the state were announced in 1973. The main opposition leader Lhendup Dorji was in a sort of exile in Europe. He was very eager to stage a comeback to the state but the charges of sedition against him were hanging over his head like the sword of Democles. He was sure to be put behind bars and disqualified for elections, the moment he stepped into Sikkim.

However, the Indian and some other diplomats of democratic countries persuaded the Chogyal to drop the charges against Dorji and allow him to contest elections. Though reluctantly, the Chogyal acceded to the request. On reaching Gangtok Kazi found that his party had almost neared extinction. Some of his earlier supporters and confidants had joined other parties, including the newly-formed Janata Congress. The Sikkim State Congress which had vouched the integration of Sikkim in the Indian Union had become non-existent. At that time there were only three political parties to be reckoned with, viz. Sikkim National Congress, Sikkim National Party and Sikkim Janata Congress.

While Sikkim Janata Congress and Sikkim National Party had respectively pro-Nepalese and pro Lepcha-Bhutia leanings the Sikkim National Congress exhibited near secular character. Obviously the atmosphere in the state became communal and such tendencies and the tacit support of the palace elements whose interest lay only in communal strife. Thus the election were "rigged" in the sense that the principle of "one man one vote" was thrown to winds. Such an arrangement suited the Sikkim National Party which alone captured 7 out of 18 assembly seat.

The other parties openly charged the Chogyal for rigging the elections an demanded repoll on the basis of "one man one vote" principle. K. C. Pradhan the Sikkim Janata Congress Chief was arrested. This led to protests, agitation and hunger strikes on the very lawn of the palace. The Chogyal on the other hand cared for such movements and instead started making war-footing preparations for his Golden Jubilee Celebrations to be held on April 4, 197, on his fifteenth birthday.

Kazi Lhendup Dorji persuaded the Sikkim Janata Congress to join hand: with his party and form a joint Action Committee to spearhead a long battle against the Chogyal. Kazi himself became the Chairman of the joint Committee. The Committee presented a charter of demands with an ultimatum that if the demands were not met within the stipulated time, the people would work for stopping the Golden jubilee celebrations. The Chogyal, on the other hand, stuck to his stand. On April 3, 1973 people from all corners of the state started converging on the lawns of the palace to prevent the conduct of festivities.

Although barriers had been created in different parts of the city, people arranged to reach the Palace lawns. For some time a war of attrition continued between the police and protestors but two fire-shots by the policemen escalated the situation. The Bhutia-dominated police used teargas shells and in the resultant melee many persons were wounded. The agitators were pushed back to Ran Paul, a distance of a dozen of Kilometres from the Palace. The retreating agitators were chased by the police and Prince Tenzing personally. The Prince who wanted to prove more loyal than the King fired some shots wounding two women and some men.

This further aggravated the situation. On the other hand, of all the wounded persons six succumbed to their injuries. The agitators now changed their line of strategy. They spread themselves in the villages and aroused the sentiments of the village folks against the theocratic monarchy and the high-handedness of the ruling junta. The Chogyal was now cornered to such an extent that he was compelled to hand over the administration to the Dewan on May 8, 1973. The agreement arrived at between the Chogyal and Dewan envisaged the setting up of fully responsible democratic government, independent judiciary, rule of the law, more powers to legislature and executive and adult franchise on the principle of one-man one-vote.

Again the general elections were announced as a result of which all the political parties started making preparations. The part agitation had helped two political parties of the state, Sikkim National Congress and Sikkim Janata Congress to come together. Their ideologies also got integrated. Thus both the parties decided to merge together. This way a new and vigorous society, Sikkim Congress came into being. The elections were held for all the 32 seats of the Assembly and the Sikkim Congress by winning 29 seats seeped the polls.

The party President Kazi Lhendup Dorji and two of his very close associates were returned unopposed. All these developments convinced the world that the days of the acrotic monarchy were over and people expected that the Chogyal by burying the past would extend a hand of friendship towards the emerging leadership, but the Chogyal refused to read the writing on the wall. He was adamant and considered himself as a living symbol of the Sikkimese identity. He was an over-ambitious man who at all costs desired to be a monarch of Sikkim like his neighbours in Bhutan and Nepal. Not only that, he even got his case internationalised through his American wife and some other associates.

On the other hand the opponents of the Chogyal and the newly- elected members were also bent upon putting a complete end of the monarchy and usher in a new era based on democracy, in Sikkim. This way their intention was to "teach a lesson to the erring stubborn Chogyal". The Chogyal too was not sitting idle. He had been conspiring with some forces whole he was using for his vested interest. With the help of intrigues, he again committed the same blunder of getting a political party floated that could espouse his cause. He got a new party Sikkim Prajatantra Party organised by his own brother-in-law Sonam Gyatso. Chogyal's eldest can Tenzing organised Lepcha Association with ulterior motives.

All such fastly moving events rent the atmosphere highly surcharged with tension, suspicion, commotion and mistrust. On May 10, 1974, under such a tense atmosphere. Chygyal executed his constitutional duty of inaugurating the State Assembly passed, as head of the state.

On May 11, 1974, the Assembly passed the resolution offering formal vote of thanks to the Maharaja and in another resolution reaffirmed its faith in the principles, purposes an provisions of the 8th May, 1973 agreement signed by the Chogyal, Government of India and the political parties of the state.

However, the political organisations seething with rage against the Ruling junta for such a long period could not be satisfied by mere resolution. They desired some effective steps and concrete outcome in the desired direction. They were impatient to have "people's rule" in the statement and a "democratic constitution" to govern the people.

Thus the Government of India sent G. R. Rajagopalan a constitutional expert, to Gangtok to lend a helping hand to the administration for speeding up the job. In the very first meeting of the experts with the elected representatives of the Sikkimese people, the members of the Legislative Assembly made in categorically clear that they were least satisfied with the prevailing arrangement and they wanted a Constitution where all powers are vested in the hands of the elected representatives of the people and not in the hands of Chogyal, who could be nothing more than a figure head.

For this purpose a special session of the Assembly was called on June 20, 1974 so that resolutions to desired changes could be passed. The Chogyal got unnerved who wanted to spare no effort to stall the meeting. Chogyal's private guards made a strenuous but unsuccessful attempt on problems and the ruling house there too has realised its position vis-a-vis the aspirations of the masses. On the other hand favourable reactions calve from many countries including the United Kingdom, United States of America, United Arab Republic, Union of Soviet Socialist Russia, Iran, Sri Lanka, Japan and African Countries.

Chogyal no doubt had eaten the humble pie, but the underhand support and whispering counselling he was receiving from the anti-Indian forces always spurred hire to act, react and overact. Small wonder Chogyal, even at this stage tried to internationalise the issue with the sole purpose of staging a comeback as "Divine King" of the Sikkimese. His American wife, through American and European contacts and the abetment of some of India's hostile neighbours pleaded at some fora to accord an international status to Sikkim. Though some of his well-wishers advised him to remain reticent, unruffled and composed at such a critical juncture yet as usual he behaved more as an advocate rather than a statesman. He did not want any opportunity to be missed for uttering his "grievances".

In February 1975 he was invited to the investitute ceremony of the King of Nepal. Keeping in view the adverse reaction of Nepal on the democratic set-up in Sikkim, the state Cabinet did not approve Chogyal's visit to Kathmandu. To the surprise of all, he included in his entourage only those bureaucrats who continued to be loyal to him and had been flaunting the authority of the Chief Minister. In Kathmandu, instead of taking part in the ceremony and festivities, he started meeting the foreign diplomats and dignitaries and started explaining his point of view in a manner that against the wishes of his subjects, a great injustice had been done to him. He picturised himself as a martyr, who had been espousing the cause of real democracy in Sikkim.

He further explained that democracy in Sikkim existed in name only. In a press conference he did a lot of mud-slinging over India and its "handmen" running the "so-called democracy" in Sikkim. He further stated that he would take the issue to the UNO and would take all steps to keep a separate identity of Sikkim and preserve its international status.

On his arrival back at Gangtok, Chogyal was mobbed by thousands of Sikkim Congress workers who raised slogans demanding his abdication from the throne. In the melee that resulted there, Chogyal's personal guards opened fire at the mob injuring many demonstrators, including a State legislator R. C. Pondyal forming his Cabinet. Before doing so he visited New Delhi along with all elected members of his party to thank the Government of India for taking effective steps to resolve the deadlock in a fair manner.

The Legislators were assured by New Delhi of unstinted support to the democratic government for building a strong and viable politico-economic base in the fabled Himalayan region. On July 23, 1974, chogyal Palden Thondup Namgyal as constitutional head of the state administered on oath of office and Secrecy to the five-member Cabinet, headed by Kazi Lhendup Dorji Khangsarpa, as the first democratically elected Chief Minister. No country except China, Pakistan and Nepal offered adverse comments on the initiation of a democratic political set-up in Sikkim.

China and Pakistan for obvious reasons, being then on very hostile terms with India had no other option than to condemn New Delhi, even if she had moved in a right and desired direction. The monarchy in Nepal sensed threat to its existence also and thus she too had to criticise, the rise of the democratic power in her neighbourhood. China compared the event to the "Soviet troops marching into Czechoslovakia in 1968 and labelled it" as bullying of small countries by big ones, although the consequent developments have proved that nothing of this sort had occurred.

The murmur in the neighbouring Kingdom of Nepal was understandable since the Monarchy there had been facing similar protests. As late -1989-90, Nepal was confronted with such Executive, in whom were vested the powers of the Chairman of the Assembly to finalise the Bill. The meeting was held on June 28, 1974.

The Assembly again passed the Bill unanimously and showed its determination to go ahead with the proposed progressive reforms, no matter how did the Chogyal or the Government of India reacted to it. The Government of India, on its part however, counselled the Chogyal to be wise and prudent to act in accordance with the wishes of the Sikkimese people.

Nonetheless, Chogyal was still adamant and he started interpreting the tripartite agreement in a manner which suited his self-interest. Contrary to the advice tendered to him by New Delhi he desired the political controversies to be kept alive. He hoped that the United Nations and some of the super powers would come to his rescue to save his theocratic monarchy. This way he came into conflict with the Government of India also, who again counselled him to give a fair trial to the new political arrangement.

Finding no support coming to him from any of the super powers and international fora, Chogyal accorded his consent to the Bill on July 4, 1974. While Chogyal was still nursing his hurt ego and injured pride, Kazi Lhendup Dorji, the leader of the majority party started attending to the issue of that day to bar the entry of the legislatures to the Assembly Hall.

Such a move alienated even the members of the so-called opposition. The net result was that the bill reducing Chogyal to mere figure head and handing overall powers to the elected representatives was passed unanimously. The passage of this resolution dealt a very severe blow to the Chogyal who was apprised of the reality that his writ ran no longer in the state. However, how sad it was that the Chogyal and his henchman refused to read the writings on the wall and they started organising protest demonstrations against the bill. Such a provocation was a sufficient reason for the elected representatives to organise massive protests and rallies against the palace clique in all parts of the state.

Obviously such moves and counter-moves led to direct clash between the pro-Chogyal and anti-Chogyal forces. The Chogyal lost his nerves, got panicky and in haste proceeded to New Delhi on an unscheduled visit without according his consent to the controversial bill.

The May 1973 agreement had provided that in case of "any difference of opinion, between the Chief Executive and the Chogyal, it shall be referred to the Political Officer in Sikkim who shall obtain the advice of the Government of India which shall be binding". When Chogyal left for New Delhi, the majority of party appealed to the Government of India to take necessary action as per the provisions of the agreement. Kazi, the leader of the majority party requested. B. S. Das, the Chief thereafter, Chogyal dragged the political battle to the legal arena. He sought an induction on the issue of electing two members to the Indian Parliament by the State Assembly and the resolution upholding the Sikkim Act 1974 as the highest law of the land and further passed that the validity of the Act could not be challenged in any court of law.

On the other hand even in the court Chogyal lost his case. He forgot that "revolutionary political changes evolve their own constitutionality." In a way the Chogyal proved a worst enemy of himself. Barring a handful of his henchmen who kept revolving around him within the palace, Chogyal completely lost the sympathies of all legislators, people of Sikkim and even the majority of the Sikkimese employees. As a reaction to his revengeful activities the legislative assembly also started moving quite swiftly. In a specially-convened session of the State Assembly on April 10, 1975 a resolution was passed to abolish the institution of Chogyal in Sikkim.

The State was henceforth declared as an integral constituent unit of the Indian Union. To strengthen their case, the state-government conducted a referendum on the issue just four days after over whelming majority of the people (more than 97%) supported the resolution under reference. The events thus proved that it was Chogyal himself who axed his own foot.

The entire Cabinet visited New Delhi to apprise the Government of India of the latest developments. The delegation also appealed and urged upon New Delhi for accepting the offer of the Sikkimese people extended through their elected representatives for the merger of Sikkim as a full fledged State in the Union of India. The delegation returned to Gangtok only when assured by the Prime insider of India in unequivocal terms that the wishes of the Sikkimese people shall certainly be honoured.

The Parliament of India resolved the thirty-eighth amendment of the Indian Constitution on April 26, 1975 and integrated Sikkim as then twenty-second state in the Union of states and Union Territories of India. The related act stipulated a separate Governor, separate High Court, a State Legislative (unicameral) assembly and a Council of Minister headed by a duly elected Chief Minister.

However, in view of the strategic location of the state, some special powers were extended to the Governor of Sikkim. The President of India accorded his assent to the Bill on May 15, 1975. On the same day, B. B. Lal who had till then been functioning as Chief-Executive, was elevated as Governor of Sikkim. Rajinder Sachar a Delhi High Court judge was sent as the first Chief justice of the newly-created High Court of Sikkim at Gangtok. Morarji Desai, who became the Prime Minister of India in 1977, thought that although the merger of Sikkim with India had become complete, final and irrevocable yet it had been done in an undesirable way.

In the year 1977, when there blew a Janata wave in the country and particularly Northern India, Kazi Lhendup Dorji simply walked out of the Congress fold along with all his party colleagues and joined the Janata Party. Much water has flown since then in

Sikkim also. It once again showed a favour for the Congress but in the elections conducted in 1990 it is the Sikkim Sangram Parishad which has stolen march over other parties.

Even in the 1985 elections this political party was at the helm of affairs in the state. The reins of administration have now been in the hands of a very dynamic, progressive and forward looking man Nar Bahadur Bhandari, who adorns the office of the Chief Minister in Sikkim.

Further Developments

An impressive feature of the Sikkimese economy has been the overwhelming share accorded to developmental activities in the state's overall expenditure, especially in the last decade. The share has touched a high of 80 per cent. In Nagaland, during the same period, this proportion never exceeded 65 per cent. Within the developmental expenditure also, the share of social services went up sharply from about 30 per cent in 1983-84 to 45 per cent in 1992-93.

In a State where cultivable land is hardly 16 per cent and where agriculture has been the mainstay of 80 per cent of the population, the need for land reform measures is obvious. The land question has remained potentially explosive. The highly skewed character of land distribution, in favour of certain echelons of the tribals, has spelt an increasing alienation of others.

However, no political party seems to be guided by a long-term development strategy. In this crucial respect, all the parties seem to be incoherent and contradictory. A glaring example is the fact that no one has even put a word on the critical issue of resource mobilisation in an economy always starved of resources. No one has put forward a sound agenda for employment generation in the public and private sectors. No one even provides an inkling of what is going on in the national economy in their manifestos, let along ideas for Sikkim's coordination with it. The parties take scant note of the fact that planned development has had its own adverse fallout in Sikkim. As in many other parts of the country, managers of the economy have been primarily bureaucrats and not the polished professionals. This has made the growth prospects not only limited but also lopsided. The need for professional managers becomes more striking and imperative in a State like Sikkim for its narrow manoeuvrability. It cannot afford to try and always fail.

The development debate in Sikkim should first address itself to the question of who should manage the economy, given the experience and perspective of the last 45 years. The answer can lie in the creation of a State-level planning authority.

Significant Events

Talking to newsmen at New Delhi on July 9, 1974, Kazi Lhendup Dorji asserted, *inter alia*, that his team consisting of all the thirty-two elected members would seek protection from the Government of India for their nascent democracy. Narrating Sikkim's special relationship with India he stated, "We intend to make it closer in the interests of our people to safeguard our democracy and further our progress. He declared, "Our destiny is safe with India."

According to him, long-term interest set for Sikkim has been "the establishment of a fully responsible government of Sikkim with a more democratic Constitution, the guarantee of fundamental rights, the rule of law, an independent judiciary and greater legislative and executive powers for the elected representatives of the people.

The historic Government of Sikkim Act, 1974, consequential to the Tripartite Agreement of May 8, 19732 provided a constitutional framework within which a democratically elected government is to function. In a nation's life evolution of constitutional government is always a long and tortuous process. Sikkim is not an exception.

Constitutional Development

Proclamation of 1953: A Dyarchy: Though monarch obtained in Sikkim, the ruler shared powers with popularly elected Sikkim Council under Sikkim's Constitution under the Maharaja's Proclamation of 1953 and its subsequent amendments. Under the Constitution, the executive structure of the state had been built up on the basis of two-fold considerations: partial devolution of authority upon the popular representative inexperience of the leaders owing to political backwardness of the people. Accordingly, by the device of dyarchy, the functions of the government were divided into two groups, viz., reserved and transferred.

Section 14 enumerated the reserved subjects consisting of eight items, including external affairs, home and police and finance. The list of transferred subjects included, *inter alia*, education, public health, excise, press and publicity and public works, transport, bazar and forests under Section 21.

Obviously, the guiding principle of this division was that within the transferred list those departments had been included which required local knowledge and social services, those in which mistakes, if any, would not be beyond the scope of remedy. Departments which were primarily concerned with law and order, and land revenue had been kept within the fold of the reserved list. Transferred subjects were administered by the elected members of the Executive Council individually responsible to the Sikkim Council while reserved subjects were under the supervision of the Secretaries responsible to the Maharaja.

Section 2 provided for "a State Council for the state of Sikkim." Section 3 stated the composition of the 24-member Council, of which 6 members were to be nominated by the Maharaja. Out of 18 elective seats 14 were distributed among the principal communities of Sikkim, namely, the Lepcha-Bhutias and the Nepalese. Amity and Harmony between them remained the only guarantee of peace and progress of the state. A note appended to the proclamation of 1958, had stated:

"... it is the desire of His Highness that the government should be carried on equally by the two major groups of Bhutia-Lepchas and Nepalese respectively without the one community imposing itself or encroaching upon the other. It is to this end that His Highness has endeavoured always to direct his government, so that with a Constitution based on equality and justice, the communities should be in harmony with each other and that such harmony may be always maintained for the good of all his people."

The General and the Sangha constituencies used to elect 3 members and one respectively. The Council thus constituted was empowered "to enact laws for the peace, order and government" under Section 13. According to Section 16, the Council was empowered to pass budget in every financial year "provided always that the event of any demand in the budget estimates being rejected by the State Council the Maharaja shall have the power to certify it and thereupon such demand shall become part of the sanctioned estimate." Section 15 laid down that matter relating to the Maharaja and the members of the ruling family, external relations of the state, including relations with India, the appointment of Dewan, etc., would not come within the purview of its discussion. The election was held in early part of 1973 to Sikkim Council; but see thing discontent among the communities centering on it came to the surface.

Extension of Constitutional Democracy

After a ten-day orgy of riot, arson and looting in the Himalayan Kingdom of Sikkim, which could, according to Crown Prince Tenzing, erupted into bloody civil war but for the Indian army's timely intervention at his father's request, a tripartite agreement (popularly known as the Gangtok Agreement) was signed on May 8, 1973. The Agreement provided for a future constitutional framework with a view to ushering in political development.

Accordingly, the Government of Sikkim Act, 1974, has been passed. Under Article 2 of Part II of the Agreement provision was made for an Assembly in Sikkim, popularly elected after every four years: Article 3(1) laid down that the Assembly "shall have power to propose laws and adopt resolutions for the welfare of the people of Sikkim" on matters relating to education, public health, excise, press and publicity, transport, bazar, forests, public works, agriculture, food supplies, economic and social planning (including state enterprises), home and establishment, finance and land revenue. The cumulative effect of these provisions is a significant advancement in the field of self-government.

The provision "the Assembly shall have power to propose laws and adopt resolutions for the welfare of the people of Sikkim" clearly signifies wider powers the under section 13 of the Proclamation of 1953 empowering the Council to enact laws relating to "peace, order and good government." And the number of subjects on which the Assembly is now competent to enact laws has increased from eight to fourteen. Significantly three subjects;

namely, home and establishment, finance and land revenue which were "reserved" earlier have been shifted to the "transferred" list.

During the working of the government under the earlier Constitution it might have been felt that no experimentation of self-government could be possible without these vital departments. Similar experience had been shared by the responsible government partial as it was, under the Government of India Act, 1919, The Sikkim Congress had been critical in the past regarding the handling of economic and financial matters of the state. As a bold step, in keeping with its aspirations, these subjects have been transferred to the popular ministry. So far as social and economic planning is concerned, it has added significance for Sikkim.

Till recently, progress reports on the implementation for the plan used to be drawn up every six months by the financial adviser who was an Indian officer on deputation. "Criticism of the administration is, in fact, criticism of along chain of senior Indian civil servants who now hold high office at home." A hiatus of opinion existed between the Government of India and the Chogyal on the technique of planning; the former wanted to stress upon "horizontal growth" while the latter was keen on "self-generating economy'" based on more revenue-earning schemes.

No wonder, such a situation impeded the economic progress of the state for long. The present popular set-up, it is claimed, would enable Sikkim to travel along the path of economic prosperity under the aegis of the Planning Commission of India. The reserved subjects remain outside the purview of the Sikkim Assembly. These are:

- the Chogyal and the members of the ruling family;
- any matter pending before the court of law;
- the appointment of the Chief Executive and the members of the judiciary; and
- any matter relating to the responsibilities of the Government of India under any other agreement between Sikkim and India.

Thus reserved subjects, which were eight under the previous Constitution have been reduced to three in the Government of Sikkim Act, 1974. An analysis reveals that there exist two distinct reserved spheres: that of the Maharaja or the Chogyal and that of the protecting state, *i.e.*, India. In the erstwhile set-up the former was predominant both in dimension and degree; but this has been reversed in the extant Act.

The Act constitutes an epoch-making event reducing the monarch to a constitutional ruler. Article 6 of the Tripartite Agreement of May 8, 1973, provided, "The Chogyal shall perform the functions of high office in accordance with the Constitution of Sikkim as set out in this Agreement." Under the Constitution it is laid down that "the Chogyal shall take precedence over other persons in Sikkim and shall continue to enjoy the position of honour and other personal privileges as may be benefiting his office."

Further, it has been stated: "all executive actions of the Government of Sikkim would be expressed to have been taken in the name of the Chogyal." The intent of these provisions is undoubtedly to establish the Chogyal as a constitutional ruler denuding him of real powers as monarch although Article 10 entitles him to exercise real powers over palace administration and the Sikkim guards only. But it was no easy task to accomplish. The Chogyal as the constitutional ruler was reluctant to accept the Government of Sikkim Bill, 1974, which, *inter alia*, heralds such drastic changes. And it was only after "further consideration" that he gave his assent to it. On his approval, the first written Constitution providing for a responsible popular government came into force in Sikkim on July 4, 1974.

Welcoming it Mr. Kewal Singh, Indian Foreign Secretary observed, "We are glad that as a result of the advice given to him (the Chogyal) he has now agreed to work in the spirit of the new situation." Understandably without enlisting cooperation between the elected representatives and the Chogyal, popular democratic system cannot survive.

Executive Council

The Executive Council envisaged under Section 20 of the 1953 Act was responsible to the Sikkim Council. Section 21 stated that Councillors were individually responsible to the Council. All of them were chosen by the Maharaja who had been armed with the power to "veto any decision made by the Executive Council and substitute his own decision therefore" under Section 26. So far as the choice of the Councillors was concerned, it did not confine to any single party. To quote the Chogyal, "We have managed quite well with coalition governments."

Thus, he had been successful in disarraying the opposition and maintaining harmonious equation between the country's original Bhutia-Lepcha community and the overwhelming majority of the Nepalese immigrants. To a careful observer, it would be evident that the affiliations were strictly observed on the eve of elections only to vanish with the publication of election results. Those who were nominated to the Executive Council automatically set together on the treasury benches while their party colleagues who did not hold offices became the opposition.

It was thus a peculiar form of executive based on national consensus. MacIver characterised the built-in structure of government in Sikkim as a Cinciliar Oligarchy. But almost all the parties pleaded for the establishment of a fully responsible popular government.

The tripartite agreement did provide for the executive council but did not clarify the mist whether it would be an advisory body or a full-fledged Cabinet with its legislative trappings, namely, the majority rule, and legislative responsibility. But the elections were fought for full responsible government by all the parties including the Sikkim Congress. The Act of 1974 provides for the Council of Ministers "to aid and advise" the Chogyal.

The Chief Minister and other ministers are to be appointed by the Chogyal on the advice of the Chief Executive who would be nominated by the Government of India. In keeping with this provision all the ministers including the Chief Minister have been appointed from the Sikkim. Congress which has got majority in the Sikkim Assembly. It would have had all the characteristics of the Cabinet system had the Chief Executive not been fitted into it.

Officers of the Executive

The institution of the Chief Executive was an interesting feature of the Executive Council under the previous constitution also. As stipulated in India-Sikkim Agreement, "the Government of India may require the Maharaja of Sikkim to appoint as Dewan (Sidlon) an officer nominated by the Government of India for such periods as may, after consultation with the Maharaja, be considered necessary." Again, under the provision of Section 24 he was the President of the executive council. Even though other councillors were to retire from office at the commencement of a new council, the Dewan used to continue in his office.

As President of the Cabinet his functions as stipulated in the tripartite agreement, fall into categories: firstly, he has to act in consultation with the respective minister-in-charge of the department; secondly, he acts as a link between the Cabinet and the Chogyal; he has to obtain prior approval of every administrative act. In addition, he is required to discharge "special responsibility" relating to proper implementation of constitutional and administrative changes, smooth running of administration, enjoyment of the basic rights by the people, etc...

For the discharge of these duties he shall be advised by the Political Officer and ultimately by the Government of India. Any case of dispute, arising out of the implementation any of the aforesaid matters between him and the Chogyal, shall be referred to the Political Officer also shall resolve and obtain the advice of the Government of India, if necessary. Excepting the "special responsibilities" the Sidlon or the Chief Executive used to enjoy almost identical powers under the previous constitutional framework. Besides positively laying down his powers and functions, under the present set-up, attempts have been made to remove certain vagueness that persisted with his office.

The earlier arrangement, because of its laconic character, generated some sort of an estrangement between the Chogyal and the Government of India. After the departure of I. S. Chopra from Gangtok the Chogyal's reluctance to fill the vacancy was a sharp pointer to this fact. At that time the question arose if the Chogyal was obliged to have a Sidlon: if so, is there any time-limit for fulfilling the obligation? Should the incumbent be an Indian?

Although office of the Chief Executive is derived from the Constitution, the Act leaves such questions unanswered. This flexibility would be desirable if rational decisions can periodically be taken on realistic assessment of conditions. When mistrust clouds the vision these provisions may lead to interminable controversy and escalation of tension in the present system.

Electoral System

In terms of the Tripartite Agreement of May 8, 1973, the Sikkim Assembly is to be elected for the first time on the principle of universal adult suffrage. It has also been incorporated in the Constitution as detailed in the Act of 1974. But, there is an apparent contradiction between "equitable representation of all sections of the people on the principle of one man one vote" and the desired goal that "no single section of the population acquires a dominating position due mainly to its ethnic origin" in the context of Nepalese majority.

The last movement's explosive temper does not warrant the suggestion for reserved seats or weightage for Bhutia-Lepchas-Sikkim's original but positively inarticulate inhabitants. The scope of working out checks and balances in a country where parliamentarism has not struck root is irrelevant. Probably, it is the sore point with the communities inhabiting Sikkim. That explains the proclamation of December 21, 1966 (abrogated by tripartite agreement) providing for multiple voting system. It is said to be the world's most complicated electoral system.

According to it, a successful candidate must not only secure a majority of votes from his community but at least 15 per cent votes from others or he must poll votes 15 per cent more than that of his nearest rival. In fact, it reflected durbar's anxiety for promoting communal integration. But it failed to create symphony of communal amity concord, devoid of which no nation can look forward to prosperous future. If administrative wisdom can evolve an electoral system on the basis of communal parity, peace is sure to dawn upon the nascent democracy in Sikkim.

The Constitution as set out in the Government of Sikkim Act, 1974, provides for a democratic set-up modelled after Indian democracy; it unfolds panorama of constitutionalism largely under Indian 'protection'. Till the other day, autonomy that prevailed centred on the monarch with "limited" participation of the masses.

The new order combines the widest possible participation of the masses with the "functional" role of the Chogyal as the titular head. The office of the Chief Executive, as it is engrafted in the system, has wider ramifications sharpening the criticisms from various quarters. As the allegation runs, till recently there had been a duet between the monarch and the Indian Government, now the Sikkim Congress had replaced the monarch to be' its partner.

Justifying India's "association" with the new order in Sikkim, Swaran Singh, the then Minister of External Affairs, stated in the Rajya Sabha that it would strengthen India's "endeavour to create conditions in which democratic forces operate." This refers to India's relations with Sikkim for ensuring the latter's steady political development.

Political Development

Early Vicissitudes: Bounded by four lands, namely, Nepal, Bhutan, Tibet and India, Sikkim had to come in contact with all of them in the course of its history. Its social and cultural life at first bore the predominant influence of Tibet though later its contacts with the other three also made a considerable impression upon the way of life of the Sikkimese population.

We should remember that before India came in a big way into the picture of Sikkim's relations with neighbours, the others were already there. Howsoever, we might desire, we cannot wish away the influences Sikkim absorbed from the other neighbours. In fact, Indo-Sikkimese relations suffer till this day from constraints such influences have left on the situation.

Sikkim's political history can be authentically traced since 1641 AD when Penchu Namgyal, the founder of the existing ruling dynasty, was enthroned under the blessings of three Lamas of Tibet. In 1706, the Bhutanese attacked and overpowered Sikkim but Tibet helped the then ruler of Sikkim Chador Namgyal, against the Bhutanese menace. Not so happy was Sikkim's fortune when next came an invasion from Nepal. China took interest on this occasion. But, ultimately under Chinese grace both Nepal and Tibet gained territories which formerly belonged to Sikkim. These vicissitudes since 1641 do not allow us, however, to presume the sufferance of sovereignty of Sikkim. The position began to change as soon as this Himalayan State had to run into intercourse with the British power operating in India through the East India Company.

Treaty of Titulia

Sikkim attracted notice from the British East India Company governing India in the beginning of the last century. The Company considered it important to have an easy passage for its officers and traders through the tracts and passes of Sikkim to have direct trade links with Tibet and also to have a firm foothold for its armies in Sikkim so as to strengthen its combating capacity vis-a-vis Nepal and Bhutan.

The Company's earliest endeavours for these objectives came in the form of friendly gestures towards the Rajah of Sikkim as early as 1814. These gestures produced the first Indo-Sikkim Treaty of Titulia in 1817. The Governor-General of India, on behalf of the East India Company, and the Rajah, on behalf of Sikkim, agreed under this treaty to have some part of Nepalese territory (ceded to the Company under the 1814 Treaty of Segaulee) placed under the peaceful possession of the Rajah of Sikkim. The considerations for this gift to Sikkim were among others, the undertakings:

- that Sikkim would submit all its quarrels with other states to the arbitration of the British Governments and would "abide by the decision of the British Government;" and

- that the Rajah would afford protection to merchants and traders from the Company's provinces and would not levy duties on the transit of merchandise beyond the established custom.

Though this treaty cannot be interpreted to have taken away the attributes of sovereignty of Sikkim, it must not be missed that what the Rajah gained through a physical extension of his territory had to be paid for by a delusion of the real powers over his own State.

Way to the Treaty of Tumloong: The next treaty between India and Sikkim was signed on March 28, 1861. But in the intervening period Indo-Sikkimese relations did not remain where they were in 1817.

During this period, the Company and its zealous officers used in relation to Sikkim all kinds of tactics which characterised the operations of the Company in all territories wherever it set its foot as a trader and ultimately became a political sovereign. In regard to the taking away of Darjeeling from Sikkim into the Company's possession and in the matter of paying compensation therefore these tactics showed themselves in the most deplorable dimensions.

Unhappy relations ensued, the cunning and unfair treatment meted out to the Rajah from the East India Company's officers in the Government of India ever since 1835 and tension points became more numerous in the decades following until in November 1860 a small British force took entry into the territory of the Rajah and involved the Company in a battle inside Sikkim. In this battle, the Company's force had ultimately to retreat.

This was avenged by the Company in February-March, 1861 by an armed expedition into Sikkim which the Rajah could not withstand at all. From this reinvigorated position of strength on behalf of the Governor-General in Council of India an envoy and Special Commissioner Mr. Ashley Eden made the Treaty of Tumloong with Sekeong Kuzoo, the Maharajah of Sikkim in 1861.

Thus, very soon after the Crown assumed direct power of governance in India replacing the East India Company, Indo-Sikkimese relations entered a new phase when the British were no longer ready to confine their objectives in Sikkim within the bargains of trade. They displayed both sword and flag as the emblems for Sikkim to respect.

Treaty of Tumloong

While generally confirming the assurances Sikkim had given to the Company in 1817, this new treaty incorporated a few important undertakings on Sikkim's part. These were:

- that British Government could track down into Sikkim territory for any criminals, defaulters or other delinquents, if the Sikkim Government delayed in delivering up such persons on demand;
- that ex-Dewan Namguay or his blood relations would not be allowed to set foot in Sikkim nor to hold office under the Maharajah or his family;

- that British Government would be allowed and assisted by Sikkim Government if the former decides to construct roads inside Sikkim or to make topographical or geological survey there;

- that Sikkim Government would not cede or lease any part of its territory nor allow the armed forces of any other country to pass through Sikkim without the approval of the British Government; and

- that the Maharajah would transfer the seat of his Government from Tibet to Sikkim, stay in Sikkim for nine months in a year and also accredit a vakil of his Government to reside permanently at Darjeeling which "became the observation post of the British in the Himalayas."

Even though the form of the Tumloong treaty may appear to be the result of two willing sovereign states, the contents are unmistakably the evidence of both humiliation and subjugation that Sikkim suffered at the hands of the other partner to the treaty. Mr. Ashley Eden, who signed this treaty on behalf of the British Government in India wrote to the Government of Bengal on April, 8, 1861, to explain why it was considered not advisable to annex Sikkim: "Nepal is tributary to China, Tibet is a tributary to China, and Sikkim and Bhutan are tributaries to Tibet and therefore, secondarily to China." Apart from the question of injuring Chinese susceptibilities, the British realised the importance of maintaining Sikkim as a buffer state between Nepal and Bhutan and instructed accordingly the expeditionary force entering Sikkim in December 1860. This explains why Sikkim was not reduced immediately to a part of the British Empire.

Protectorate State

Relations between the Governments of Sikkim and India continued to be governed by the Treaty of 1861 while further erosion occurred to the inherent authority of the Government of Sikkim to administer its territories freely on its own. Transactions of trade and other questions increasingly furnished proofs of Sikkim's subordination to the Government of India.

The British authorities in India were ultimately led to presume that "Sikkim is a part of the Indian Empire." The Government of India no longer deemed it necessary to have an agreement with Sikkim on the question of its status and relationship with India. In fact, this relationship was described for the first time as that of a protectorate in a Convention between Great Britain and China concluded on March 7, 1890 concerning Sikkim and Tibet which were not parties at all to this Convention.

Convention Stated in Article II

"It is admitted that the British Government whose protectorate over the Sikkim State is hereby recognised, has direct and exclusive control over the internal administration and foreign relations of that State and except through the permission of the British Government, neither the ruler of the state nor any of its officers shall have official relations of any kind, formal or informal with any other country."

This Convention also delineated the boundary of Sikkim and Tibet. Afterwards till India was under British rule, internal administration of Sikkim was interfered with by the Government of India on its own evaluation of necessity and to any extent it deemed fit. Only the considerations which weighed against formally annexing this small Himalayan State in the middle of the 19th century probably stood held good and Sikkim was allowed all the years following to retain its distinct identity under the long line of hereditary rule that started in 1641.

Whenever, however, any Maharajah showed tendencies of which the Government of India did not approve, the latter took quick actions either to make him refrain from showing such tendencies or to replace him with another member of the royal family. Maharajah Tashi Namgyal who became the ruler of Sikkim in 1914 continued to hold the royal seat till his death in 1963. His long rule till the end of British rule in India was marked by good relations between himself and the Indian Empire of Great British. Being fully confident that under his rule, British interests would not come to mischief in any way, the Sikkim Government's sphere of autonomous administration was enlarged.

It is important to note that the British Government as the paramount power studiously followed till 1935 a policy of distinguishing Sikkim from about 560 princely states of India. Though the instruments by which British power operated its paramountcy over these states were not quite dissimilar, with regard to Sikkim the British Government did not pose or recognise the problem of fitting it into one general scheme of constitutional development in British India, as was done with regard to the Princely states.

The political platforms of the people of British India or the people of Sikkim too did not pose any such problem. As early as in 1921, a Chamber of Princes was established with membership offered to the Indian Princely states. No such offer was, however, extended to Sikkim.

As for why this difference was maintained by the British rulers in India we may make a pertinent conjecture on the basis of the following official view expressed in the Report of the Indian State Committee, 1928-29, on the question of sovereignty of the Indian states:

"It is not in accordance with historical fact that when the Indian states came into contact with the British power they were independent, each possessed of full sovereignty and of a status which a modern international lawyer would hold to be governed by the rules of international law. In fact, none of the states ever held international status. Nearly all of them were subordinate or tributary to the Moghul Empire, the Mahratta supremacy or the Sikh Kingdom and dependent on them.

Some were rescued, others were created by the British." Obviously, Sikkim does not fall in this category. Sikkim held an international status, or at least, it was tributary to other powers which British power could not reduce to its formal or informal subjection.

Had the British authorities been consistent, they would have continued to respect this difference to the end of their rule in India. But to an imperial ruler virtues like consistency in respect of equality and sovereignty of other nations are frequent casualties. It was not otherwise when under the Government of India Act, 1935, one seat was allotted to Sikkim in the proposed second chamber of the federal legislature.

It was the obvious intention of the British Government to integrate Sikkim along with the princely states of India into one federal framework. The federal part of the Government of India Act, 1935, was still born because certain conditions stipulated in the Act had not been fulfilled. That is why the attempt of the British authorities to effect formal annexation of Sikkim and to integrate it into the Indian Empire of Great Britain proved an abortive exercise.

Hence, incidentally, Sikkim continued to be a protectorate of British India till the British withdrew from India. The interests of the Indian Government in Sikkim were looked after through a Political Officer posted at Gangtok to act under the External Affairs Department of the Government of India. Before we proceed further to recount the evolution of Indo-Sikkimese relations, it is necessary to make out the substance of the protectorate status in international and domestic law. This cannot be done without remembering the origin of this status for certain nationalities. An observation made in a Soviet book deserves quotation:

> "International protectorate is a form of dependence by which one state, on the basis of a treaty concluded with another, hands over the management of its foreign affairs and usually receives an advisor (Resident) to deal with internal affairs. A protectorate agreement is an unequal treaty, concluded in violation of the rights of self-determination. It is used by the ruling class of the protector power to intensify the exploitation of the protectorate population."

The book further says, "Despite the incompatibility of the protectorate system with the UN Charter in which the principles of equality and self-determination are recognised in terms of international law, imperialist member states still enforce protectorate over a number of dependent countries..."

It must be admitted that Sikkim's position as a protectorate in relation to British India very well conforms to the above observations made in general about protectorates in Asia and Africa under European powers.

Not very different are the observations of British experts on international law. While discussing, "Treaty Relations of British Overseas Territories" J. E. S. Fawcett made certain observations regarding the status of a protectorate under international law. He accepted that the protectorates of the United Kingdom in Asia and Africa were neither British possessions nor part of the British dominions but foreign territories. It was held that the local rulers handed over responsibilities for the conduct of their external relations to the Crown.

Under British constitutional practice, the relations of the UK with such protectorates were regarded as "a source rather than a derivative of international law." Fawcett discards the view that such relations are determined by international law. He emphasises that the territory of protectorate is not foreign in the sense that it can be annexed at any time by the Crown. Actually Kenya and Southern Rhodesia, formerly protectorates, were annexed in 1920 and 1923 respectively. Fawcett concludes, ". . . that the United Kingdom and its overseas territories (which among others include protectorates) form a system which is governed in the relation between its parts by domestic law, and which constitute in international law a unitary state of which the Crown of the United Kingdom is the representative head."

From these observations of both antagonists and protagonists of imperialism we may conclude that the protectorate status of a state is the product of imperial practice and the rules governing the relations between the protecting state and its protectorates have their legal sanction in that practice.

Relations with Free India

India's independence after division of the country into India and Pakistan made the question of state succession complicated. Pandit Jawaharlal Nehru, however, asserted. ". . . both from a practical and a legal point of view, India as an entity continued to exist, that certain provinces and parts of certain provinces now sought to secede. . . seceding areas were free to have any relation which they liked with foreign powers. . ." This view was ultimately accepted by the United Nations Organisation in accepting the automatic membership of India after her independence. Hence, it could be presumed that India succeeded also to the British Indian relations with Sikkim after August 1947. However, to remove all confusions in this regard India and Sikkim entered into a standstill agreement in 1947 to retain their respective rights and obligations, which the British rulers had evolved earlier through treaties and practice.

This was not a happy position for India. She herself had suffered the curses of imperial domination for too long a period and had to sharpen all her material, intellectual and moral arsenals to fight its oppressions. The leaders of this struggle had to take avowed stands of disowning the inheritance of imperialist privileges of any sort in their relation with any other people. Jawaharlal Nehru referred to the common cause of India with other countries of Asia in the First Asian Relations Conference in March-April 1947.

In his inaugural address he said, "The countries of Asia can no longer be used as pawns by others; they are bound to have their own policies in world affairs.' It is in this tenor that Article 51 of the Constitution of India also directed the state to endeavour to "maintain just and honourable relations between nations."

Hence, the framers of the Constitution found no method consistent with its ideological postures to provide in itself a framework within which Indo-Sikkimese relations, as they were, could be fitted. To suggest that Article 1(3)(c) providing for the acquisition of territories was incorporated with an eye on Sikkim would be a gross over-statement. This clause was a provision for contingencies in general and perhaps more relevant to the possibility of Princely states of India (not Sikkim) joining the Indian Union in future.

It may be noted that the Sikkim State Congress petitioned to the Maharajah of Sikkim as early as in December 1947, among other demands of democratisation, for immediate accession to India. This demand was countered by the Sikkim National Party in a resolution adopted on April 30, 1948. This resolution urged Sikkim under no circumstances to accede to the dominion of India.

When, however, the former party surrounded, the palace of the Maharajah to press for the acceptance of its demands on May 1, 1949, the Indian army came to the protection of the Maharajah. From this, it may be understood what a quandary the Government of India was in.

Gangtok Treaty of 1950

On December 5, 1950 came the India-Sikkim Treaty of Friendship signed at Gangtok. The first article of this treaty cancels formally all previous treaties between the British Government and Sikkim which were in force before that date. This suggests that by the standstill treaty of 1947 the legacy of British imperialism was continued but the treaty of 1950 sought to undo that legacy.

The treaty of 1950 made a few gestures to place the Governments of Sikkim and India on an equal footing as is common among two sovereign and equal states agreeing for mutual benefit. Quite unlike the British Indian treaties with Sikkim, this treaty placed equal obligations on the two governments to seize and deliver up fugitive offenders from the territories of each other. It placed Indian nationals within Sikkim and the subjects of Sikkim within India under an equal obligation to be governed by the laws of the country in which they remain.

Indian nationals and Sikkimese subjects were equally allowed rights to carry on trade and commerce and to acquire, hold and dispose of movable and immovable property in each other's territories. The two governments agreed equally not to levy import duty on goods brought from each other's territories. Finally, the treaty mentioned expressly that the Government of India had in mind the friendly relations existing between Sikkim and India and wanted to strengthen them further.

While noting this marked improvement in the friendly attitude of India towards Sikkim in this treaty, it must be admitted that India was unable to evolve a new mechanism or a fundamentally new legal framework so that Indo-Sikkimese relations could grow completely breaking away from the legacy of the past. Article II of this treaty affirmed the continuance of Sikkim as a protectorate of India. India undertook the responsibility of Sikkim's defence, territorial integrity, and external relations whether political, economic or financial. These responsibilities were naturally accompanied by certain rights for India in the Treaty.

These included: the right to initiate measures considered necessary inside or outside Sikkim for its defence, stationing of troops in Sikkim, the exclusive rights of constructing, maintaining and regulating the use of railways, aerodromes, navigation facilities, posts, telegraphs, telephones and wireless installations in Sikkim, the rights of constructing in Sikkim roads of strategic importance and for improving communications with other adjoining countries and the right to appoint a representative to reside in Sikkim. Correspondingly, Sikkim was prohibited by this treaty to import arms, ammunitions and military stores, etc. without previous consent of the Government of India to have any dealings with any foreign power; to construct railways, aerodromes, etc. without the consent of India. Finally, in Article XII, it was provided that in all disputes about the interpretation of this treaty the decisions of the Chief Justice of India should be final. This shows that India's experiment of friendship with Sikkim did not find a suitable model to work upon. The model used still smacked of the legacy of the past.

This treaty mentioned Sikkim's "autonomy in regard to its internal affairs" subject to the provisions of the treaty (Art. II) and also India's desire to assist Sikkim in its "development and good administration." The treaty was, however, conspicuously silent on Sikkim's prospect of attaining self-government or democracy. This is particularly striking because the Indian people had to pay in blood for telling the British rulers that good government was no substitute for self-government.

Redefinition of Indo-Sikkimese Relations

The tripartite agreement of May 1973 coming in the wake of rocking convulsions in Sikkim's political life, was a new experiment to make amends for the lacuance of the Gangtok treaty. The demands of politicised sections for a democratic polity could no longer be ignored. So far as India is concerned, the agreement in no way diminished her control-the Assembly and the Council of Ministers as the two institutions of arch importance for newly emerging democracy remained under India's control.

At the same time, the emerging political forces, particularly the members of the newly elected Assembly expressed their eagerness to have their representation in Indian Parliament. All this enabled the Government of India to find a device for affording a place to Sikkim under the Constitution of India.

To suppose that increasing association of Sikkim with India has little or no odds to overcome might, however, be a one-sided and short-sighted appraisal. The Chogyal's assertion of rights and privileges against the wishes of the Assembly and the loyalties of some sections of the people to the palace are odds obviously directed against development of democratic institutions in Sikkim. But opposition to the roles assigned to the Indian Political Officer and the Chief Executive nominated by the Government of India is not apparently incompatible with democratic development but directed primarily against the control India has had over Sikkim all these years.

The policies and actions of the Government of India in this context might be interpreted to mean that India has no objection to development along democratic lines implying the reduction of the Chogyal's office to a non-entity provided the people of Sikkim so demand, and India has no objection either to bring to an end the historical legacies of the protectorate system provided Sikkim agrees progressively to be integrated with India.

Though the Thirty-sixth Amendment to the Constitution of India may be meaningful in this context, it cannot be regarded as anything better than a make-shift arrangement in the absence of a clearer objective. In spite of the small size of Sikkim's territory and population, a careful approach is necessary on India's part in view of the historical context and Sikkim's peculiar geo-political significance. The success of Indian policies will not depend on the legality of Indian actions because legality in this context being the product of imperial practice may not command the respect of all who matter. Success will squarely depend on how far all important sections of the Sikkimese population appreciate the compatibility of their democratic aspirations with Sikkim's abiding association with India.

Total Merger

The situation in Sikkim at the time of Nehru was different. The proposal about merging Sikkim with India was turned down by him before the Chinese aggression. After the aggression the situation had changed. Mr. Morarji Desai expressed his personal view saying that merger of Sikkim had not been a desirable step. But this was not his view as the President of the Janata Party or as the Prime Minister. He had very much accepted the merger of Sikkim with India and had sent me as the sole representative of the Central Janata Party to give a report about which of the different factions claiming to be the Sikkim Janata Party be recognised.

The factors which lead Mrs. Gandhi to merge Sikkim with the Indian Union are various. The geo-political situation, of course, must have been in her mind but an overwhelming majority of the people of Sikkim also wanted to merge. Some leaders and may be the Chogyal had not liked the idea. He was toying with the idea of some kind of an adjustment with America which would ultimately have led to a reaction on the part of China, the next-door neighbour. So it was a prudent step to merge Sikkim with India.

The arguments used by the Chogyal were the same as those by some of the native Princes who had initially tried to remain outside India. But the pressure of the people of those States and a good sense and foresight that prevailed amongst most of the bigger Princes and with Sardar Patel's leadership the states were merged with India. Legally of course, the position of Sikkim was not exactly similar to the other 500-odd Indian native States but then even amongst the Indian States the position of everyone was not exactly the same.

It is not fair to say that the Sikkimese consider Indians outsiders. Some demonstrations at the funeral of the Chogyal were held but those were not really anti-Indian. The Chogyal had wanted to remain independent and had his personal following. The demonstrations were held by those people and not by the mass. The agitation before merger was two-fold, one for the merger with India and the other for the end of the feudal rule. But the Chogyal himself was quite popular. The main political agitation was against the Chief Minister, Kazil Lendhup Dorji. The merger of Sikkim with India has been a wise step because, otherwise, super powers and the powerful neighbour across the border would have created problems, and the security of India might have been in danger. I don't think that the Central assistance to Sikkim is extra large because many of these small States get proportionately much larger aid than the bigger ones.

The feeling that Sikkimese and Indians are different is not true. In the Northeastern Region like Nagaland, Mizoram or even Meghalaya, as a matter of fact, the population on the surface may look ethnically different from the other Indians. But then the people of Tamil Nadu look very different from the north Indians. They also have their own ethnic problems. So it is not merely a question of bringing the Sikkimese closer together. National integration implies that all sections of Indian opinion should be brought together.

We have so many languages, so many different cultures, we dress differently, our food habits are so different. It is a very peculiar situation of ours where there is a basic unity beyond tremendous diversity.

It was not fair to the Chief Minister, Mr. Bhandari, to say that he was anti-Delhi. The local leaders of many States have used anti-Delhi rhetorics. The Chief Minister of West Bengal uses much stronger anti-Delhi rhetorics when he is in his own State. But when he went to Delhi or spoke on international issues or Indo-Soviet friendship then he is a strong supporter of the Delhi line. Mr. Bhandari need to have used anti-Centre rhetorics to get more support and aid for his State. But when he belongs to the same party that is ruling at the Centre it is not possible for him to use anti-Delhi rhetorics in that sense.

The per capita aid given to Sikkim is much larger than the national average. But the aid given to Mizoram, Arunachal or Meghalaya is also much more than the national average. Even amongst the major States the Central and varies from State to State. The smaller the state the more it has to depend on Central assistance. For instance, the union territory of Delhi gets huge Central assistance which is much higher than the national average. The Central Government's per-capita expenditure on Delhi is higher than Sikkim. I am not sure that 16 per cent of Sikkim's annual budget is spent on motor vehicles. But then Sikkim is a mountainous State and many of the areas are inaccessible and it requires high-power jeeps and other vehicles to reach them.

Why should the Centre freeze its aid to a strategically important small State like Sikkim where the population has been neglected for a long time by the feudal Government. Sikkim has a large bureaucracy but a strategically important backward State like it requires the same. When its own industries start growing from the present take-off stage the amount of aid may become less, because it will develop its own resources by that time. The problem of the Sikkimese Nepalese and the interests of the Sikkimese 'Bhumiputras' are in a way similar to the problem of the 'Ahoms' in Assam. The Nepalese in Sikkim are in a majority and the Bhumiputras claim that they are the original inhabitants. There are so many States where the original inhabitants are neglected. Then the problem may come as to who are the original Indians. If that question is seriously taken up then possibly an overwhelming majority of the Indians will be called the *new-comers*.

The Nepalese speak a different dialect while the Bhumiputras speak a different one. They are ethnically different. But then to the plains people it is often difficult to distinguish them. This sort of a problem is emerging in many bigger States also. For instance, in Bihar the caste problem is there. Whether it is an ethnic or a caste issue we most often find that the root cause is economic where a particular section feels neglected. In the hills areas of Darjeeling district Gorkhas are numerous though in a minority. But in Sikkim the Nepalese are in majority so the question of the demand for Gorkhaland may not be there. I feel the Sikkimese Nepalese would not like to join a Great Gorkhaland theoretically because then they may be in larger area than they are but may loose the dominance they enjoy in Sikkim.

The Sikkimese students do come to other States for obtaining professional degrees because the facility in Sikkim is limited. The problem of Sikkim is very much an economic one. Supporting Sikkim economically will go a long way in balancing the Sikkimese psyche. The situation in Punjab was different as there was a strong movement for separation from India. The Gorkhaland movement too is one for a separate Statehood. Sikkim already is a State and the problem does not arise there.

4

Geography

On April 26, 1975 consequent upon popular demand expressed through a special referendum of the people of Sikkim the Constitution of India was amended (thirty-eighth amendment) to integrate the erstwhile Indian Protectorate as a full-fledged State of India. Prior to this merger the Union of India comprised 21 States and 9 Union Territories. Thus Sikkim became the Twenty-second state and at that time besides being the youngest state of the country Sikkim was also the smallest state. Now with Goa assuming the status of the smallest state of the Indian Union, Sikkim has stepped up by one rung with Delhi was also accorded statehood then Sikkim shall be the third smallest state of the country with first position going to Delhi.

This small state covers only 0.21 per cent of the total geographical area of the country. In area besides the state of Goa, the Union Territories of Lakshadweep, Dadra-Nagar Haveli, Daman-Diu, Pondicherry and Delhi each cover lesser area than Sikkim. However, the Union Territory of Andaman and Nicobar islands is larger in a real coverage than Sikkim.

The second smallest State of Sikkim is bounded by Nepal on the west (an independent Hindu Kingdom), Bhutan on the east and Tibet (a mighty province of China, although still claimed as a separate country by the Tibetans living in India and other foreign countries) in the north. In the south it shares its inter-state boundaries with West Bengal. Bounded by two foreign countries on two sides and one Indian Protectorate on one side, the state of Sikkim is characterised by a very high strategic value out of all proportions of its small size and relatively quiet history. On the map one finds that Bhutan and the Indian State of Sikkim share a common frontier only for a very short stretch.

Elsewhere both these political units are separated by the Chumbi valley. This valley was a part and parcel of Sikkim in the past but was later on occupied by Tibet. Obviously, after forcefully occupying Tibet, China entered this valley and thus the valley has assumed a very strategic location. After Chinese aggression on India in 1962, the valley is continuously being occupied by the Chinese forces and thus the valley has assumed a very strategic position for the two neighbouring countries.

In terms of longitude the state of Sikkim is bounded by 88° 00' 58" East and 88° 55' 25" East of longitudes (east of Greenwich) while in its latitudinal extent the state lies between 27° 04' 46" North and 28° 07' 48" North, latitudes, *i.e.,* North of equator. In its area, extent the state roughly stretches for about 112.70 kilometres in north-south direction and for about 64.0 kilometres in its east-west direction. The total geographical area of the state as per Census of India is 7906 square kilometres.

Physical Features

The "thimble sized" State of Sikkim is almost an irregular rectangle in shape. With no worth mentioning flat tract of land, Sikkim is an extremely rugged and mountainous state. The river valleys too limit themselves to the courses through which they flow with rare exceptions of tiny level patches found here or there. The streams and rivulets, in fact do not flow through generally concerned valleys but through gorgeous channels, at places resembling to mini canyons.

The territory falling within the state of Sikkim, technically speaking runs through the inner Greater Himalaya, where these mighty snow-clad mountains appear to be projecting Southward. In the words of an another Grover, "The whole Sikkimese landscape provides a sweeping panorama of mountains, sky and emerald lakes cupped in the towering folds of rock-walls." Since the Himalayan mountains today stand oil areas formerly covered by the spread of the vast Tethys Sea, there are bound to be lakes scattered over the entire length and breadth of these mountains. There are lakes dotting many places, including the Mansarovar, the Dal, the Nagina the Nainital, the Mansar, the Suinisar, the Dharmshala Dal and numerous other big and small lakes found from Kashmir to Kohima.

During the organic, *i.e.* "mountain building" process as a result of compressional forces the stratified sediments of the Tethys Sea were folded. However, the places which were least affected by the buckling up forces were not drained out and thus became reservoirs of water. They are being fed over the centuries by the snow-melt waters provided by the surrounding snowy ranges. The Green Lake found in the northwestern section of Sikkim is one instance of such lakes.

The State of Sikkim is separated from the neighbouring foreign lands, *i.e.,* Bhutan, Tibet, and Nepal by way of wall like steeply rising mountains which range in their elevation from 3,600 metres (10,000 feet) to 9,100 metres (28,000 feet) above mean sea level. It is only in the south that it has so such physiographic barrier which separates it from its sister state of West Bengal. In the words of Waddel, "It may be viewed as a stupendous stairway out of the Western Border of Tibetan Plateau by glaciers and great rivers and leading down to the Indian plains." In a way the otherwise secluded and isolated region on three sides slowly and steadily gets merged into the Indian territory.

The mighty hoary peaked Singahla range forms the international frontier between Sikkim and Nepal. This range is an offshoot of the Greater Himalaya which takes off from the Kanchenjunga massif and is crossed through the Chaibhanjan Pass (located at an elevation of 3,450 metres, i.e. 10,320 feet above the mean sea level) all the Sikkim Nepal Border on the west of the state. The northern crest of the Singalila range remains perpetually snow covered. The Singalila peak with an altitude of 3,679 metres above mean sea level is found on the tri-function of Nepal, Sikkim and the Indian State of West Bengal.

The Dongkya range is found on the eastern side and forms a section of the Indo-Tibetan Border and gradually passes southwards along the Indo-Bhutan frontier. On an average, its altitude hovers around 5,000 metres above mean sea level but its loftiest elevation culminates in a peak, located in its northern part characterised by a 7,134 metres high peak, above the mean sea level. This wall-like steep Orographic feature on the east is negotiable through the strategic passes of the Nathula (4,750 metres or 15,512 feet), Jelepla (4,450 metres or 13,254 feet) and Wangkurla (4,320 metres or 12,998 feet above mean sea level) passes.

Some other important and noteworthy passes of Sikkim towards China are the Tsohla, Thangkarla, Say Sayla and Changrala. It is interestingly to know that all along the Himalaya the suffix la refers to a pass; as for instance Shipkila on the Himachal Pradesh and Western Tibet border, the Changla and Larala on the Kashmir-Tibet border, the Molingla on the Uttar Pradesh-Tibet border and the Bomdila in Arunachal Pradesh. The Nathula and Jelepla were in news during the Chinese aggression of 1962. It was through these passes that the Chinese forces tried in vain to thrust into the Indian territory.

The northern international frontier in this section, along Tibet roughly coincides with the axis of the Central or Middle Himalaya running between the mountain peaks of Kanchenjunga (8,598 metres above sea level and the second highest peak of India and the third highest peak of the world — K2 or Austin Godwin which is 8,611 metres in elevation above mean sea level located in Jammu and Kashmir but under the illegal occupation of China is the highest mountain peak of India) and Chomolhari (7,314 metres above mean sea level) on the Tibeto-Bhutan border.

About 67 per cent of the total geographical area of Sikkim is highly rugged and lofty consisting of very high peaks and almost perpetually snow covered mountain ranges and from these snow-clad mountains take out avalanches and glaciers. Though there are numerous glaciers moving in different directions yet the Zemu and the Talung glaciers are two major glaciers of the region. Resultantly one finds many features gouged by the erosive and transportational actions of glaciers. Cols, glacial cleavages, serrated ridges, nunataks, glacial grooves, tarns, cories, roche moutonnes, etc. are some of the significant features seen in these glacial affected areas.

Many of the streams flowing through Sikkim are streams that originate from the melting snows of the glaciers. These lofty areas are without any permanent human habitation although some of the accessible parts are visited by the trans-human nomads with their yaks and sheep during the summer phase of their year round movement.

The most noteworthy and significantly magnificent group of mountain ranges in Sikkim is that group which is dominated by the Kanchenjunga, the third loftiest peak of the globe and the towering rather crowning glory of Sikkim which, as already described, attains an altitude of 8,598 metres or 28,140 feet above the mean sea level. The Kanchenjunga (a corrupted form of the local nomenclature of Khwigchcridzodnga) is still referred to as "climbed but virgin still peak." Five gigantic summits always covered with snow are termed as five treasures of the Kanchenjunga. Above the gentle mists that continue to curl and writhe over mountain ranges, the five summits can be identified distinctly.

A mountaineering expedition with the objective of scaling the third highest peak of the world reached here successfully in 1955 but spared the last couple of metres of snow untrampled in deference to the popular Sikkimese belief that the Khangchendzodnga is both a god and an abode of the god. This Britain sponsored and British expedition was headed and led by the world reputed mountaineer, hikker and trekker Charles Evan. He succeeded in putting the members of the expedition on the peak through the southern easier route from Nepal's side.

The Indian Army Expedition at a later date decided to follow the difficult Eastern ridge route to the Summit from Sikkim's side. Following the untrodded path Major Prem Chand and Naik N. D. Sherpa succeeded in scaling the Kanchenjunga on May 31, 1977.

They also held the Sikkimese belief in high esteems and planted the Indian Tri-colour nearly six feet (1.8 metres) short of the pointed tip of the peak. They did not go further to even touch the peak. Thus they succeeded in scaling the second loftiest peak of India through a route long considered an impossible task by the mountaineering world. Small wonder the Kanchenjunga continues to be referred to as a climbed but still a virgin peak that affords some of the most magnificent ice and snow scenario in the world.

Other noteworthy and significant mountain peaks of Sikkim are the Kinchinjahan (6900 metres or 22,700 feet), the Siniolchu (6,815 metres or 22,620 feet) and the Chorniome (6,800 metres or 22,386 feet) above the mean sea level, located on the Sikkimese Greater Himalaya. In between the loftiest mountains on the eastern and western sides of Sikkim, are located many deep, narrow and Canyon like gorgeous valleys with the Valley of Teesta as the Principal Valley of Sikkim.

Towards the south as one approaches the state of West Bengal the mountains become lower and lower in height and these lower mountains are those parts of the state which have borne the brunt of the human wrath in the form of unscientific removal of its floral wealth. They are the part and parcel of the Shiwalik ranges that extend as the foothills of the Himalaya throughout their entire extent.

Conclusively it can be inferred that Sikkim is a region with varied elevations ranging from 220 metres or 800 feet at the southern foothills to more than 9,300 metres or 28,000 feet above the mean sea level along the northern and northwestern parts.

Mountains

Jongsong Peak

Jongsong Peak is a mountain in the Himalayas. At 7,462 metres (24,482 ft) it is the 53rd highest in the world. Its peak forms a three-way boundary between India, China and Nepal. The peak is dominated by Kangchenjunga, just 20 km (12.2 m) to the south. Between its first ascent by an expedition led by G. O. Dyhenfurth in 1930 and the first ascent of Nanda Devi in 1931 it was the highest-climbed peak in the world.

Mahabharat Lekh

The Mahabharat Lekh or Range is a major east-west mountain range with elevations 1,500 to 2,700 metres (5,000 to 9,000 feet) along the crest, paralleling the much higher Great Himalaya range from the Indus River in Pakistan across northern India, Nepal, Sikkim and Bhutan but then the two ranges become increasingly difficult to differentiate east of Bhutan as the ranges approach the Brahmaputra River. The Mahabharat range also parallels the lower Siwalik or Churia Range (Outer Himalaya) to the south.

Southern slopes of the Mahabharat Range are steep and nearly uninhabited due to a major fault system called the 'Main Boundary Thrust". The crest and northern slopes slope gently enough to support upland pastures and terraced fields. Nepal's densely populated Middle Hills begin along the crest, extending north through lower valleys and other "hills" until population thins out above 2,000 metres and cereal-based agriculture increasingly gives way to seasonal herding and cold-tolerant crops such as potatoes.

Most ethnic groups found along the Mahabharat Range and northward into the Middle Hills have Tibeto-Burman affinities including Newar, Magar, Gurung, Tamang, Rai and Limbu, however the most populous ethnic group is indo-european Hindus called *Paharis*, mainly of the upper Brahman and Kshatriya or Chhetri castes. Lower terrain south of the escarpment was historically malarial and inhabited by apparently aboriginal peoples with evolved immunity, notably the Tharu.

The Mahabharat Range is an important hydrographic barrier crossed by relatively few rivers. Drainage systems have evolved candelabra configurations with numerous tributaries flowing south from the Himalaya through the Middle Hills, gathering immediately north of the Mahabharat Range and cutting through in major gorges as the Karnali in the west, the Gandaki or Narayani in central Nepal, and the Kosi in the east.

With temperatures persisting around forty degrees Celsius in the plains of India from April until the onset of the summer monsoon in June, but ten to fifteen degrees cooler atop the Mahabharat Range, Hill Stations were developed as alternate capitals and resorts for the hot season by India's Mughal and British rulers. There are no hill stations *per se* in Nepal, Sikkim or Bhutan since the capital cities are high enough to avoid extreme heat.

Mount Pandim

Mount Pandim is a Himalayan mountain located in Sikkim, India.

Siniolchu

Siniolchu is one of the tallest mountains of the Indian state of Sikkim. The 6,888 m (22,598 feet) mountain is considered to be a particularly beautiful mountain, having been described by Douglas Freshfield as "the most superb triumph of mountain architecture and the most beautiful snow mountain in the world". It is situated near the green lake adjacent to Mount Kangchenjunga, the highest peak in the state and third highest in the world. Siniolchu's summit was first scaled in 1936 by the German climbers Karl Wien and Adi Gottner. Later Sikkimese Everest climber, Sonam Gyatso, also scaled the top.

Kangchenjunga

Kangchenjunga is the third highest mountain in the world (after Mount Everest and K2), with an elevation of 8,586 metres (28,169 ft). Kangchenjunga translated means "The Five Treasures of Snows", as it contains five peaks, four of them over 8,450 metres. The treasures represent the five repositories of God, which are gold, silver, gems, grain, and holy books. Kangchenjunga is called *Sewalungma* in the local Limbu language, translates as 'Mountain that we offer Greetings to'. Kanchenjunga or Sewalungma is considered sacred in the Kirant religion.

Three of the five peaks (main, central, and south) are on the border of North Sikkim district of Sikkim, India and Taplejung District of Nepal, while the other two are completely in Taplejung District. Nepal is home to the *Kangchenjunga Conservation Area Project* run by the World Wildlife Fund, in association with Government of Nepal. The sanctuary is home to the Red Panda and other montane animals, birds and plants. India's side of Kangchenjunga also has a protected park area called the *Khangchendzonga National Park*.

Although *Kangchenjunga* is the official spelling adopted by Douglas Freshfield, A. M. Kellas, and the Royal Geographical Society that gives the best indication of the Tibetan pronunciation, there are a number of alternative spellings which include *Kangchen Dzonga*, *Khangchendzonga*, *Kanchenjanga*, *Kachendzonga*, *Kanchenjunga* or *Kangchanfanga*. The final word on the use of the name *Kangchenjunga* came from His Highness Sir Tashi Namgyal, the Maharaja or chogyal of Sikkim, who stated that "although *junga* had no meaning in Tibetan, it really ought to have been Zod-nga (treasure, five) Kang-chen (snow, big) to convey the meaning correctly". Following consultations with a Lieutenant-Colonel J. L. R. Weir (HMG political agent to Sikkim), he agreed that it was best to leave it as Kangchenjunga, and thus the name remained so by acceptance and usage.

Until 1852, Kangchenjunga was assumed to be the highest mountain in the world, but calculations made by the British Great Trigonometric Survey in 1849 came to the conclusion that Mount Everest (known as Peak XV at the time) was the highest and Kangchenjunga the third-highest. Kangchenjunga was first climbed on May 25, 1955 by Joe Brown and George Band of a British expedition. The British expedition honoured the beliefs of the Sikkimese, who hold the summit sacred, by stopping a few feet short of the actual summit. Most successful summit parties since then have followed this tradition.

Geography: The five peaks of Kangchenjunga are as follows:

Name of peak	Height (m)	Height (ft)
Kangchenjunga Main	8,586	28,169
Kangchenjunga West (Yalung Kang)	8,505	27,904
Kangchenjunga Central (Middle)	8,482	27,828
Kangchenjunga South	8,494	27,867.
Kangbachen	7,903	25,925

The huge massif of Kangchenjunga is buttressed by great ridges running roughly due east to west and north to south, forming a giant 'X'. These ridges contain a host of peaks between 6,000 and 8,000 metres. On the east ridge in Sikkim, is Siniolchu (6,888 m/ 22,600 ft). The west ridge culminates in the magnificent Jannu (7,710 m/25,294 ft) with its imposing north face. To the south, clearly visible from Darjeeling, are Kabru North (7,338 m/24,075 ft), Kabru South (7,316 m/24,002 ft) and Rathong peaks (6,678 m/21,910 ft). The north ridge, after passing through the minor subpeak Kangchenjunga North (7,741 m/ 25,397 ft), contains The Twins and Tent Peak, and runs up to the Tibetan border by the Jongsong La, a 6,120 m (20,080 ft) pass.

Kangchenjunga is known for its famous views from the hill station of Darjeeling. On a clear day, it presents an image not as much of a mountain but of a white wall hanging from the sky. The people of Sikkim revere Kangchenjunga as a sacred mountain. Permission to climb the mountain from the Indian side is rare, but sometimes allowed.

Because of its remote location in Nepal and difficult access from India, the Kangchenjunga region is not much explored by trekkers. It has, therefore, retained much of its pristine beauty. In Sikkim too, trekking into the Kangchenjunga region has just been permitted. The Goecha La trek is gaining popularity amongst tourists. It goes to the Goecha La Pass, located right in front of the huge southeast face of Kangchenjunga. Another trek to Green Lake Basin has recently been opened for trekking. This goes to the northeast side of Kangchenjunga along the famous Zemu Glacier.

The Kangchenjunga Conservation Area (KCA) covers 2,035 sq km surrounding the mountain on the Nepalese side.

Singalila

The Singalila Range is an enormous spur of the Great Himalayas. The crowning glory of this range is the 8596 m elevated summit, of Mount Khangchendzonga. This peak — the third highest in the world, is a difficult mountain to climb, because of unpredictable weather and winds. The Sikkimese believe that it is not meant to be climbed, but only worshipped, as it is the abode of five treasures of the snows. In deference to local sentiments, no expedition has set foot on the summit — but remained a few metres below. For those of us who cannot attempt the climb, the 5000 m high viewpoint at Goechela (the Lock Pass) offers a superb alternative. A depression, between Mount Pandim, and a spur of the Kabru Peak form the pass. It looks down into the Talung Valley, with the mighty Talung Glacier, winding its way down below. One is surrounded by great white peaks — Khangchendzonga (8,596 m), Simvo (6,811 m), Siniolchu (6,888 m), Pandim (6,691 m), Kabru (7,338 m) and Rathang (6,087 m). The awe inspiring sight, instills a feeling of standing in the very lap of Khangchendzonga, and gazing up at its face.

Glaciers

There are many glaciers in Sikkim among which the most important ones are Zemu Glacier, Rathong Glacier and the Lonak Glacier in North Sikkim.

Zemu Glacier

The Zemu glacier is the largest and the most famous glacier of the eastern Himalayas. It is 26 km in length and is situated in a large U-shaped valley at the base of the Khangchendzonga massif in northwestern Sikkim. The Teesta River rises from the snout of this glacier.

Many tributary glaciers feed the trunk glacier. The side valleys in which these glaciers lie open into the main Zemu Valley from different directions. Icefalls and waterfalls have formed at the junction of the tributary glaciers with the Zemu glacier.

Rathong Glacier

The Rathong Glacier is an important glacier situated in Sikkim. The source of Rangeet River flows from the Rathong Glacier.

Rathong Glacier, near Kanchenjunga, the third highest peak in the world, is in West Sikkim District. River Rangit — a major tributary of River Teesta — originates from this glacier. The glacier is an ideal trekking base. The Chaurithang falls is at the Rathong Glacier. The Goecha Pass is also nearby.

Lonak Glacier

Lonak Glacier, at an altitude of about 4,720 m, is in North Sikkim District. It is one of the three major glaciers of Sikhim, in the Himalaya range in North east of India. The other nearby glaciers include Zemu Glacier and Rathong Glacier.

Rivers and Water System

The drainage pattern of Sikkim is dendritic in nature. It means that the criss-crossing streams of the region appear like a tree wherein the Teesta river in its lower course is the trunk, whereas, other streams, rivulets and torrents are the branches, sub-branches, twigs and leaves, Moreover, genetically the drainage pattern of Sikkim is consequent. In other words, the river, streams and rivulets of Sikkim are post-Himalayan in origin. They have come info existence after the uplift of the Himalayan mountains from the sea.

There are no pre-Himalayan or antecedent rivers like the Brahmputra and the Indus in Sikkim. Still from another angle the streams of Sikkim are young rivers who contribute more to erosional morphology than depositional morphology. Small wonder none of the streams is fit for navigational purposes although many of them at many places are fit for the harnessing of hydroelectricity. In fact, the state has vast potential of water power which if properly harnessed can completely revolutionise the economy as well as the society of Sikkim.

As already narrated, the Teesta is the principal river of Sikkim although there are a number of streams in the state. Winding its way through the region, the Teesta divides the state into two parts in north-south direction. The Teesta is the Ganga or the life line of the state of Sikkim, since an overwhelming number of its villages are found in the main as well as tributary valleys of the Teesta.

In fact the settlement pattern of Sikkim is also dendritic in nature, as villages everywhere in the region are located along the river banks only. It is but natural that in a region characterised by extreme ruggedity, lofty elevations, snow clad peaks and inhospitable physical landscape, the usable flat patches fit for human settlements can be available only along the banks of the drainage lines.

Teesta, the trunk and major river of Sikkim originates as a snout (a stream coming out of the melting water of a glacier) out of the Zemu glacier north of the Lachen gonlpha. Two important streams flowing from the northern direction and joining the Teesta as right hand tributaries are the Lhonk and the Lachung.

The latter rises from Pauhunri and meets the Teesta at Chunlthang while the former rises partly from the area lying in the vicinity of the Green Lake which is itself located in the northwestern section of the state. The observation made by Bose in respect of the Teesta river system is worthy of note here.

"There is a striking contrast between the deep gorge bottom of the Teesta and the enclosing mountains including the Kanchenjunga group within a few Kilometres of the rise of the Teesta from the Zemu glacier snout, its drop to 1,000 metres near Singhik and Mangan in Central Sikkim."

The Teesta drainage system itself is a tributary system to the Ganga-Yamuna drainage net. After traversing through the state of Sikkim the Teesta enters the Bengal Tarai and reaches Jalpaiguri in northern West Bengal through Siliguri. The Teesta has always been a sorrow of southern Sikkim and Northern West Bengal. It is always in spate (flooded) during the rainy period and often floods the nearby areas. As a result of its menacing floods a huge loss is caused to life, including human life, and property inclusive of standing crops.

Now with the passage of time a concern is being voiced in this regard. Check on mass felling of trees, controlled grazing and reforestation as well as afforestation hold the key along with the construction of small check dams at suitable sites on the Teesta and its tributaries.

Among the significantly important tributary streams of the Teesta are included the Ranjit, the Rongni Chu, the Talung, the Ragpo and the Lachung. All these streams are snow-fed rivers. Sikkim primarily forms the catchment area of the Teesta drainage system.

The trunk as well as tributary valleys are southward-sloping valleys. Near their origin, obviously near the higher snow fields the river courses are relatively wide but as soon as they start flowing along the steep slopes, as a result of the gradient promoted excessive erosive power the valleys become deep and narrow. In this section, it is the vertical erosion that far excels the lateral erosion.

The rapidly flowing streams besides creating gorge-like valleys also result in the formation of hanging valleys. The Ranjit, a major tributary of the Teesta comes out of the Middle Himalaya, courses through western Sikkim and has its confluence with the Teesta in the forested tract of Peshok near Kalimpong in northern part of the state of West Bengal.

So much is the significance of the Teesta and Ranjit in the social, cultural and economic life of the Sikkimese people that the rivers have been immortalised in the folklore and literature of Sikkim. Once their flooding postures are controlled and their waters properly used and harnessed for irrigation and hydroelectricity the Teesta and all its tributaries shall come to enjoy much more significance for the people of Sikkim.

The Plants

As a result of copious rainfall making adequate moisture available to the soil and air, the natural vegetation in Sikkim is fairly dense and highly luxuriant. Sikkim is one of those regions of the whole world which as a result of immense vegetable luxuriance and a large variety of floral species are renowned as pockets of prized and rich floral wealth. Though it is highly surprising but strikingly true that the tiny region contains more than 4,000 species of plants.

As per Imperial Gazetteer of India published in 1909 the collection of Hooker's (a world-famed botanist of his period) alone consisted 2,902 Sikkimese plants when one enters the forests of Sikkim he finds then as luxuriant as they appear to be endless. There is also a particular reason for the dense and luxuriant growth of vegetation besides heavy and copious rainfall. Sikkim is one of those portions of the earth which experience regularly very frequent lightning during the summer rainy period for about five months.

Small wonder in many descriptions Sikkim has been referred to as "land of lightning". The frequent and excessive occurrence of lightning leads to the addition of fair amounts of nitric acid to the soil as well as air. The nitric acid present in the soil helps in the growth of dense and luxuriant vegetation while the nitric acid present in the air aids the expansion and growth of leaves, branches, twigs and other parts of the foliage. A variety of flowers with different blues, colours, shapes and sizes spreading fragrance all around make Sikkim the Garden of Eden.

The natural forests of Sikkim broadly fall in three categories, *i.e.*, sub-tropical wet forests, temperate forests and Alpine forests. The temperate forests further fall in three sub-types, *i.e.*, wet temperate forests. Natural vegetation has very often been employed as a criterion of dividing Sikkim into physical divisions. The sub-tropical wet forests extend to an average elevation of 1,600 metres (about 5,000 feet) above mean sea level. Orchids, panel anus, ferns, tree ferns, some deciduous trees and a variety of bamboo dominate the floral scenario in this zone. Sal, a valuable tree from more than one angle, is also found in this belt.

This zone covers a very thin belt in the southern-most part of this landlocked tiny state but it is quite surprising that even within this narrow belt as many as twenty different varieties of bamboo alone are found. In the world as a whole, so far, about five thousand different varieties of Orchids have been found and studied botanically. Nevertheless, out of this total number nearly 600 varieties (twelve per cent) have been spotted in Sikkim alone.

For many decades the botanists claimed this number but in the year 1965 when the last princely ruler (Chogyal) of Sikkim had to be coronated, Tseten Tashi an indefatigable orchidician succeeded, in laying his hands upon an altogether new variety of the orchid. Thus his discovery added one more type raising the total number of Orchid varieties, so far spotted in Sikkim to 601.

After the name of the last Chogyal this chaste white orchid has been mined as Cyrn Ni Mon Ebnrnewn Varl Delizoilg Chogyal. This bewitchingly attractive orchid has rosy specks as well under surface of its petals with a bright yellow spot on its lips. Similar to the tropical rain forests, *i.e.*, equatorial type of forests, one comes across dense undergrowth and bush vegetation in these forests. Leechas, which have been described as "cure of tropical moist forests" have also intruded in this vegetation zone of Sikkim.

A major part of the state of Sikkim is covered by temperate forests. Depending upon latitude, altitude above sea level and the amount of precipitation (rainfall and snowfall) the temperate forests of the state are divided into three sub-categories, *i.e.*, wet temperate forests, moist temperate forests and dry temperate forests. The wet temperate forests are found north of the subtropical wet forests. In this sub-zone the amount of rainfall exceeds that of the snowfall. To the north of this sub-belt is located the belt of the moist temperate forests wherein the amount of annual snowfall has and edge over the yearly amount of rainfall.

Beyond this sub-category of forests towards the north are found the dry temperate forests. This is an area which falls in the rainshadow zone and thus is characterised by the dry temperate forests. Most of the northern sections of the major river valleys are found within the temperate zone. Oak, chestnut, giant flowering magnolia, exhibitionist rhodendron, cherry maple, laurel maple, pine, fir trees and fern trees characterised by branches appearing like curled tongues of the giant moths, dominate this forest zone of the state. Above an average altitude of 2,610 metres (8,000 feet) above mean sea level, rhodendron, the pride and glory of Sikkim, grow majestically in abundance. About thirty varieties of this floral species are found in Sikkim alone.

The Nepalese call it by the name of qurans while the Kumaonls have named it burans or baries. During spring when the rhodendrons flower, the entire landscape presents a bewitching scenario laden with flowers of different shades and hues. With increasing altitude the tree goes on getting dwarfer. It is a medicinal tree and the juice of its flower is recommended to persons who suffer from hypertension and related cardiac disorders. Now in some Himalayan towns, particularly Shimla, where also rhodendron dominates the landscape "Rhode Squash" is prepared out of the flowers and it has been welcomed by the consumers Sikkim too has a large potential for this activity.

The northern most and the loftiest zone of Sikkim contains Alpine forests which carry coniferous trees, *i.e.*, the trees which have their canopies in the form of cones. Cypress and giant cedars are the common-most trees found in this zone. Dwarfing in size with increasing altitude, these forests continue right up to the snowline, where they bow to the icy winds. With rising elevation the coniferous trees halt their upward and north ward advance but the Junipers and multi-coloured but short-statured shodendrons persist and appear to be engaged in a grim battle against climatic odds for their existence.

Meadows, pastures and a mantle of alpine flowers afford an appearance of a natural carpet which spread right up to the snowline. The snowline occurs at an average elevation of 5,000 metres (about 1,000 feet) above mean sea level. In and around the snowfield snowman (yeti) has also been spotted" by some persons, prowling in the snowy wilderness. The gentler slopes at these heights are very often found to be covered with a flower mantle of the Primula species which undoubtedly add a touch of glorious hue to the sombre grandeur of these lovely mountains. In the neighbouring Himalayan States of Sikkim and Bhutan the Primula flower is held in reverential eastern.

Botanically Sikkim is the richest floral pocket of India, if not of the world. It may not be an exaggeration to state that perhaps other country of equal or larger size presents such a wide variety of floral wealth." Besides trees, creepers bushes and other non-flowering plants, about 4,000 varieties of flowering plants and shrubs are found in the state of Sikkim.

The Animals

As has been noted above Sikkim is a storehouse of orchids. Orchids afford the greatest and fascinating attraction to the butterflies. No wonder, Sikkim is lepidopterist's (a student of butterflies and mots) paradise. If the botanists (more particularly the orchidists) have found out 601 varieties of orchids, the lepidopterists have not lagged behind and they have succeeded in discovering as many as 631 varieties, of butterflies. The butterflies although about in areas characterised by warmer climate yet in Sikkim the attraction extended by the Orchids is so bewitching that butterflies of different colours are found right up to 2,500 metres (8,000 feet) above sea level. In forested valleys characterised by the dominance of orchids the butterflies swarm in unending flocks. The pleasant pastures, mountains, meadows, varying slopes, verdured valley walls, undulating foothills, dense undergrowth and numerous floral species constitute rich haven for a variety of birds, creepers, animals and insects.

About 600 types of birds 2,000 varieties of creepers and insects have been found in the state of Sikkim. Eighty-one species of mammals (the animals which suckle and feed their young ones on their own milk) alone have been found in this region.

The black and the dreaded brown coloured bears are mostly found in forested areas lying at elevations ranging between 1,250 metres to 3,400 metres (4,000 feet to 11,000 feet) above mean sea level. Musk deer is a common animal in areas characterised by an average altitude of 2,800 metres (9,000 feet) above mean sea level. Tiger, sambhar, leopard, panther, leopard cat, marbled cat, barking deer and large-sized squirrel are by and large confined to the subtropical wet forests.

The snow leopards had been quite common in the highest elevations of Sikkim but uncontrolled hunting of this highly- prized animal led to the fast dwindling in its numbers, Yak, panda, otter goral, wild boar, ovis, nahure, byhang-linig (wild sheep) and bhyang-gra (wild goat) are another major wild animals which are found in the higher reaches of Sikkim. Otter is a prized animal. The brocaded fur caps worn by some Sikkimese are prepared from the fur bearing skin of Otter. In the snowfield, roaming around glaciers and snowy slopes has been found the snowman (called Yeti internationally) locally named Nee guyed. On higher elevations tailless mountains rats, rock lizards and predators like snow-fox are also found.

If Sikkim is a paradise for the lepidopterist and orchidist, it is no less for an Ornithologist, *i.e.*, students of birds. Numerous species and varieties of birds ranging from the gigantic Imamergeyer to the miniscule flower pecker abound in the forests of Sikkim. The rich ornithic wealth offers a lifetime of work and delight to any dedicated ornithologist. Some of the principal bird varieties include thrushes, babblers, Himalayan cuckoo, barbet, eagles, teals, quails, ducks, doves, partridges, and flamboyant pheasants.

The Tibetan black crow with rosy paws has also been found in Northern Sikkim. The mini wet or the "Red King" of Nepal which is red bright coloured is also found in Sikkim. Crap and trout fish are found in plenty in the rivers and lakes.

Natural Wealth

Copper, lead and zinc are the major mineral resources of the state. The surveys conducted by the Geological Survey of India also revealed that there existed reserves of graphite, coal and limestone. Iron ore and pyrite deposits have also been located in the region. There is sufficient evidence, historical as well as archaeological, to assert that copper mining and copper smelting were traditional arts with the Sikkimese people. However, no factors have been, so far, unearthed which show as to why and how this traditional vocation came to an end.

Before the state of Sikkim was made an integral part of the Indian Union, the Government of India actively collaborated with the princely rule of Sikkim for ushering in an era of socio- economic development for the Sikkimese people. In the year 1960 the joint venture of Sikkim Mining Corporation was set up to investigate and extract the mineral resources of the state.

Copper deposits have been found at Dikchu, Bonglichu, Rhenock Lingui Zondok, Rangpo (Beyang), Rattokhari Barmiak, Tukkhni, Rinch Napong Pakyong and Rorathang. Tamlog is the possible copper ore location. Coppee veins are quiet widespread and contain a rich content of copper. It is hopefully surmised that the richest copper ore mines shall come to be developed at Bhatang and Pachikhani. The copper Mining Corporation had earlier been working in the surrounding area of Rangpo.

The State Government, later on, created the Department of Mines and Geology. The basic aims and objectives of this Department are the studies of the mineral wealth of Sikkim from economic angle and also to assess and evaluate the surface and subsurface features of relevant places from engineering point of view.

In tackling problems of landslides under the aegis of this department a Mineral Exploration and Geo-Chemical Laboratory was set up. This organisation has acquired a diamond core drill machine which is being used not only in exploring the mineral ores but also for foundation testing of bridges, buildings as also for grouting the destablised pockets for preventing the occurrence of rock series and landslides on roads and elsewhere.

A pilot rock cutting and polishing plant is in the process of establishment at the premises of the Sikkim Mining Corporation at Rangpo. The plant shall study the commercial values of the Himalayan marble and other associated rocks. The feasibility of establishing a full-fledged rock cutting and polishing plant for commercial purposes alone is also being currently studied.

The Department of Mines and Geology has set up an economic deposit extraction centre for the extraction of silica rich quartzites and talc at Mangsari, Tharpu. This centre has already been leased out while the quartzite deposits in other areas are being investigated and samples are being side by side sent to the Central Glass and Ceramic Research Institute, Kolkata, for qualitative analysis. The geological evaluation on utilisation and future prospects of the low grade coal of Namchi and Ranjit valley in consultation with the CMPDIL, were completed. Studies, in consultation with the Regional Research Laboratory, Bhubaneshwar, Orissa, for evaluating the physical feasibility and economic viability of the low grade graphite ores at Chitra are in an advanced stage. Detailed traverse mapping of Legship-Naya Bazar Road section on the scale of 1:500 had been completed and now the estimation surveys of coal and dolomite are in progress. The dolomites of different grades have been delineated on the basis of their chemical composition. The geo-chemical analysis of about 200 samples had already been completed. Preliminary investigative geological surveys on the sillimanite deposits found along the upper reaches of Rottak Khola carried out in western Sikkim. The techno-economic feasibility study on the dikchu copper and zinc deposits were completed. It has proved that the deposits at Dikchu are of better grade than the deposits at Rangpo.

Forestry

Sikkim, a Himalayan State located in a geologically fragile and ecologically sensitive hilly terrain, has over 81 per cent of the total geographical area of the state under the administrative control of Forests, Environment and Wildlife Department. The forest cover has increased from 37 per cent to 44.1 per cent of the total geographical area of the state during the last two decades.

Biodiversity: There are five types of forests in Sikkim. They are:

- Tropical Dry Deciduous Forests,
- Sub-Tropical Semi-Evergreen Forests,
- Temperate Broad Leaved Forests,
- Sub-Alpine Mixed Coniferous Forests, and
- Alpine Scrubs.

Sikkim harbours over 400 species of flowering plants, 300 species of ferns and allies, 11 species of oaks, 8 species of tree ferns, 40 species of Primulas and 20 species of bamboo, 550 species of Orchods, 36 species of Rhododendron and 9 species of conifers A large number of medicinal herbs and shrubs are found in Sikkim. The faunal wealth of Sikkim comprises of 144 species of mammals, 600 species of birds, 550 species of butterflies and moths, and 33 species of reptiles and 16 species of frogs.

Mountain Peaks, Lakes, etc.: There are 28 number of mountain peaks, 28 glaciers, 180 lakes and 104 lakes and streams.

State Policy of Environment Forests and Land Use: The State Legislative Assembly passed Resolution on State Policy of Environment, Forest and Land Use 2000 vide No. 764/F/ENV & WL dated 18th March 2000.

Activities and Achievements: Forestry and Wildlife Sector:

- *A Forestation:* A forestation is one of the major activities of the Department. Although afforestation was being carried out since inception of this department, it took pace with the announcement of the year 1995 as Harit Kranti Year by the government. Since then the Government of Sikkim has given top priority for creating more and more green cover in forests as well as in private wastelands. Since then, over 45,000 ha of degraded forest lands and about 15,000 ha of private land has been covered by tree, fodder, fuelwood and ornamental plantations and by aided natural regeneration.

- *Forest Protection:* Of late, protection of forests have become the challenging task for the department. With the explosion in population, the hunger for more and more timber and other forest produce has risen.

  — *Establishment of Wireless Communication Network:* To protect forests from illegal felling and theft of forest produce, the department has established Wireless Communication Network connecting the Blocks with the Ranges, Subdivisions, Divisions and Circles of both the Territorial and Wildlife Wings.

  — *Amendment Sikkim Forests, Water Courses, Road Reserve (Protection and Preservation) Act, 1988:* The Act has been amended to make room for stringent punishment to the offenders. Royalty, especially of timber for constructional purposes in Gangtok and other urban areas has been revised upwardly but the royalty of timber for bonafide use in villages have been kept at a highly subsidised and affordable rate.

  — *Ban on Felling of Green Trees and Commercial Exploitation of Medicinal Plants in Reserved Forests:* The Government of Sikkim has banned felling of green trees in reserved forests except from the project sites which are cleared by the

Ministry of Environment and Forests, Government of India for setting up of projects for socio-economic development of the state and the Nation. There is no commercial extraction of timber from the forests of Sikkim and export of timber outside the state has been banned by the State Government. Commercial Exploitation of medicinal plants too has been banned in the reserved forests.

— *Removal of Cattle Sheds from the Reserved Forests:* The Government of Sikkim has taken decision to remove the goths (cattle sheds) from the reserved forests. In East, South and West Districts eviction the cattle sheds is under progress to be followed in North District.

— *Control and Management of Forest Fires:* Forest Fire is the regular phenomenon in the forests especially in Teesta and Rangit valleys. Fire watchers are being engaged during the fire seasons and fire fighting equipment are being provided to fire fighters. Fire watchtowers are also being constructed for prompt detection of forest fires. Patrolling vehicles during fire seasons are provided to the Territorial Divisions with wireless sets for prompt action.

— *Empowerment of Forest Officials:* The Forest Officers especially of the Territorial and Wildlife Wing have been provided with the powers to deal with the forest offences under Sikkim Forests, Water Courses, Road Reserve (Protection and Preservation) Act, 1988 and Wildlife Protection Act, 1972.

— *Formation of Joint Forest Management Committees and Watershed Committees:* Notification No. 202/F was issued on 26.06.1998 and Joint Forest Management was introduced in Sikkim to obtain maximum participation of the people for protection and management of forests. So far, 121 Joint Forest Management Committees have been constituted. Besides, for implementation of Integrated Watershed Development Programmes, 31 Watershed Associations have been formed and registered under Societies' Registration Act.

— *Strengthening of Territorial and Wildlife Circles:* The Department has strengthened these two circles by posting of maximum number of forest guards in these Circles. Over 70 forest guards and 40 Block Officers have been appointed in between 1995 and 2000 and posted in Territorial and Wildlife Circles for effective protection and management of forests and wildlife in the state.

Wildlife Management: Over 30 per cent of the total geographical area of the state is being maintained as protected area network and managed in the form of Wildlife Sanctuaries and National Park.

Wildlife Sanctuaries: There are 6 wildlife Sanctuaries in the state which are set aside for protection and conservation of the endangered flora and fauna.

	Name of Sanctuary Location/District	Area
1.	Shingba Rhododendron Sanctuary, North Sikkim	43.00 sq km
2.	Fambonglho Wildlife Sanctuary, East Sikkim	51.76 sq km
3.	Kyongnosla Alpine Sanctuary, East Sikkim	31.00 sq km
4.	Moinam Wildlife Sanctuary, South Sikkim	34.35 sq km
5.	Barsey Rhododendron Sanctuary, West Sikkim	104.00 sq km
6.	Pangolakha Wildlife Sanctuary, East Sikkim	208.00 sq km

This sanctuary is recently proposed and is located in the Eastern part of the East District of the state which forms the wildlife corridor with West Bengal and Bhutan. Notice for proclamation has been issued and further action is being taken.

Kanchenjunga National Park: The initial area of this National Park was 850 square kilometres. The park area was extended to 1784 square kilometres for conservation of high altitude flora and fauna of the state.

Kanchenjunga Biosphere Reserve: Kanchenjunga Biosphere Reserve with the core area of 1784 square kilometres (Kanchenjunga National Park) and buffer zone of 835.92 square kilometres was declared by notification issued by the Ministry of Environment and Forests, Government of India on 7th February 2000. State Level Biosphere Reserve Committee and Biosphere Reserve Implementation Committee (local committee) were constituted vide Notification No. 369/F, ENV & WL dated 16th December 2000. The Management Plan of the Biosphere Reserve for the year 2001-02 with the financial target of Rs. 101.72 lakhs has been submitted to the Ministry of Environment and Forests, Government of India.

Himalayan Zoological Park: The Himalayan Zoological Park located at Bulbuley near the town of Gangtok has an area of 205 hectares. The initial project cost of establishment of the zoological park was Rs. 467.00 lakhs. Infrastructure development of the zoological park started in the 8th Five Year Plan. The project was revised in the year 2000-01 with the financial target of Rs. 1060.00 lakhs.

The Environment

Notwithstanding the fact that Sikkim is a part of the Indian subcontinent, the weather and climatic conditions enjoyed by this region cannot be simply described as "monsoonal" or "Tropical moist". Although the valleys with least elevation and relatively southern location do experience tropical moist climate largely affected by the in blowing monsoons particularly during the summer season, yet elsewhere and at other places the climatic conditions are contrastingly different. In the state besides there being latitudinal variations there are experienced altitudinal variations too.

In fact these are the extreme elevational variations over space which lead to extremely varied climatic conditions in Sikkim. In accordance with the normal lapse rate and adiabatic changes (caused by the rising relief), the temperatures in the bottoms of the valleys situated at lower elevations, particularly during summers, are similar to the monsoon type of climate. Thus all those valleys characterised by elevations of less than 600 metres above sea level experience moist tropical or humid tropical climate.

Thereafter as one climbs up, the temperatures start falling and areas lying between 600 metres to 2,000 metres above sea level enjoy cool temperate climatic conditions. Further up, it is cold temperate climatic conditions which prevail in area having elevations between 2,000 metres to 3,000 metres above mean sea level.

Higher still the temperatures rapidly fall and coldness increases till the snowline is reached which itself is determined by altitude and aspect. The climatic conditions in this zone (above 3,600 metres from the mean sea level) change from the Arctic to Polar. In this small state a traveller can experience different climatic conditions, particularly in the context of temperatures just during his journey of one day.

The areas which have elevations of more than 5,000 metres above sea level have perpetually snow-clad peaks and ranges and obviously they enjoy Arctic type of climate. In the words of Frederick, "It comprises every kind of exquisite scenery — from the rank tropical luxuriance of the lower valleys to the magnificence of its great snowy peaks, of which there are no fewer than fourteen, all above 20,000 feet (around 6,500 metres) on its northern borders."

Only in the lower valleys located in the southern section of the state, summer heat in right sense is experienced. Thus, the foothill zone adjacent to the West Bengal border experiences relatively high temperatures during summer. Elsewhere the summers are pleasant or cool or cold. For instance in Nayabazar located in the southern-most section of the state the summer temperatures are as high as 40°C. However, when one moves northward with rising relief, there Namchi enjoys summer temperatures around 35°C. These are however, the maximum temperatures during the summer season and the minimum temperatures may fall by 5°C.

Nevertheless, while moving further north when the altitude too progressively rises the summer maximum as well as minimum temperatures fall appreciably. For instance in the capital city of Gangtok the summer maximum and minimum temperatures are recorded at 23.3°C and 21.3°C respectively.

The amount of rainfall depends upon the aspect and altitude. Since the rainfall is mainly caused by the monsoon winds and the depressions travelling along with them the south-facing slopes get more rainfall than the north-facing slopes which being under the rain shadow impact receive lesser amount of rainfall. It is particularly so in case of the highly elevated parts.

On the whole average amount of rainfall varies between 125 cm to 500 cm. As per Imperial Gazetteer of India, "Sikkim is the most humid place in the whole range of the Himalayas, because of its proximity to the Bay of Bengal and direct exposure to the effects of the moisture laden southwest monsoon, from which the ranges east of Sikkim are partially screened by the mountains on the south flank of the Assam valley."

As elsewhere in the country, except the Andhra Pradesh and Tamil Nadu coastal regions, a major part of the rainfall in Sikkim is received during the months of May to September.

Although the monsoonal rains begin in May yet they are at their climax in the months of June, July and August. In September with the initiation of the retreat of the summer monsoons the amount of rainfall decreases. Nevertheless, the monsoonal rainfall is not only uncertain but erratic too.

Sometimes the rainfall is too heavy, sometimes too low, sometimes the rainfall is too early and sometimes too late. Many a tune longer spells of dryness and sunshine are experienced even during the rainy period.

Sometimes the rains get prolonged to October while in some years the rains rapidly come to an end in September. At other times, there is too much of rainfall in the concluding part of the rainy season. As far as the areal spread of the rainfall is concerned the moisture-laden monsoons penetrate deep into the interior areas of Sikkim through the Teesta valley thereby extending the humid belt right up to the lower reaches of the snow capped mountains. Gangtok receives about 360 cm of annual rainfall while Namchi and Nayabazar respectively receive 155 cm and 140 cm of annual rainfall. During winters a sizeable part of the state receives copious snowfall. After the first snowfall the winds blowing from the mountains to lower valleys bring cold spells and cold waves. The gravity winds catching up in the afternoon whip up snow storms and blizzards in many snow-covered parts of the state.

5

Society

It is traditionally accepted that the Lepchas are the autochthonous tribe of Sikkim. After them came the Bhutias, from Tibet, followed by the Nepalese and finally the Indian business community from the plains. However, before one goes into the ethnic composition of Sikkim, it needs to be said that the Sikkimese, irrespective of the tribe, class or community they belong to, are essentially simple folk. Like most hill-tribes, the Sikkimese is thus far relatively untouched by consumerism. Cliched though it may sound, the Sikkimese truly exemplify how different communities can exemplify how different communities can coexist in peace and mutual.

The Sikkimese can be broadly classified into the Lepchas, the Bhutias, the Nepalese and the plainsmen (mostly businessmen from elsewhere in India). Communities, cultures, religions and Customs of different hues intermingle freely here in Sikkim to constitute a homogeneous blend. Hindu temples co-exists with Buddhist monasteries and there are even a few Christian churches, Muslim mosques and Sikh "Gurudwara". Although the Buddhists with monasteries all over the state are the most conspicuous religious group, they are in fact a minority constituting only 28 per cent of the population.

The majority, 68 per cent profess Hinduism. The predominant communities are the Lepchas, Bhutias and the Nepalis. In urban areas many plainsmen — Marwaris, Biharis, Bengalis, South Indians, Punjabis — have also settled and they are mostly engaged in business and government service. Because of development and construction activities in the state, a small part of the population consists of migrant labourers from the plains and from Nepal: plumbers, masons and carpenters from Orissa, Bihar and West Bengal and Sherpas who are hired by the army to maintain the roads at high altitudes. There are also a few thousand Tibetan Refugees settled in Sikkim. Cultural and economic forces are reshaping the way of life of the Sikkimese. This can be seen by taking a walk down the

M. G. Marg of Gangtok, boys and girls sporting the latest fashions probably picked up from a new Hindi movie or BBCs Clothes Show gaily tromp up and down. An open Jeep carrying jubilant footballers who have won a match passes by — they are singing Daler Mehndi's popular Punjabi song "Bol Ta Ra Ra" at the top of their voices.

The cable TV is definitely attempting to remould the cultural landscape of Sikkim. You should not be Surprised if you come across a village girl some where in the wilderness dressed in a Punjabi Kurta Pajama singing a Hindi number "Didi tera dewar diwana" while tending to her herd of cattle. In spite of such powerful external influences, Sikkimese has proved to be resilient accepting the benefits of progress while retaining their ethnic identity.

The Lepchas: The original inhabitants of Sikkim are said to be Lepchas. They existed much before the Bhutias and Nepalese migrated to the state. Before adopting Buddhism or Christianity as their religion, the earliest Lepcha settlers were believers in the bone faith or mune faith. This faith was basically based on spirits, good and bad. They worshipped spirits of mountains, rivers and forests that was but natural for a tribe that co-existed so harmoniously with the rich natural surroundings.

The Lepcha (Zongu) folklore is rich with stories. The Lepcha population is concentrated in the central part of the Sikkim. This is the area that encompasses the confluence of Lachen and Lachung rivers and Dickchu believers in the bone faith or mune faith. This faith was basically based on spirits, good and bad. They worshipped spirits of mountains, rivers and forests that was but natural for a tribe that co-existed so harmoniously with the rich natural surroundings. The Lepcha (Zongu) folklore is rich with stories. The Lepcha population is concentrated in the central part of the Sikkim. This is the area that encompasses the confluence of Lachen and Lachung rivers and Dickchu. The Lepchas, in appearance, have slightly accentuated Mongoloid features, are fair and boast a bigger build than their neighbours.

Docile and peace loving, the original inhabitants of Sikkim have now become a minority and have a reservation earmarked for them in the Dzongu region of North Sikkim. Here, one and still find families living by age-old customs and manners- untouched by the rapid strides into development that the rest of Sikkim has taken. Despite their unassuming nature, the Lepchas are highly refined lot. Their language (also known as Rong) is highly developed and one of the few tribes to recognise the value of education and, even today, boast of some highly educated individuals.

The Lepchas or Rong pa, literally the "ravine folk" are fast dwindling in numbers. The Lepchas are very intelligent, samiable and extremely hospitable. They love sports and games and are sociable. They are peace-loving people who avoid quarrels. Many of them are concentrated in the Dzongu valley in northern part of Sikkim.

The Lepchas mostly live by trade or on agriculture. Paddy, oranges and cardamom are their favourable crops. The Lepcha house or 'li' usually 4 or 5 feet above the ground, is usually rectangular in shape. They are usually made of woody stems of bamboo. Life in a Lepcha hut is very simple. Lepchas are excellent weavers and make fine tribal cloth. They are also adept in bamboo and cane weaving. A traditionally dressed Lepcha would be found wearing half pajamas, under a robe made of striped cotton resembling a loose jacket the whole ensemble is called a *pagi*.

The robe, which comes to the knees, is pinned on the shoulder and tied around the waist. Accompanying him would be a ban or payak, the traditional Lepcha knife. Apart from their reserve Dzongu, the Lepchas can be seen sporting their traditional dress at archery competitions (in which they are very good) or during special occasions like festivals and marriages. The Lepcha lady wears a two-piece dress — a full-sleeved blouse called *tago* and a skirt called *domdyan*. A scarf round the head is also a common feature.

The Lepchas are also the best people to have around if you are lost in the forest. Their close link with nature had led them to possess a tremendous and unparalleled vocabulary. They have names and terms for every fern, bush, moss and mushroom. They also know what is the best to eat in the forest. The delicacy of bamboo shoots is, after their offering to world cuisine.

The Nepalese: The Nepalese appeared on the Sikkim scene much after the Lepchas and Bhutias. They migrated in large numbers and soon became the dominant community. The Nepalese now constitute more than 80 per cent of the total population. The Nepali settlers introduced the terraced system of cultivation. Cardamom was an important cash crop introduced by the Nepalese. Except for the Sherpas and Tamangs who are Buddhists, the Nepalese are orthodox Hindus with the usual caste system.

The Nepalese form the majority constituting about 70-80 per cent of the Sikkim's total population. The Nepalese are a conglomeration of different ethnic groups, socially self-contained. The Nepalese are excellent farmers and soon after their migration and settlement in Sikkim they introduced terrace cultivation, which brought a productive method of farming to the mountainous terrain. Dasain is the biggest and most important festival celebrated by the Nepalese Hindu.

It falls approximately in the month of October and is concurrent with the northern Indian celebration of Dussehra. The Nepalese decorate their house doors and pillars with banana leaves and strings of marigold flowers and say prayers for the goddess Durga. On the eighth day or Ashtami, many families sacrifice goats or buffaloes and on the tenth day or Vijayadashami, the elder family members smear the foreheads of the younger members with tikas and relatives visit each other seeking blessings from the older members. Tihar festival is celebrated 15 days after Dasain with great gaiety and enthusiasm.

The Nepalese worship Goddess Laxmi on the first day. During the evenings thousands of butter lamps are lighted and crackers are burst to celebrate the festival of light. On the third day is Bhai-Tika when sisters put tikas on their brother's forehead and pray for their well being. The Sikkimese Nepali is the inheritor of the legacy of Hindu traditions. The language spoken by Nepalese is understood and spoken by people all over the state. The Nepalese woman wears 'Chobandi cholo' as blouse and sari complete the outfit. The men wear 'dowra suruwal'.

Many Nepali folk dances and songs are connected with cultivating and harvesting seasons. One such popular dance is 'Dhan Naach' performed to project a rich cultural heritage of this community. 'Maruni' is one of the oldest dances in which young girls embellished with colourful costumes and rich ornaments perform dance in an extremely graceful and lyrical style on festive occasions. The Nepalese community consists of several tribes. Among them are the Gurungs, Limbus, Tamangs and Rais.

The Bhutias: They are the people of Tibetan origin. They migrated to Sikkim perhaps somewhere after the fifteenth century through the state of Sikkim. In Northern Sikkim, where they are the major inhabitants, they are known as the Lachenpas and Lachungpas. The language spoken by the bhutias is Sikkimese. Bhutia villages are as large as those compared to those of Lepchas. A Bhutia house called "Khin" is usually of rectangular shape Lachenpas and Lachungpas have their own traditional legal system called "Dzumsa" (meaning meeting place of the people) headed by "Pipon" (Village headman).

Even with the abolishing of Mondal Systems (A system where village headman called Mondal collects revenue from public and submits to government and also settles minor disputes) in other parts of Sikkim and coming up of Panchayati system, the Dzumsa of North Sikkim has been given full protection by the government by deeming a status of Panchayat ward and the Pipon, a status of Panchayat. The Bhutia aristocrats are called Kazis and they were the part of Chogyal government before 1975 when Sikkim state was an independent Kingdom. The Bhutia traditional dress called "Bakhu" which is a loose cloak type garment that is fastened at the neck on one side and near the waist with a cotton belt.

Male members put 'Bakhu' with a loose trouser. The ladies use 'Bakhu with a silken full sleeve blouse called "Honju" a loose gown type garment fastened near the waist tightly with a belt. In the front portion they tie a loose sheet of multi coloured woollen cloth made of special design. This is called "Pangdin" and is a symbol of a married woman. The ladies are very fond of heavy jewellery made of pure gold. Bhutias usually take rice with animal fat fried vegetables or meat. The other foods are "Momo" (steamed samosa with meat inside) and Thukpa (Noodles). "Zhero" and "Khabzay" are beautiful salty tusks prepared from flour during the festivals like Losar/Loosong.

Demographic Features

Sikkim is a fabulous Himalayan State, characterised by a unique physical charm and bashful cultural beauty, which is inhabited by people professing different faiths and who hail from different ethnic stocks. Before it that the varying sociocultural traits of the major populace groups are described in terms of demography it is worth while as well as quite meaningful to narrate the composite population characteristics of the state.

Demographic Attributes

Sex ratio (number of females per thousand male population) is an important demographic characteristic influencing some other attributes and social welfare. Sikkim has a sex ratio of 875 against the all-India sex ratio of 935. These figures pertain to the 1981 census.

A decade ago in the year 1971 when India had a sex ratio of 830 Sikkim was characterised with a sex ratio of 863. Two conclusions become crystally clear. Not only did Sikkim had ages-old relations with the polyandrous Tibetans but a section of the Sikkimese population, particularly the Bhutias have been polyandrous. The decline in the sex ratio during the present period when quite a large influx of the business bound floating population was necessitated corroborates the repeated findings of the demographers that the business bound immigration and emigration are sex selective and male dominated.

In the state of Sikkim as per 1981 census 29.02 per cent of the people belong to scheduled tribes and scheduled castes. Like all other Himalayan (more particularly the areas located in the Higher Himalaya) regions, the natives living here are by and large scheduled tribes people. Nonetheless, among the immigrants who are primarily from the Hindu dominated parts of India, there are people hailing from Harijan communities and are thus categorised as scheduled caste people. On the whole only seven per cent of the people living in Sikkim belong to this category. In the population of Sikkim there are people professing Hinduism, Buddhism, Islam, Christianity and Jainism. However, in numbers the Hindus and Buddhists dominate the populace.

In view of the ever-changing definition of a worker from census to census, it has become very difficult to present a comparative pictures of the working population. In the year 1971 about 56 per cent of the populace consisted of working population.

However, in the year 1981 as a result of changed definition, as elsewhere in the country, the percentage of the working population has come down to 45 per cent. Among them the agriculturists and those who pursue "other services" dominate the related scenario. A region where out of necessity every able-bodied person has to be pressed into one or the other activity, irrespective of age or sex (having very young children) take out a precarious sustenance the Labour-force is likely to be proportionately higher than the general picture of the country.

Moreover, a large influx of the workers from other parts of the country who enter the state mostly without their spouses and other dependants, the ranks and ratios in the working force shall get swelled.

After having peeped through the major demographic characteristics of the people of Sikkim, it is worthwhile to have a glance over the anthropological and sociological aspects of the major communities living in Sikkim.

The People

As per 2001 census the total population of Sikkim was 5,40,493 persons. It had risen from 2,09,843 persons in 1971 showing a decadal variation of 50.77 per cent or 5.07 per cent per year. In the year 1961 the total population of Sikkim was 1,65,189 persons.

In other words the increase in population during the census decade of 1961-71 was of the order of 27.03 per cent or about 2.7 per cent per year. It means the growth of population has been phenomenal, rapid and unprecedented during 1971-81. This means that much of the growth has been the outcome of immigration which was obviously required to man and manage the numerous plans, projects and schemes initiated, after Sikkim's merger in the Indian Union, for the socio-economic amelioration of the people of Sikkim.

Earlier to the merger Sikkim was only a protectorate of the Indian Union. No doubt India had been extending grants, subsidies, loans, assistance and support to the Sikkim Chogyal for initiating plans and policies aimed at the social uplift and economic development of the Sikkimese people but after the merger it became a sacred duty of the Union Government of India to bring about socio-economic changes on war-footing for the welfare of the people of Sikkim who had thrown their lot with India.

Naturally for opening hundreds of schools. Dispensaries, Public Health Centres, Hospitals, Veterinary Centres, Research-cioii — Training Centres, Banks and Cooperative Societies; Building Roads, Bridges, Houses for the People; Harnessing Water Power; Building and setting up small and medium scale industries; expanding existing infrastructural facilities; initiating many schemes for the development of villages and uplift of the down trodden of the society, expansion of establishments and the like the technocrats, bureaucrats, skilled workers, experts and others had to be immigrated to Sikkim. Such people who were taken to work in Sikkim for years together had to take their families along with them.

No wonder the rate of natural increase of population in the wake of expanding public health facilities was bound to rose. Resultantly the rate of population growth during the decade under reference was bound to be high and unprecedented.

Nonetheless, as a result of the local people trained in many vocations and the completion of certain vital projects the immigration rate of the floating population has relatively abated and it is expected that the growth of Sikkim's population in 1981-91 decade shall come down and the total population of the state in 1991 shall be around four lakhs. The tiny State of Sikkim covers only 0.2 per cent of the total geographical area of the Indian

Union and it carries only 0.04 per cent of the fatal population of the country. She ranks 24th among the State and Union Territories, of India as per area and 28th as per population.

As far as the arithmetic density of population is concerned, she has 45 persons on the average living in one square kilometre of her area. The States of Mizoram (23 person per sq km), Arunachal Pradesh (8 persons per sq km) and the Union Territory of Andaman and Nicobar island (23 persons per sq km) are still at lower rungs of the ladder. Nonetheless, vis-a-vis the national picture (221 persons per sq km), Sikkim does not appear to be an over-populated region. But when one views the issue in the context of the population distribution he realises the reality.

In fact only the southern and eastern parts of the state are inhabited. Even in the higher reaches of these sections, human settlements are found only along the river valleys and that too far and between in dispersed form.

Elsewhere the human settlements are few and far between. Vast stretches of land are characterised by steep slopes, inhospitable climate conditions, increasing incidence of snow mantle, snow storms, glaciers and avalanches. One does not find even the trace of Homosapiens for hundreds of kilometres. Hence, in the southern and southeastern densely populated parts of the state the human pressure on land is quite heavy.

In Gangtok, the average density crosses even the figure of one thousand. Thus whereas, the thickly peopled areas are over-populated and suffer from population problem the remaining parts in relation to present technology, do not seem to be potentially fit for human settlements and may be termed "non-acumen" of the demographers.

Urban Settlements

Against the 23.31 per cent of the total Indian population living in cities, towns and other urban areas, in Sikkim only 16.15 per cent of the people live in urban settlements. As many as eight states and Union Territories, *viz.*, Arunachal Pradesh (6.56%), Dadra and Nagar Haveli (6.67%), Himachal Pradesh (7.61%), Assam (10.29%), Orissa (11.52%,), Tripura (12.34%), Bihar (12.47%) and Nagaland (15.52%) are characterised by lower degrees of urbanisation. Till the census enumeration of 1941 Sikkim had no urban area. Only in the census operation of 1951 Gangtok was accorded urban status. For another two decades Gangtok was the lone urban settlement of Sikkim.

During the census enumerations of 1971 half a dozen new towns were identified. These were Singtam, Rangpo, Mangan, Gyalshing, Jarthang, Nayabazar and Namchi. After that when the immigrants swelled the population numbers of some other settlements and particularly the numbers of persons engaged in non-agricultural activities the number of census towns was likely to rise still further. However, till 1971 nearly two-third (68 per cent) of the urban population of the state continued to live in the capital town of Gangtok only.

Style of Living

The people of Sikkim and particularly the ruralites live in small houses scattered in villages. The houses by and large are similar to primitive dwellings anywhere. However, the Bhutia and Lepcha houses are different than the Nepalese houses. The Lepcha and Bhutia dwellings are constructed on taller stone foundations and they are often supported by poles made up of tree-trunks. Partially enclosed, basements of these houses are used for tethering animals at night. The Kiratis and Nepalese erect their houses on foundations that go deep underground. They construct separate apartments for their animals. These houses have thatched roofs but their walls are often made up of mud-clay materials. Nepalese take a pleasure in giving colour wash to their houses. Sometimes a Nepali house is multicoloured. The interiors of their dwellings are kept neat, clean and tidy by the Nepalese.

Every year, after the rainy season is over, the floors and walls of the houses are given a new look through a plaster made up of clay, cow dung and straw. The houses and their courtyards are enclosed by stone walls. Inside the courtyard every household maintains a small kitchen garden in which vegetables, fruit plants and vines (grape) are raised. The Nepalese and Kiratis also utilise this space for growing tobacco.

Apart from a small fraction the Sikkimese are a non-vegetarian people. Drinking of Liquour is quite common among the males. Raki and Chharlg are the popular local brews made out of rice and barley respectively. Before taking liquor the Sikkimese sprinkle few drops of it in the air to appear evil spirits. Among dishes Chhau-Chhau, a Sikkimese parallel of the Tibetan Chow-meen is taken on all festive occasions. It is a mixture of vegetables and noodles.

The three principal communities dress up in their own and different fashions. The Nepalese women folk tie a cloth around their waist for a skirt and cover the upper torso with a blouse. The headgear is called *majetro* which is a two metre long dupatta. This dress in the Gurkhali dialects is referred to as Gunyu Cholo or Fariya Cholo. Shirt, payjama (trousers), coat and a Nepali cap constitute the dress for male Nepali. The Lepcha and the Bhutia women dress up themselves in Bakkhu, a long double-breasted gown. This gown is fitted to the body with the help of along cloth piece tied along the waist.

Inside the gown a loose blouse with long sleeves is put on. The married womenfolk carry a long apron-like cloth hanging from the waist. This cloth is often brocaded on both the corners. The women of older generation still put on embroidered caps. On festive occasions Oonjiyoo, i.e. a silken coat is put on by those who can afford it. The Bhutia man too wear Bakkyiu with long sleeves. They put on trousers also. The Lepchas use the dress similar to the Naga dress.

In all probability, since they came to Sikkim after having settled in Nagaland for generations they stuck to their old dress. A cap carrying multicoloured feathers of different birds is their head dress. However, with the passage of time it has become difficult to identify people from their dresses since many Nepalese flaunt Bhutia dresses and vice versa.

Moreover, with increasing contact with the people from other parts of India, salwar kameez shirt, pantaloon, coat, neck-tie have made enroads. Educated people now prefer to dress themselves in the Western fashion. The Educated female now often support bobbed cut hair. Shukla is right when he says, "Thus Sikkim these days is a big cultured laboratory, where different blends are being mixed up and a synthetic culture part Bhutia, part Nepali and part Indian is coming up."

Sikkimese women love jewellery. The Bhutia womenfolk have a preference for Tibetan type of ornaments. Necklaces carrying costly stone heads steal the show. The Nepali woman like golden necklaces studded with costly stone heads. In remoter areas large earrings looking like bracelets are still used. The woman on the whole are soft spoken, laborious and attractive. In Sikkim there is no seclusion for women and they work shoulder to shoulder with man. Marriage ceremony is a gala festival for the Sikkimese. Earlier this ceremony was spread over eighteen days but now it has been limited to three days only. The maternal uncle of the bride holds a very prestigious position in matrimonial affairs. At the time of bethrothal (engagement) unless his consent is obtained no deal can be stuck. Obviously he is the first to receive gifts including money and liquor. Only after he has accepted the gifts the engagement stands binding, irrevocable and final. After engagement, the would be bridegroom is required to work with his prospective in-laws. On the day of wedding the would be couple and their parents gather together on a watir spring sprouting from beneath a massive monolith. At this spot the bride and bridegroom are blessed and it is prayed that the marriage may be as stable as the massive rock and the couple should have offspring continuously like the flow of the spring. Bride price has to be paid.

The price usually consists of a milch cattle, a calf, bronze and brass utensils, ornaments, a pony or a horse. The bride is taken to her in-laws a year after the wedding ceremony. On all these occasions the relatives of both the sides are feasted on delicacies and liquor. Till recently divorce had no sanction in this region. Chogyal Tashi Namgyal's wife lived separately but the King could not divorce her.

On the whole the Sikkimese are an honest, laborious and well-looking people. They are well behaved and hospitable. As Singh has commented "once you are in Sikkim you will be surprised at the grace, courtesy, easy laughter and the joie de vivre of the people. If you are any Sikkimese household to be initiated into the mystique of Chhang."

Festivals

Two festivals are occasions of special importance all over Sikkim. One occasion is dedicated to the deity Kanchenjunga and the other to Lossoong the Sikkimese New Year Day.

Kanchenjunga: The two day festival of dance performed during the worship of snowy range of Kanchenjunga (Khang-chen-dzod-nga) is a dance peculiar to Sikkim alone. It is celebrated in September. The third Chogyal of Sikkim, Chador Namgyal (1686-1716) introduced this dance about two and a half centuries ago as a result of a vision.

Kanchenjunga is about 40 km from Gangtok and is the most unifying force in the myth and identity of the state. Khang-chen-dzod-nga means the five treasures represented by five summits of this gigantic mountain. According to tradition the five treasures are salt, precious stones, religious scripts, medicines and grains and invincible armour.

The natural environment in which the Sikkimese live have made them to revere, fear and worship this mountain. They believe that their prosperity even their lives depend on the good humour of the deity, for he has the power to destroy human habitations with devastating floods and avalanches, wash away their bridges and ruin their crops by sending terrible hail storms down the valleys.

Kanchenjunga is portrayed as a fiery red — countenanced deity with a crown of five skulls, riding the mythical snow lion and holding aloft the banner of victory. Esoteric masks, flashing silks, opulent brocades and embroidered boots are the costumes of the dancers. The dancers are all male. In this warrior Dance the warlike pomp and panoply, the war deity resplendent the flaming robes, the fantastic Snow lion, comprise the essence of the dance. This mask dance is termed as Singhi Dance, i.e. Lion Dance by Nepalese. They visualise the ferocious god of Kanchenjunga riding over a lion and hence call this dance as Singhi Dance.

Lossoong: On Lossoong, the Sikkimese New Year Day, Black Hat (kali topi) Dance demonstrating the triumph of good over evil is demonstrated. This masked dance is also performed by male dancers mostly the Lamas. The dance revives the old story which narrates that about twelve centuries ago King Land-Darma was slain for suppressing Buddhism in Tibet. The King was slain by a Lama wearing a fantastic black robe lined with white and riding a white horse blackened with soot.

Health Care

The Department of Health and Family Welfare has made a considerable progress in providing basic health care services to the people of the state. It has already achieved the national norms of establishment of 1 Primary Health Centre per 20,000 and 1 Primary Health Subcentre per 3,000 population and can today boast of having one of the best rural infrastructure in the country.

All these centres have trained medical and Paramedical staff, capable of rendering the basic health care services. Although greater stress has been given to primary health care, the curative aspect of health has not been neglected. To augment the curative services, sophisticated equipments and specialised services in different fields have been made available at STNM Hospital, Gangtok. Super-speciality in Cardiology with Intensive Coronary Care Unit and a State Level Blood Bank and Transfusion Unit with facilities for HIV screening has also been set up at STNM Hospital, Gangtok. A 500-bedded Central Referral Hospital has also been completed in the capital in collaboration with Manipal Foundation Group for providing advanced tertiary level curative services.

The District Hospitals are also being upgraded at a rapid pace to provide better health care services to people residing in remote areas of the state. The Namchi District Hospital has already been equipped with latest sophisticated equipments under the bilateral scheme with the French Government.

Review of the basic health indices like Crude Death Rate, Crude Birth Rate, Infant Mortality Rate, etc. indicate a significant improvement in the health status of the people of the state through the years. All these health indicators are well below the national averages, however, they need to be improved further to achieve the desired goals.

Efforts are also being made to deal with diseases posing as major public health problems in the state. Tuberculosis has been one of them. The State, besides the grants provided by GOI, has been providing substantial financial assistance and other inputs to detect as many TB cases as possible and treat them with the latest regime of drugs. A new WHO strategy called 'Directly Observed Treatment (DOT) Course has been initiated in the state with the objective of achieving cure rate of more than 85 per cent.

The department has also been successful in bringing down the number of cases of Iodine Deficiency Disorders/Goitre to a substantial low level in the state. The prevalence of Goitre as per the sample survey conducted by ICMR in 1976 was 56 per cent. The sale of non-iodised salt has been banned throughout the state since 1985.

Significant achievements have also been made under various national Programmes like FW & MCH Programme (now known as Reproductive and Child Health Programme), National Leprosy Eradication Programme, National AIDS Control Programme, National Programme for Control of Blindness, etc. The performance under FW & MCH Programme has increased tremendously since the time, which is less than 1 case per 10,000 populations. The recorded prevalence rate of Leprosy as of March, 2001 is 0.91 per 10,000 population.

To combat the spread of Human Immunodeficiency Virus (HIV), an 'Aids Cell' was established in the state in 1992. Since then, a significant progress has been made in bringing about mass awareness among the people. So far, 13 HIV positive and 2 AIDS cases have been detected in the state. Besides these, State has been organising special eye and plastic surgery camps in collaboration with foreign agencies on regular basis. A special camp for physically handicapped was also organised in the state in 1996 and a total of 336 handicapped persons were provided with various types of aids.

The State Government is also able to provide free medicines and diet in all the hospitals and PHCs including other health related facilities. Treatment for ailments for which facilities do not exist in the state are being referred outside and the required financial assistance are being provided by the State Government.

A State Illness Assistance Fund has also been created with, the funding on sharing basis between the State Government and Govt. of India in the ratio of 75:25 for persons Below the Poverty Line (BPL) to make them avail the best referral services in institutions outside the state. The State Government has also brought out a Notification in June, 1996 waiving all charges on investigations and ICCU admissions to senior bonafide citizens (above 65 years).

A number of health related Acts and Notifications have been enforced or brought out in the state. Some of the important Acts brought out or enforced are "The Sikkim State Prohibition of Smoking and Non-Smokers Health Protection Act, 1997", "Pre-Natal Diagnostic Techniques (Regulation and Prevention of Misuse) Act, 1994", Bio-Medical Waste (Management and Handling) Rules, 1998, etc. The State Government has also established health cadres for the benefit of doctors, nursing and paramedical staff. A 'State Commission on Population' has also been constituted to implement the National Population Policy, 2000 in the state effectively.

The future programmes of the department are also encouraging, both from the point of preventive and curative aspects. The department hopes to achieve 'Health for All' by 2015. The State Government has also recently approved the proposal of upgrading and modernising the STNM Hospital of the capital. In view of the increasing number of accident cases in the state, a 'Trauma Centre' is also being established at STNM Hospital Gangtok with the financial assistance from the Government of India. A De-Addiction-cum- Treatment Centre for drug addicts and alcoholics has also been established at STNM Hospital and two more such centres are being constructed at Namchi and Gylashing.

To further strengthen and consolidate the health system and infrastructure, extra financial assistance is being sought from European Commission under European Commission Health and Family Welfare Sector Programme in India. The Australian Agency for International Development (Aus AID) has also agreed to provide financial assistance for capacity building (training) in Bio-Medical Waste Management under India-Australia Training and Capacity Building Project and other science activities by the students.

Sports and Games

A full-fledged Department of Sports and Youth Affairs was established on the 4th July 1995. This was an acknowledgement by the government of the importance of Sports and Youth Programmes in the development of our youth to promote physical fitness and through this to fight the menace of drugs, and to provide the facilities and exposure for the talented to excel.

At the school level all institutions are provided sports equipments. Inter School competitions at the district and the state levels are organised on a regular basis in a few chosen games. Inter School women's' football was introduced in 1999 and this was not with great enthusiasm by the fairer sex. The state championship in 2000 was won by the West District. Inter School football for the West District also won boys.

Participation of Sikkim in the National School Games been revived and the state school team participated in the 2000-01 National championship in Table Tennis (Gujarat) and Football (Jammu) in the month of December 2000. For promoting excellence a 'Search More Bhaichung' Programme was launched in 1999. Under this scheme a statewide talent hunt for the best under 14 year old footballers was carried out. In all over 6,000 players were screened and a final selection of 26 players was made.

A 'Sports Hostel' at Namchi has been started that houses for boys. Board and lodge is provided and the players are coached by the senior state coach of the department. The Sports hostel team took part in the 'sub-junior' Subroto Mukerjee tournament held at Delhi in November 2000. The team did well in reaching the semi finals of the tournament where it lost to the 'Steel Authority of India' football Academy. On the initiatives taken by the department, the Sports Authority of India has established a 'Sports Training Centre' at Namchi under its Special Area Games Scheme. The SAI Training Centre has the following three disciplines of:

- Football;
- Boxing; and
- Archery for promotion.

Preliminary work of setting up a Sports Academy at Gangtok has been initiated through short listing of talented juniors in Football, Table Tennis and middle distance running. Sports for the general public is organised and promoted through the different state sports associations. Although autonomous bodies most have been formed and established on the initiative of the department. The activities and programmes of these bodies are fully supported by the government through use of the various infrastructural facilities, the use of equipments and the technical support of its district sports officers and coaches.

There are now a total of 13 state associations and 3 district sports associations. These are listed below:

- Sikkim Archery Association,
- Sikkim Amateur Athletic Association,
- Sikkim Basketball Association,
- Sikkim Body Building Association,

- Sikkim Amateur Boxing Association,
- Sikkim Badminton Association,
- Sikkim Cricket Association,
- Sikkim Football Association,
- Sikkim Tae Kwon Do Association,
- Sikkim Amateur Tae Kwon Do Association,
- Sikkim Karate Association,
- Sikkim Table Tennis Association,
- Sikkim Veterans Association,
- South District Sports Association,
- West District Sports Association,
- North District Sports Association,
- Sikkim Olympic Association.

The Major competitions and tournaments organised and conducted by these associations include:

- "The Chief Ministers. Gold Cup Archery Tournament" initiated in 1999.
- The Vijay Merchant Cricket Tournament.
- The Kanchenjunga Invitational Boxing Tournament.
- "The Eastern India and Mr. Sikkim" Body Building Competition.
- "The Open Marathon" Competition.
- The All India Sikkim Governor's Gold Cup Tournament.
- "The 10th North Eastern Sports Festival" organised by the Department. Apart from these highlights all the associations conduct league and state championships on a regular basis.

The past few years has seen the state team/players making their mark at the National and International level.

- The state junior Football team was runners-up in the Junior National Championship's held at Manipur in 1998-99.
- Tae Kwon Do championships, held at Hong Kong in 2000.
  - Shri Heera Pradhan represented India and Shri Trilok Subba was chosen as the national coach for the competition.

The bestowing of the 'Arjuna Award' on Shri Bhaichung Bhutia was a matter of great pride to all Sikkimese. The year 2000 has ended on an encouraging note when recent National Championships for Tae Kwon Do, held at Bangalore on the 29th, 30th and 31st December, Sikkim bagged a total of 20 medals. To include: 4 Gold Medals, 10 Silver Medals and 6 Bronze Medals. To make a mark at the National level, the Department of Sports has acquired the services of 3 international sports-persons, all from Sikkim and employed them as coaches of the Department. They are:

- Shri Jaslal Pradhan (Arjuna Awardee) — Boxing.
- Shri Jigmee Youzer — Archery.
- Shri Thupden Rongkup — Archery.

So as to encourage sports and sports-persons the government has been pleased to issue two notifications:

- Facilities of leave as duty for sports-persons, technical officials and judge for recognised state zonal, Inter-state and international competitions and
- Cash Award incentives for athletes, players and teams for winning medals in recognised national competition.
- Under the Government of India incentive scheme scholarships at Rs. 5.400 per student/annum is provided by the Sports Authority of India for deserving sports-persons. The selection is based on performances registered at the district, state and interstate competitions. 72 such scholarships to include 16 National level scholarships at Rs. 7,200 per annum were awarded to Sikkimese boys and girls for the year 1999-2000.

Under its Programmes of infrastructural development the focus of the government is on the up gradation of the Paljor Stadium into a modern sports complex. The sources of funding have now been tied up and the work is in full progress. Under its youth Programme schemes, two of the major ones that are organised on an all India Basis by the Government of India, i.e. the National Service Scheme and the National Cadet Corp. Sikkimese youth are provided the opportunity to participate in activities that inculcate discipline, a sense of responsibility towards the society, a sense of national 'ONENESS' through integration camp Programmes as also to compete and excel.

The main activities were as under:

- Basic Leadership Course-mountaineering, conducted in association with the 'Sonam Gyamtso Mountaineering Institute'.
- A major integration camp with the participation of 700 youths from all over the country was organised at Rangpo in November, 2000. The Camp was held for a total of 10 days.

6

Education

Literacy in Sikkim is 69.68 per cent, which breaks down into 76.73 per cent for males and 61.46 per cent for females. There are a total of 1478 government-run schools and 471 private schools. Twelve colleges and other institutions in Sikkim offer higher education. The largest institution is the Sikkim Manipal University of Technological Sciences, which offers higher education in engineering, medicine and management. It also runs a host of distance education programmes in diverse fields. There are two state-run polytechnical schools, Advanced Technical Training Centre (ATTC) and Centre for Computers and Communication Technology (CCCT) in Sikkim which offer diploma courses in various branches of engineering. ATTC is situated at Bardang, Singtam and CCCT at Chisopani, Namchi. Sikkim University a central university, began operating in 2008 at Yangang, which is situated about 28 km from Singtam. Many students, however, migrate to Siliguri, Kolkata, Bangalore and other Indian cities for their higher education.

In a Special Category State like Sikkim, the role of education assumes special significance both in terms of human resource development and the resultant socio-economic advancement. Sikkim witnessed a massive expansion of schools in the last two decade of its merger into the Union.

The growth so far has been quantitative and it is about time that quality is induced in the existing system in order to ensure that the huge State investment yield return in the form of productive human resources. The State Government has adopted several measures towards that end. The teaching qualification has been upgraded and professional training made essential for fresh recruitment and training to in-service teachers is being planned out in phased manner. The State is also encouraging reputed private training institutes by providing them financial support in the form of grants-in-aid.

With the view to ensure that there is an equitable distribution and growth of schools in every corner of the state, 15 new school building are being constructed under BADP in the less accessible locations in the remote border areas of the state. Another 198 new school buildings are being constructed from the non-Lapsable Pool funds. A total of 6,557 sets of 3 seater desks and benches have been made from funds provided under BADP, NLP and PMGY. Free Textbooks, Exercise Books, Uniforms and Midday meals are being provided up to the Class-V level as added incentives to foster more enrolment and to curb dropout rates. There are no tuition fees for all students in the state from the Pre-Primary stage right up to the Degree level. As on 30.9.2000, there was a total enrolment of 1,52,249 students in Government and Government aided schools in the state. A school now exists within walking distance of every child in Sikkim. In the field of higher education the state has 6 colleges. The State Degree College, Tadong (East District) now offers Honours Courses in Physics and Geography in addition to its existing curriculum.

In the current session, the State Language, Lepcha, Limboo and Bhutia have been included in the curriculum. The Namchi Degree College (South District) was established in 1995 with the view to provide rural students access to higher education.

The Loyola College, Namchi provides B.Ed. Courses to which the Education Department annually sends a batch of in-service teachers. The Teacher Training Institute of the Carmel Sisters is a useful auxiliary to the DIET and SIE The Manipal Foundation has established an Engineering College. There is also a regional IGNOU Study Centre in the Capital Gangtok. In the area of professional and technical education, the government has established two Polytechnics:

- The Advanced Technical Training Centre at Bardang (East District).

- Centre of Computers and Communication Technology at Chisopani, South District.

(Both are established in technical collaboration with Nettur Technical Training Foundation, Bangalore).

The Centrally sponsored project CLASS is being successfully implemented in 16 Senior Secondary Schools in the four Districts. Five of these schools are equipped with the latest configured computers.

The Centrally Sponsored Scheme of Sarva Shiksha Abhiyan is being implemented in the West District to achieve the goals of Universalisation of Elementary Education. Pre-Project implementation of Sarva Shiksha Abhiyan in the remaining 3 District is currently under way. The Education Department envisions a future where every child in the state is well equipped with the knowledge, skills and the confidence that are the ingredients in ensuring a meaningful and purposeful life.

The Himalayan Kingdoms (Sikkim was so before its merger in the Indian Union) were traditionally governed by monarchies and the Kings who literally enjoyed the "divine rights". Whereas, Nepal was governed by an autocratic monarch till recently, the Kingdom of Bhutan continues to be ruled by a monarchy.

So was the system of governance in Sikkim till about a decade and a half ago. Since the ruling systems in Bhutan and Sikkim were influenced by Tibet, itself ruled by a Dalai Lama, it was but natural that these states should have also gone the way in which the ruler was not merely a temporal head but a spiritual head also.

Such a system was bound to last long in areas inhabited by simple and ignorant folks who were otherwise separated in small groups from other groups by high mountains and highly unfavourable physical environment. Nevertheless, in today's world closely and continuously interlinked by fast developing media, the days of such monarchies wherein the absolute power rests with one person are almost over. No wonder Sikkim started feeling political turmoil shortly after India attained freedom from the British yoke. And it was this turmoil that gave birth to political parties.

The first political party of Sikkim, *i.e.*, the Sikkim State Congress came into existence in the year 1947. To counter the movement and struggle waged by this party the vested interests in Sikkim floated another political party under the banner of the Sikkim National Party. When because of some omissions and commission, though unintentional, the role and character of the Sikkim State Congress came under clouds Lhendup Dorji Khangsarpa laid the foundations of the Sikkim National Congress.

However, when Dorji had to go in self-imposed exile in Europe, his party came under a scathing attack. The Chogyal through fair and foul means, of course more of foul means, succeeded in dividing the ranks and files of the Sikkim National Congress. In his absence it was the Sikkim National Party that started benefiting from this division. One more party, the Sikkim Janata Party, emerged out of the political confusion created by the intra-party feuds and inter party-strives. With the return of Dorji to Sikkim, the political events took sharp turns and a very hectic situation came to the forefront.

The political organisations had to wage a "do and die battle" for the ouster of the theocratic monarchy. In this struggle the Sikkim National Congress and the Sikkim Janata Congress came so close to each other that ultimately they merged to form a more formidable party, *i.e.*, Sikkim Congress. It was the Sikkim Congress that achieved ultimately the objective of Sikkim's merger with India and the replacement of the theocratic monarchy by a democratic set- up.

However, in the year 1977 when the newly constituted Janata Party routed the Indian National Congress from the political scenario in the Centre the Sikkim Congress also switched its loyalties. The Sikkim Congress also became a provincial organ of the Janata Party. Nevertheless, with the return of the Indian National Congress in the Centre the Janata Party in Sikkim also confronted a crisis. Some people founded Congress I also in the state. Once again the changing permutations and combinations led to political confusion and chaos in Sikkim.

Only at this juncture some Sikkimese politicians characterised by far-sight as well as foresight inferred that in Sikkim, until and unless a regional party oriented towards the local sociocultural milieu gets a stronghold there lay no political salvation for the region. Thus was born the Sikkim Sangram Parishad. During the last two general elections the Sikkim Sangram Parishad has literally been sweeping the polls in Sikkim and constituting the government. Even the lone member to the Parliament from Sikkim during these elections has been the representative of this party.

In Sikkim the state is governed by a Government headed by the leader of the majority party. The Governor in Sikkim is appointed by the President of India, who in turn invites the leader of the majority party to form the government. It is, however, the prerogative of the Chief Minister to choose the members of his Cabinet. The Chief justice to the Sikkim High Court is appointed by the President of India in consultation with the Supreme Court. The same procedure is adopted for the appointment of other Judges of the High Court. It is the Chief Justice who appoints Judges of the Subordinate Courts. The Chairman and the Members of the State Public Service Commission are appointed by the Governor.

The State comprises four districts. Each district is headed by a Collector or Deputy Commissioner. The Deputy Commissioner is lent a helping hand by the Subdivisional Officers, Tahsildars land Naib Tahsildars in the day-to-day administration. In some remote areas still the village headman and tribal chief enjoy more power and authority. The system of modern Panchayats has also started becoming popular in certain parts of the state. These Panchayats besides looking after the developmental works also dispense justice to the villagers. Patwari is the lowest but very powerful revenue official in the village, assisted in the discharge of his duties by the village watchman. The Village-Level Worker, *i.e.*, the Gram Sewak has now become a friend, philosopher and guide to the ruralites who advises them on the choice of seeds, implements, fertilizers, etc.

Sikkim is the state where departments were started and strengthened on the advice of the Government of India when Sikkim was an Indian Protectorate. In the administrative annals of the state, very often one comes across narrations which describe that a particular department was initiated on the counsel of the Government of India. At present there are about three dozen departments which look after the administration, development, welfare and justice. Among them the important ones are the departments of agriculture, animal husbandry, local self government, forests, tourism, power, law, public works, industries, health, education, cooperation geology and mining, printing and Stationery, food and supplies establishment, planning and development, rural development, scheduled tribes and scheduled castes welfare. Police, land department is peculiar to only some states in India and among them Sikkim enjoys an important place.

It is the department which looks after the religious institutions in the state. A region suffering from terrain difficulties and climatic hospitalities rather hostilities is bound to have deeply religious people.

Obviously in such a region there shall be shrines, monasteries and nunneries. Thus it is very essential that the State Government has a department which provides support and helping hand to these institutions and also keeps an eye on the management of such institutions.

Education System

The thumb-shaped and bantam state of Sikkim has revealed in the tremendous evolution in the arena of education that it has achieved since the last decade or so. There has been an abundance in the number of fresh schools along with colleges that are being erected in order to procure an impetus to Sikkim education. There are numerous esteemed schools within the proximity of Sikkim, that are either affiliated to the ICSE or CBSE Board of education which is an epitome of the augmenting standards of Sikkim education. But the major resurgence has been in the field of higher education owing to the fact that entire caboodle of colleges are being established to meet the ever increasing demands of the career-minded pupils. This much needed impulsion in the field of education of Sikkim, has refurbished the entire structure of the state as well. The major colleges that have upgraded the touchstone of education across Sikkim includes the Sikkim Government College in Gangtok, Loyola College of Education at Namchi, Manipal Institute of Technology, Industrial Technique Institute in Rangpo, Research Institute of Tibetology, Manipal Institute of Medical Sciences, Institute for Handicrafts in Gangtok, SHEDA Institute of Tibetology, Damber Singh College in Deorali.

All these above-mentioned organisations epitomise the level of education across Sikkim and has increased the opportunities presented to the youth of the state. The entrance examinations along with the computer learning academies constitute another integral wing of the education within Sikkim. Thus, if you are dwelling in Sikkim, you will not have to invest too much time in searching the most apt institute for your child.

Schools

With the advent of the 21st century, the Sikkim schools have undergone a major transition, as a result of which the pupils are bestowed with many different sorts of facilities that one dreams of. As a matter of fact, Sikkim schools have beyond a shadow of a doubt lifted up the standards of education in this state and continues to get even better. The major schools across Sikkim which have taken it to their responsibility to nurture the youth of the state and procure them with a platform so that they can excel in any field of their choice, are mentioned below:

Tashi Namgyal Academy (TNA): Previously dowered with the designation of 'Nepali-Bhutia School', this school is so spacious that it can accommodate a maximum of 1747 students without any major hindrance. The ICSE board from Delhi has granted affiliation to this esteemed school.

Sa-Valle-Row Academy: Ever since its erection in the year 1995, this school can house a total of 300 students at a time. This school has obtained its affiliation from the CBSE Board and includes 4 non-teaching staff.

Children's Preparatory School (CPS): Regarded as one of the most cost-effective schools, the Children's Preparatory School has however made no compromise with the quality of education that it imparts to its students.

Holi Cross School: Amongst all the missionary schools at Sikkim, the Holi Cross School is regarded as the most reputed and has a capacity to accommodate 1,300 students.

Army School: This is one of those few schools of Sikkim, that aims towards procuring education to the heirs of the army personnels.

- Tashi Namgyal Academy, Gangtok.
- Namchi Public School, Namchi, South Sikkim.
- St. Joseph's School, Martham.
- Tashi Namgyal Higher Secondary School (boys), Gangtok.
- Kendriya Vidyalaya School, Gangtok.
- Palzor Namgyal Girls School, Gangtok.
- Bahai' School, Gangtok.
- HDFS School, Chongey.
- Deorali Girls Senior Secondary School, Gangtok.
- Enchey Senior Secondary School, Gangtok.
- Holy Cross High School, Gangtok.
- Modern School, Gangtok.
- Kyi-de-Khang School, Gangtok.
- West Point Senior Secondary School, Gangtok.
- St. Xaviers School, Pakyong.
- St. Francis School, Jorethang, South Sikkim.
- Tendong Academy, Namchi, South Sikkim.
- Don Bosco School, Malbasey, Soreng, West Sikkim.

Colleges and Institutes

Among all other Northeastern States of India, Sikkim has the best educational infrastructure. In last few years, there has been a phenomenal growth of education in Sikkim. The state has quite a few pre-primary schools and CBSC affiliated Senior Secondary

Schools. Unsurprisingly, Sikkim has won the title of 'Best performing small state in Education' in 2004 and 2005 and also the 'Skoch challenger award for best use of Information Technology'. Higher education in Sikkim has been smoothened by the rapid growth of various colleges and institutions in Sikkim.

Sikkim Government Law College

Established in 1977, this college offers honours courses in English, Nepali, Political Science, Accountancy, History, Geography, Zoology and Botany and also Law course

Namchi Degree College

Here honours courses in English, Economics, Education and Nepali are taught along with pass courses in English, Geography, Nepali, Sociology, Economics, Political Science and Education.

Damber Singh Degree College

Set up in 1944, this college teaches only pass courses in English, Political Science, Sociology and Education.

Loyala College of Education

This college is specifically for B.Ed. Course.

Apart from these colleges in Sikkim, Sikkim colleges and institutions also include Government College at Rhenock, Harkamaya College of Education at Deorali, Pakim Paletine College at Pakyong, Himalayan Pharmacy Institute at Mazitar. There are management Institutes in Sikkim like Sikkim Manipal Institute of Technology, Polytechnic institutes like Advanced Technical Training Centre, research centre like the National Research Centre for Orchids. There is scope for hotel management studies in Sikkim, at Institute of Hotel Management, Tadong.

Universities

Sikkim universities allow the students to opt for higher studies within the territory. The universities of Sikkim provides a peaceful academic atmosphere for the students, so that the students of Sikkim can be keep abreast with the latest technologies.

Sikkim universities helps the students within the territory of Sikkim to pursue a higher degree at the tertiary level. Moreover, it is noteworthy that in Sikkim, universities witness a large variety in the population of the students, who enrol in the universities at Sikkim to pursue their higher studies. Apart from students from within the territory, Sikkim also witnesses a large number of students from the neighbouring countries who come to Sikkim to harness their future. The Sikkim Manipal University is one of the renowned universities of Sikkim that is helping the students to strengthen their prospects in life.

Universities are the career shapers. After completing 10 + 2 level of school education students join some university, or any college affiliated with a university in general or technical discipline for completion of under graduate courses, which opens the door for the real job market as well as for higher studies at post-graduate and research level.

When students pass 10 + 2 level of examination they are required to submit application form for different universities/university colleges to join a course. The selection is normally made on the basis of merit in last qualifying examination or on the basis of entrance test conducted by the university or on the basis of both. In some cases interview is also conducted. Generally students are required to submit separate application form for individual university or University College. At same time pupil require detailed and up to date information about a university/university college like about the university, courses offered or admission details, etc. And gaining know-how about individual institute or university is a rigorous task.

To make the work of aspiring students easier our team of educational researcher at National Network of Education (NNE) has collected detailed information about the university in Sikkim.

Moreover, the Sikkim University Bill, 2006 also seems to be instrumental in the development of the universities in Sikkim. According to this Bill, there should be a university in Sikkim under the name of Sikkim University. The Bill further states that the Sikkim University must be given certain powers which are as follows:

- To provide instructions to the institutions under the Sikkim University.
- To grant diplomas and degrees to the students on the basis of examinations.
- To undertake and extend extramural studies and trainings.
- To provide the facilities such as distance education and correspondence education.
- To provide Principalships, Professorships, etc.

Thus, we can see that the universities of Sikkim largely help the students of Sikkim to strengthen their prospects in future.

7

Language and Literature

In Sikkim at present there are people, as employees, from different parts of India. Among them are people who profess to faiths like Islam, Christianity, Sikhism and Jainism. However, they constitute a fractional minority in the total population of the state. The natives of Sikkim have been Buddhists and Hindus.

Among these people, the demographic scenario consisted of three major communities, *i.e.*, the Lepchas, the Bhutias and the Nepalese, Since these three communities, in minute details, have different sociocultural backgrounds, they speak different dialects also. The relatively original inhabitants, *i.e.*, the Lepchas or Rongpos speak Rongkye, *i.e.*, the language (Kye) of the Rongs or Rongpas.

But this tongue is spoken by those Lepchas who live away from Gangtok and particularly in isolated, remote and inaccessible rural areas. The Lepchas who have been living in Gangtok and southern Sikkim for a long time, naturally came in contact with the physically very active and mentally alert Nepalese who have dominated trade, commerce, business, agriculture and pastoral activities.

Thus these Lepchas who have come under the closer contacts of the Nepalese obviously wished and preferred to learn the Nepalese tongues. On the other hand those Lepchas who took keen interest in the learning and propagation of Buddhism had to learn the Tibetan language and the Bhutia dialects because, whereas, most of the basic religious titles related to Buddhism are written Sanskrit, Pali, Prakrit and Tibetan language, the anchor sheet of the Sikkimese Mahayan, *i.e.*, Kanjoor-Tanjoor are written in the Bhutia tongue. Mahayana Buddhism has been the state religion in Sikkim till the state was merged in the Indian Union, when it automatically became secular and as per Constitution of India the state cannot profess or further any religion.

Nonetheless, the people of Sikkim and particularly the Lepchas and Bhutias continue to be Buddhists and under the shelter of the Indian Constitution they are free to profess, preach and further their religious faith, *i.e.*, Mahayana-Buddhism. Under such conditions, no wonder one finds the ancient literature of Sikkim, overwhelmingly religious in its character, is in Sanskrit, Pali and Prakrit languages. Even the bed-rock of the Mahayana Buddhism, *i.e.*, Kanjoor-Tanjoor in its original form was composed in Sanskrit and was later on got translated in Bhutia language.

In fact the Kanjoor-Tanjoor is that religious scripture which contains in its composed form, the Tibetan version of the discourse delivered by Lord Buddha which were originally written in Sanskrit. The Kanjoor-comprises 108 volumes of about one thousand pages each. The Tanjoor on the other hand besides containing explanations and commentaries on original scriptures comprises treatises on History, Science and Painting.

On the day of Buddha Purnima, *i.e.*, the birthday of the Lord Buddha, the Kanjoor-Tanjoor are taken out in procession and people pay their reverences, respects and homage. Barring this theological literature no other literature has so far been crated in the Sikkimese-Bhutia language.

However, during recent years and particularly after the reins of administration came into the hands of the popularly elected governments, some school level textbooks have started appearing in the Bhutia language. Certainly it is a welcome step to wipe out illiteracy from among the Lepchas of isolated and remote settlements. It is also a very happy development that with the rising rates of literacy and the gradual spread of education some gifted young poets have started composing their verses in the Sikkimese-Bhutia language. Lobjang Lama is one such poet who has created a mark on the literary scenario of this region.

For a long time the Lepcha or Kye language had no script of its own. Under such conditions no literature could have been produced in the Kye language. Nevertheless, Chador Namgyal, the third Chogyal invented a script for this language. However, no attempt could be made to develop a type for Lepcha script. Resultantly it was not possible to print books in this language. Nonetheless, some enthusiastic Lepcha zealots started bringing out a hand written magazine in this language. But because of many inherent difficulties, particularly the want of finances and patronage, the attempt had to be abandoned soon after.

As already stated about two-third of the people living in Sikkim are Nepalese; they invariably speak different Nepalese dialects. The sub-sects of the Nepalese, *i.e.*, Rais, Gurangs, Limbus, and Tamangs use their different dialects. The Nepalese language and literature have now come to flourish in Sikkim, particularly when there are no restrictions on the free expression by people in any language of one's choice. A "Nepali Study Circle" has been constituted by some Nepalese interested in the development and furtherance of their language, literature, culture and tradition.

The circle has been successfully bringing out a quarterly magazine in the Nepali language. This organ has been providing opportunities to budding Nepalese poets, story writers, essayists and journalists.

The circle also brings out a monthly in English language, but many, rather a majority, of the articles included in this magazine are by the Nepali contributors who very often write about the sociocultural spectrum of the Sikkimese-Nepalese. The monthly highlights even the problems faced by the Nepali community. Even some of the finest Nepali stories in English renderings appear in this organ, so that non-Nepali knowing people of Sikkim can be educated about the literary richness of the Nepalese.

This monthly magazine has been given the name of Premula. Tulsi Aptan, Ramdatt Lal Thakur, Raghunath Suvedi, Santosh Barweda and Shanti Pradhan are those Nepali poets of Sikkim who have made a mark in their field.

So long as the state of Sikkim was under the dominance of the feudal Bhutia monarchs, the Bhutia language was the language of the state. Nonetheless, English had been widely used and continues to be used in offices and educational institutions. However, one finds a very pleasant change with the people's rule coming into power. The three-language formula has been adopted in schools.

Besides English and a native language the school students are required to learn Hindi as well from class IV to class VIII. Such a policy is a right step towards national integration and the meaningful development of the regional languages. The State on its part takes all steps to develop all languages. The work may however become easy if the State Government goes ahead to establish a department or academy dealing with the development of languages, literature and culture of the region.

Languages

Nepali is the *lingua franca* of Sikkim. Bhutia and Lepcha are also common. English and Hindi are also spoken and understood in most of Sikkim. Other languages include Dzongkha, Groma, Gurung, Limbu, Magar, Majhi, Majhwar, Nepal Bhasa, Rai, Sikkimese, Sherpa, Sunuwar, Tamang, Thulung, Tibetan, and Yakha.

Indian English, the Official Language

Indian English or South Asian English comprises several dialects or varieties of English spoken primarily in the Indian subcontinent. These dialects evolved during and after the colonial rule of Britain in India. English is one of the official languages of India, with about ninety million speakers according to the 1991 Census of India. Fewer than a quarter of a million people speak English as their first language. With the exception of some families who communicate primarily in English, as well as members of the relatively small Anglo-Indian community numbering less than half a million, speakers of Indian English use it as a second or third language, after their indigenous Indian language(s), such as, Assamese, Urdu, Gujarati, Punjabi, Hindi, Sindhi, Pushto, Bengali, Balochi, Kannada, Telugu, Marathi, Tamil, Malayalam, etc.

Several idiomatic forms, derived from Indian literary and vernacular language, also have made their way into Indian English. Despite this diversity, there is general homogeneity in syntax and vocabulary among the varieties of Indian English.

Sikkimese

Sikkimese language, or Sikkimese Tibetan language (also known as Dranjongke (Wylie: *'bras-ljongs-skad*), 'Bhutia language', Dranjoke, Denjongka, Denzongpe Ke, Denzong Ke) belongs to the Southern Tibetan language family. It is spoken by the Denzongpa nationality in Sikkim. Sikkimese People refer to their own language as Dranjongke (Wylie: *'bras-ljongs-skad*) and their homeland as Denzong (valley of rice).

Sikkimese is written using Tibetan script.

Nepali

Nepali is an Indo-Aryan language with around 17 million speakers in Nepal, Bhutan, Burma and India. Nepali was originally known as Khas Kura and was the language of the Khasa Kingdom, which ruled over the foothills of what is now Nepal during the 13th and 14th centuries.

Nepali first started to be used in writing during the 12th century AD. It is written with the Devanagari alphabet, which developed from the Brahmi script in the 11th century AD. Three letter code for Nepali is NEP.

Nepali is spoken in eastern region and adjacent south central region of Nepal and also spoken in Bhutan, Brunei, India. People speaking Nepali are 99,00,000 in Nepal, 58.3 per cent of the population and total in all countries is 1,60,56,000 including Bhutan and India.

Alternative Names of Nepali are NEPALESE, GORKHALI, GURKHALI, KHASKURA, PARBATIYA, EASTERN PAHARI. Dialects of Nepali are BAITADI, BAJHANGI, BAJURALI (BAJURA), DOTELI, SORADI, ACCHAMI, JUMLELI (JUMLA, SINGJA, SIJALI), and DARJULA.

It is official language and *de facto lingua franca* of Nepal and is also spoken in Bhutan, parts of India and parts of Myanmar (Burma). In India, it is one of the country's 23 official languages: Nepali has official language status in the formerly independent state of Sikkim and in West Bengal's Darjeeling district. Similarly, it is widely spoken in the state of Uttaranchal, as well as in the state of Assam.

Geographically, Nepali is the easternmost of the Pahari languages, a group of related languages spoken across the lower elevations of the Himalaya range, from eastern Nepal through the Indian states of Uttarakhand and Himachal Pradesh. The influence of the Nepali language can also be seen in Bhutan and some parts of Burma. Nepali developed in proximity to a number of Tibeto-Burman languages, most notably Nepal Bhasa, and shows Tibeto-Burman influences. Nepali is closely related to the Hindi-Urdu complex (macrolanguage) and is sometimes considered mutually intelligible to some extent, yet is more conservative with more Sanskritic derivations and fewer Persian or English loan words. Nepali is commonly written in the Devanagari script, as are Hindi and Sanskrit. There is some record of using Takri script in the history of Nepali, especially in western Nepal, Utarakhand, and Himanchal. Bhujimol is an older script native to Nepal, while Rajana script is another writing system historically used.

Nepali developed a significant literature within a short period of hundred years in the nineteenth century, fuelled by Adhyatma Ramayana; Sundarananda Bara (1833); Birsikka, an anonymous collection of folktales; and a version of the South Asian epic Ramayana by Bhanubhakta. The contribution of trio-laureates Poudyal, Devkota, and Sama took Nepali to the level of other world languages. Template: Clarification The contribution of expatriate writers outside Nepal — especially in Darjeeling and Varanasi — is also notable.

Historically, the language was first called *Khaskura*, then Gorkhali or Gurkhali (after the Gurkha ethnic group before the term *Nepali* became dominant. Other names include Parbatiya ("mountain language", identified with the Parbatiya people of Nepal) and Lhotshammikha (the "southern language" of the Lhotshampa people of Bhutan). Scholars Kamal Malla and Tej. Kansakar comment of the Sanskrit derivation of Nepali: Janaka, Yajnavalkya, Valmiki, Kapila and Gautama Buddha have greatly contributed to the Sanskrit and Prakrita from which the Nepali language seeks its origins.

Lepcha

Lepcha language, or Rong language is a language spoken by the Lepcha people in Sikkim, and parts of Nepal and Bhutan. The Lepcha script (also known as "rong") is a syllabic script which has a lot of special marks and requires ligatures. Its genealogy is unclear. Early Lepcha manuscripts were written vertically, a sign of Chinese influence. Lepcha is considered to be one of the aboriginal languages of the area in which it is spoken. Total number of speakers numbers near 50,000. Lepcha is difficult to classify, but Van Driem (2001) suggests that it may be closest to the Mahakiranti languages.

Hindi

Hindi is the name given to an Indo-Aryan language, or a dialect continuum of languages, spoken in northern and central India (the "Hindi belt").

Native speakers of Hindi dialects between them account for 41 per cent of the Indian population (2001 Indian census). The Constitution of India accords Hindi in the Devanagari script as the *official* (But it is one of the official language along with English but one among the national language along with many other languages of India) language of India (English being the subsidiary official language). It is also one of the 22 scheduled languages specified in the Eighth Schedule to the Constitution. Official Hindi is often described as Standard Hindi which, along with English, is used for administration of the central government. Hindustani or Standard Hindi is also an official language of Fiji.

The term *Hindi* is used from multiple perspectives of language classification; therefore, it must be used with care. Standard Hindi and standard Urdu are considered by linguists to be different formal registers both derived from the *Khari Boli* dialect: Hindi being Sanskritised and Urdu being additionally Persianised (written with different writing systems, Devanagari and Perso-Arabic script, respectively).

Other Languages

Dzongkha Language

Dzongkha, occasionally *Ngalopkha,* is the national language of Bhutan. The word "dzongkha" means the language (*kha*) spoken in the *dzong,* – dzong being the fortress-like monasteries established throughout Bhutan by Shabdrung Ngawang Namgyal in the 17th century.

Dzongkha bears a close linguistic relationship to J'umowa spoken in the Chumbi valley of Southern Tibet and to the Dranjongke language of Sikkim. It has a much more distant relationship to standard modern Central Tibetan. Although spoken Dzongkha and Tibetan are largely mutually unintelligible, the literary forms of both are both highly influenced by the liturgical (clerical) Classical Tibetan language, known in Bhutan as *Choke,* which has been used for centuries by Buddhist monks. Choke was used as the language of education in Bhutan until the early 1960s when it was replaced by Dzongkha in public schools.

Dzongkha and its dialects are the native tongue of eight western districts of Bhutan (viz. Phodrang, Punakha, Thimphu, Gasa, Paro, Ha, Dhakana, and Chukha). There are also some speakers found near the Indian town of Kalimpong, once part of Bhutan but now in West Bengal. Dzongkha study is mandatory in all schools in Bhutan, and the language is the *lingua franca* in the districts to the south and east where it is not the mother tongue.

Linguistically, Dzongkha is a South Bodish language belonging to the proposed Tibeto-Burman branch of the Sino-Tibetan group. It is closely related to Sikkimese, the national language of the erstwhile Kingdom of Sikkim; and to some other Bhutanese languages such as Cho-cha-na-ca (*khyod ca nga ca kha*), Brokpa (*me rag sag steng 'brog skad*),

Brokkat *(dur gyi 'brog skad)*, and Laka *(la ka)*. Modern Tibetan is a Central Bodish language and thus belongs to a different sub-branch.

Dzongkha is usually written in Bhutanese forms of the Tibetan script known as Joyi *(mgyogs yig)* and Joshum *(mgyogs tshugs ma)*. Dzongkha books are typically printed using Ucan fonts like those to print the Tibetan abugida.

Dzongkha is rarely heard outside Bhutan and environs. However, the 2003 Bhutanese film, *Travellers and Magicians* is entirely in Dzongkha.

"Bhutani" is *not* another name for Dzongkha, but the name of a Balochi language. The two are sometimes confused, even in some published ISO 639 codelists.

Groma Language

Groma is a language spoken in Sikkim and Tibet. It belongs to the southern group of Tibetan languages. Its speakers identify as Tibetans.

Gurung Language

Gurung is a term used to collectively refer to Eastern Gurung and Western Gurung, nevertheless, mutual intelligibility between the two languages is limited. Total number of all Gurung speakers in Nepal is 2,27,918 (1991 census). Perhaps, a distinction should be made between Gurung as an ethnic group and the number of people who, actually, speakers of Gurung.

Nepali, Nepal's official language, is an Indo-European language, whereas Gurung is a Sino-Tibetan (or according to recent revisions-Tibeto-Burman) language. Gurung are recognised as an official nationality by the Government of Nepal.

Limbu Language

Limbu is a Tibeto-Burman language spoken in Nepal, Sikkim, Kashmir and Darjeeling district, West Bengal, India, by the Limbu community. Virtually all Limbus are bilingual in Nepali.

The name *Limbu* is an exonym of uncertain origin. Limbus refer to themselves as *yakthungba*, and their language as Yakthung Pan. It has four main dialects; Panthare, Phedape, Chatthare and Tambar Khole. Panthare dialect is the standard dialect of the Limbu language, whereas Phedape is spoken and understood by most.

Magar Language

Magar is a language spoken in parts of Nepal and Sikkim in India by Magar people. It is divided into two groups: Eastern and Western, and further dialect divisions give distinct tribal identity. In Nepal, 770,116 speak the language.

While the Government of Nepal developed Magar language curricula, as provisioned by Constitution, the teaching materials haven't successfully reached Magar schools. At least one Magar feels that failure among members of his caste to take education seriously may be the result of school instruction in Nepali language. It's not unusual for groups with their own language to feel that the "mother-tongue" is an essential part of identity.

"If we want to develop the Magar language, we should not teach our children Nepali. We have to teach the Magar language first. We have to teach learning and reading the language from the very beginning. For example, they are all Magar in Gulmi Bharsay hills. They don't know the Magar language, nobody speaks Magar but they are educated, they are rich too. But they do not speak the Magar language".

Magar language is sometimes lumped with Kham language spoken further west in Bheri, Dhaulagiri, Karnali and Rapti zones. Although the two languages have a large number of words in common, they have major structural differences and are not mutually intelligible.

Majhi Language

Majhi is a language spoken in parts of Nepal and Sikkim. Total population: 22,087.

Majhwar Language

Majhwar is an unclassified language — possibly a dialect of Asuri — spoken in parts of Nepal and Sikkim. Total population: 27,958.

Nepal Bhasa

Nepal Bhasa is one of the major languages of Nepal. It is one of roughly five hundred Sino-Tibetan languages, and belongs to the Tibeto-Burman branch of this family. It is the only Tibeto-Burman language to be written in the Devanagari script. It is spoken mainly by the Newars, who chiefly inhabit the towns of the Kathmandu Valley. Although Nepal Bhasa is classified as a Sino-Tibetan language, it has been greatly influenced by the Indo-Aryan languages.

Geographic Distribution

The language is spoken by roughly around a million people in Nepal according to 2001 census; a few thousand people outside Nepal also speak the language. In terms of speakers, it ranks similar to Jumli, another language spoken mainly in western Nepal.

- In Nepal: Kathmandu valley, i.e. (Kathmandu Metropolitan City, Lalitpur Sub Metropolitan City, Bhaktapur Municipality, Kirtipur Municipality, Thimi Municipality), Dolakha, Banepa, Dhulikhel, Bhimphedi (Makwanpur), Panauti, Palpa, Trishuli, Nuwakot, Bhojpur, Biratnagar, Baglung, Bandipur, Birgunj, Hetaunda and other chief cities.

- In India: Sikkim, West Bengal.

- In Tibet: Khasa.

With an increase in emigration, various bodies and societies of Nepal Bhasa-speaking people have emerged in countries like the United States, the UK, Australia and Japan.

Dhanwar Language (Dhanwar also known as Rai)

Dhanwar also known as Rai is a language spoken in parts of Nepal by an Indo-Aryan ethnic group. It is an Indo-Aryan language belonging to the East Central zone and must not be confused with Tibeto-Burmese Rai languages spoken by the Rai of Southern Mongoloid phenotype. Dhanwar's total population: 53,229. There are almost 150 different kinds of Rai who speak different Rai languages.

Sherpa Language.

Some grammatical aspects of Sherpa are as follows:

- Nouns are defined by morphology when a bare noun occurs in the genitive and this extends to the noun phrase. Defined by syntactic co-occurrence with the locative clitic, comes first in the noun phrase after demonstratives.

- Demonstratives are defined syntactically by first position in the NP directly before the noun.

- Quantifiers: Number words occur last in the noun phrase with the exception of the definite article.

- Adjectives occur after the noun in the NP and morphologically only take genitive marking when in construct with a noun.

- Verbs may morphologically be distinguished by differing or suppletive roots for the perfective, imperfective, and imperative. Occur last in a clause before the verbal auxiliaries.

- Verbal Auxiliaries occur last in a clause.

- Postpositions occur last in a postpositional NP.

Sunwar Language

Sunuwari is a Kiranti language spoken in Nepal by the Sunuwar people. It was first comprehensively attested by the Himalayan Languages Project.

Tamang Language

Tamang is a term used to collectively refer to a dialect cluster spoken in parts of Nepal and Sikkim. It comprises Eastern Tamang, Northwestern Tamang, Southwestern Tamang, Eastern Gorkha Tamang, and Western Tamang. Lexical similarity between Eastern Tamang (which is regarded as the most prominent) and other Tamang languages varies between 81 per cent to 63 per cent; lexical similarity between Spanish and Portuguese, for instance, is estimated at 89 per cent.

Thulung Language

Thulung is a Kiranti language spoken in parts of Nepal and Sikkim. It is also known as Thulunge Rai, Thulu Luwa, Thululoa, Thulung La, Tholong Lo, Thulung Jemu, Toaku Lwa. Total population: 33,313.

Literature

Nepali Literature

Nepali Literature refers to literature written in the Nepali language. It is not necessarily written by Nepali nationals nor all the literature written in Nepal, because it is widely used in some parts of India and Bhutan. In fact the official language of Indian state of Sikkim is Nepali. There are many prominent writers of Nepali literature from other countries, especially from India like Parijat. Also there is a diversity of languages spoken in Nepal like Maithali, Bhojpuri, Nepal Bhasa, etc.

The Nepali language evolved from Sanskrit and it is difficult to state the ancient history of Nepali literature because most scholars wrote in Sanskrit, especially religious literature. However, Nepali literature can be roughly divided into five periods.

Pre-Bhanubhakta Era

Nepali literature certainly existed in oral and folklore forms for hundreds of years. There exists no evidence of a published literary work in Nepali language before Bhanubhakta, however.

Bhanubhakta Era

Most, if not all, Nepali language speakers honour Bhanubhakta as the "ADIKAVI" (literally meaning 'first poet') of the Nepali language. Bhanubhakta's single most important contribution to Nepali literature is probably his translation of the holy Ramayana into Nepali language. Bhanubhakta wrote the Ramayana in metric form, using metres used in Sanskrit. Bhanubhakta also wrote original poems on diverse subjects ranging from family morals advocacy to satire of bureaucratic red tape and poor conditions of prisoners.

Motiram Era

Motiram Bhatta is the figure who revived the legacy of Bhanubhakta and publicised the contributions of the latter. Motiram played such a fundamental role in the legacy of Bhanubhakta that some allege that Bhanubhakta was just a fabrication of Motiram's mind.

Pre-Revolution Era

A very prolific time despite lack of freedom of expression, independent magazine "Sharada" was the only print medium available for the publication of Nepali literature. Short stories had Laxmi Prashad Devkota, Guru Prashad Mainali, and Bishweshwar

Prashad Koirala as the recognised trident force. But this was one of the most significant periods for literature development. "Muna Madan" by Laxmi Prashad Devkota shows the life of a man who leaves his wife and goes abroad to make money and while returning he dies. It also shows the life of a poor woman who suffered much without her husband. Bishweshwar Prashad Koirala introduced psychology in literature. His literary works are "Teen Ghumti", "Doshi Chasma", "Narendra Dai", etc.

Post-Revolution Era

In Muna Madan, the hero returns home from Lhasa after earning money but does not find his wife and mother. He does not die till the end of this 'khandyakavya' and we can consider him to be a tragic hero Muna Madan.

"The trope of 'building' that runs though (Indra Bahadur) Rai's novel *Aaja Ramita Chha* (1964)... must be seen not simply as materialistically aspirational, as a derivative symbol of arrival for the protagonist, but as a measure of dwelling that is at home in history."

Literacy

The rate of literacy till the influx of immigrants arrived in Sikkim continued to be miserably low. Small wonder at the time of 1971 census operation only 18.5 per cent of the Sikkim's population only consisted of literate persons. Even this total literate population was male dominated. Very few females at that time were literate. After about a decade when consequent upon the merger of the state in the Indian Union a heavy chunk of the business-bound immigrants had entered Sikkim the literacy percentage rose to 34.05 against the all-India literacy rate of 36.23 per cent.

If the numbers of the floating population are subtracted then the native literacy stands around 20 per cent only. Literacy rate in 2001 census was 69.68. The female literacy on the other hand is hardly about 10 per cent. The long domination of the feudal political order, difficult terrain, incessant rains for five months in a year, icy cold winters, fatalistic and superstitious people, agropastoral oriented economic order and the like have been those factors which impede the progress of literacy in the region.

Nonetheless, after the popular government came in power many new schools had been opened, existing schools upgraded and strengthened and the numbers of post-secondary stage schools have been increased. The stipends of poor students studying in schools had been raised. All these steps proved fruitful and it is expected that at the time of next census operation even the native literacy rate shall go up.

Media

The southern urban areas have English, Nepali and Hindi dailies. Nepali language newspapers as well as some English newspapers are locally printed, whereas Hindi and

English newspapers are printed in Siliguri. Important local dailies are the *Samay Dainik*, *Sikkim Express* (English), *Sikkim Now* (English), and *Himalibela*. The regional editions of English newspapers include *The Statesman* and *The Telegraph*, which are printed in Siliguri and available in the same day, as well as *The Hindu* and *The Times of India*, printed in Kolkata, which are received with a day's delay in the towns of Gangtok, Jorethang, Melli and Geyzing. *Himalaya Darpan*, a Nepali daily being published from Siliguri is one of the leading Nepali dailies in the region. The *Sikkim Herald* is an official weekly publication of the government. Online media covering Sikkim include the Nepali newspaper *Himgiri*, the English news portal *Haalkhabar* and the literary magazine *Tistarangit*. *Avyakta*, *Bilokan*, *Journal of Hill Research*, *Khaber Khagaj*, *Panda*, and *Sikkim Science Society Newsletter* are the registered publications in Bengali, Nepali, and English published out of Sikkim in weekly, quarterly, half-yearly, and annual periodicities.

Internet cafes are well established in the district capitals, but broadband connectivity is not widely available. Satellite television channels through dish antennae are available in most homes in the state. Channels served are the same available throughout India along with Nepali language channels. The main service providers are Dish TV, Doordarshan and Nayuma. The area is well serviced by local cellular companies.

8

Economy

- -

Sikkim's social fabric is further warped by the resentment the locals have against plainsmen, chiefly the Marwaris who dominate trade and commerce through their extensive marketing network developed both within and outside the state over several decades. Being a tightly knit community, the Marwaris can successfully dictate price to local farmers and at another level, outsmart local businessmen who have few contacts in the principal markets of Kolkata, Lucknow and Kanpur. The result, laments the Chief Minister, is that unfortunately for them, the people cannot enjoy the fruits of their labour.

However, Mr. Balchand Sarda, Gangtok's independent MLA and the first plainsman to win an election in the state, denies that traders are exploiting local agriculturists. A section of Marwaris who first settled here 70 years ago, he argues, "why can't the State Government through its cooperatives build up a monopoly?" "In fact, the State Government has been trying since 1982 to strengthen the cooperative banks for providing short-term credit. But its proving difficult to beat the decades-long traditional links between illiterate farmers and the Marwaris", says the West District Collector, Mr. T. B. Barphungha.

In a manner so similar to the practice in other parts of India, farmers find banks and cooperative alien concepts and prefer direct dealing with the traders. But interest rates are usurious and the gullible farmers almost invariably end up pledging their crops to them. "Farmers in the state would have even lost their land due to indebtedness had it not been for the official ban on outsiders buying land," says Mr. Barphungha. This problem of one community capturing the market is not new and one only belonging to Sikkim. It is a common phenomena which can be observed in the entire subcontinent. The strongest push to the local economy has come from New Delhi. The Centre has pumped in so much money that some people here have become millionaires overnight.

Plan assistance to Sikkim has skyrocketed since the merger from about Rs. 6 crores annually to Rs. 44 crores in 1985-86.

During the Sixth Plan, per capita Central assistance to Sikkim amounted to Rs. 1,209, which is not just the highest for any State but several times the national average of Rs. 80. "Sikkim's own revenue is just about Rs. 11 crore annually, whereas this year (1985) we have projected a total expenditure of Rs. 97 crore," says Mr. R. Narayanan, who has been the state's Development Commissioner since 1976. Gangtok, the capital, has changed the most. Concrete structure have sprung up on almost every vacant space shielding the green-blue hills that surrounding the town. Even to catch a glimpse of the mighty mountain-Kanchenjunga, one has to look for a vantage place. Streets are as crowded as any other place in the country. The shops display videos and other luxury items.

Such a lot of money coming to a few hands has also brought in worst of the new world corruption and graft, etc. in the land of the Lamas and the monasteries where a minor theft would have been regarded as a major deviation from the ways of Buddha even a decade ago.

Behind the facade of its apparent affluence, however, not all is well. Indeed, nemesis may be catching up with Sikkim. Barring a watch manufacturing unit set up by HMT in collaboration with the State Government, there is hardly any industry of consequence in the state. Employment is thus limited to Government jobs and public works. One out of every 18 persons is a Government employee and assuming that each of them has to take care of five persons on an average, which is often the case, then about one-fourth of the state's population lives off the government.

Furthering the problems, according, to Sunday (October 1986) the bureaucracy is again heavy, there are 21 secretaries including the Chief Secretary and one additional Chief Secretary. About 16 per cent of the state's annual budget is spent on 600 odd vehicles used by Government officials. As long as New Delhi keeps bearing the cost as it does now, Sikkim can afford the luxury of adding more people to its bureaucracy and more vehicles to the government pool. But what happens if New Delhi scales down its assistance or decides to freeze it at a particular level?

More pertinent, how long can the bureaucracy already large enough serve as a solution to the increasing unemployment in the state? Education being absolutely free up to the school learning stage, every year about 80,000 students are coming out of Sikkim's schools. And every time the Chief Minister opens a school he does not forget to mention what it means to him or would to his successors: One more headache, a fair number of students coming out of schools can reasonably hope to secure professional degree from different institutions outside the state by availing themselves of the seats reserved for Sikkim in these.

A Sikkimese can get admission in a medical or an engineering college under this system in designated institutions without sitting for the admission tests or fulfilling the admission norms set for others. But what will Sikkim do with all these doctors, engineers and MBAs? Where are the jobs for them? And if there is a job who is to get preference? A candidate of the majority Nepalese community or the native Lepcha-Bhutia community whose interests India is pledged to safeguard under the terms of Sikkim succession to India?

It further says, sooner or later the bubble has to burst. And when it does it will once again throw up the question — 'Has India been wise in annexing Sikkim?'

Economic Development

Although Sikkim is unhappy about non-fulfilment by the Union Government of its three basic political demands, the Ministry of Mr. Bhandari was firmly of the view that the his time was most opportune for launching development programme in a big way in view of the peaceful atmosphere prevailing in the state.

Today, there is not a single Central industrial unit worth mentioning in Sikkim. The State's meagre financial resources are not enough to set up big industries. This being the position it totally had to rely on central help and assistance.

The Sikkim Sangram Parishad, therefore, had asked the Centre to come in a big way to help Sikkim develop agricultural, industrial, tourism and communication sectors. "This must come at the earliest so as to catch up with the rest of the country in various sectors of economic activities.

According to Mr. Bhandari, since the objective of the Seventh Plan is to improve the standard of living, paying particular attention to the problems of poverty and underdevelopment, the State Government has decided to bring about significant increases in productivity and incomes of the poorer sections of the population by way of effective utilisation of the available resources in the state. His Government wanted to derive the maximum benefit out of Rs. 230 crores, sanctioned by the Planning Commission for the States' Five Year Plan (1985-90).

Development of Agriculture

Although the Tibetans call it 'Denzong' (the rice bowl) — only 12 per cent of the land in Sikkim is under agriculture and very little of it under rice, the staple food of the majority, which is mostly imported from other States. The simple logic should be to make the state self-sufficient in foodgrains by way of giving maximum stress on agriculture. Its agriculture policy, therefore, should be to concentrate only on value-added cash crops like cardamom, ginger, orange, strawberries and vegetable. Against the state's requirement of about 40,000 tonnes of rice the targeted production of rice during 1986-87 would be about 17,500 tonnes.

As there is no way to raise the acres of land under agriculture, Mr. Bhandari tried to better the economy of the people through horticulture and by establishing breweries and setting up a marketing system abroad for Sikkim products — tea, fruits, flowers and orchids. He claimed that floriculture could earn about Rs. 1 lakh annually from one acre. He had gone for tea cultivation in the higher reaches of western Sikkim but the Manager of tea estate says that he had only started breaking even. To make profit he had to expand his 450 acres to at least 600 acres.

There is a dedicated effort of a large section of officials and experts in forests, agriculture, animal husbandry and soil conservation to make Sikkim more productive. Sikkim at one time had nearly 450 species of orchids some of these with rare medicinal value. Unfortunately, nearly 50 species are lost for ever.

The Government maintains an orchidarium to protect the species. Forest nurseries are growing sapling and experimenting with all kinds of fast growing for fuel and fodder. More than 50 varieties of fruits, including tree tomatoes from China are being experimented for determining their suitability in the state climate. Already coffee is being grown in experimental farms and quality mangoes, hybrid mandarins and oranges, guava and even olives are being tried.

The few products that it can compete on such as canned fruits, jams, juices, alcohol and spirits had to be produced with utmost efficiency as the basic molasses or sugarcane had to be transported from as far as Andhra Pradesh. Yet the fruit canning factory at Singtam is able to maintain an inventory for four months and produces at a cheaper cost than the brands marketed by the multinationals. Unfortunately, the government factory has a marketing problem, being smaller in size it can be swayed by the Indian subsidiaries of the multinational through TV commercials and long credit.

Development of Animal Husbandry

Mr. Bhandari tried to expand the animal husbandry programme hybrid cattle are to be procured and a network of cooperatives to be set up. He was happy that the Centre's contribution to Sikkim was many times more than what it had been during the days when Sikkim was a protectorate. Now the Animal Husbandry Department is looking for other breeds which can survive in that environment. Piggety and poultries are the other options.

Taxation

Sales Tax

All small scale units will be exempted from payment of sales tax for three years from the date of their starting production. Further the small scale units who pay sales tax on purchase of machinery, equipment and raw materials, whether purchased locally or imported from outside the state are eligible for 50 per cent relief as outright grant for three years, from the date of their starting production.

Income-Tax

The industries shall be exempted from paying income-tax for five years.

Planning

Five-Year Plan

The State Government for development of sericulture in Sikkim sanctioned a project with the financial outlay of Rs. 500.00 lakhs. 1,000 farmers will be trained and provided with incentives and infrastructure in the project for silkworm cultivation. The project will be continued in the 10th Five Year Plan also.

Fisheries: The Directorate of Fisheries is under Forests, Environment and Wildlife Department. This Directorate besides propagation and conservation of river fishes has also taken up the task of propagation of trout and its introduction in the high altitude lakes. The Fish Farmer's Development Agency provides loans with subsidies for production of fishes. The Directorate has two fish farms for fish seed production:

- Singling Fish Seed Production Centre-for production of inland fish seeds like carps.
- Menmoitso Fish Seed Production Centre-for production trout fish seeds.

Awards: From the year 2000, Forests, Environment and Wildlife Department, Government of Sikkim has started giving Rajya Van Sangrakhshan Evam Paryavaran Puraskar to individuals and organisations for contribution towards protection of environment and forests. Three individuals and one Voluntary Organisation were given the award on 15th August 2000.

Forest Manual and Code: It is an important document which purports to deal with the duties, functions and responsibilities of the organisation as also those of its members. It defines and describes the powers and functions — both administrative as well as financial — to be exercised during the course of discharging various duties by its members. It profiles the Department's own sphere of activities and how they are to be conducted. The manuscript has been examined by Finance Department and is on way of vetting it by Law Department.

Schemes Funded by Ministry of Environment and Forests, Government of India: The following Schemes are being funded by the Ministry and implemented by this Department.

Integrated Afforestation and Eco-Development Project: There are two projects being implemented in the state. The projects are:

- Integrated Afforestation and Eco-Development Project Scheme in Rangpochu Watershed in East District with Financial Target of Rs. 592.29 lakhs and Physical Target of 5500 hectares. The project is in the last year of implementation and is required to be further extended in the 10th Five Year Plan.

- Integrated Afforestation and Eco-Development Project in Dzongu Watershed in North District with the Financial Target of 2000 hectares and financial outlay of Rs. 101.72 lakhs.

Non-Timber Forest Produce including Medicinal Plants Projects: There are four projects funded by the Ministry of Environment and Forestry the 9th Five Year Plan, they are:

- Non-Timber Forest Produce including Medicinal Plants in Low Altitude.
- Medicinal Plants Projects in High Altitude.
- Bamboo Plantation Project.
- Farming Project of Medicinal Plants.

The total financial target of all these projects is over Rs. 400.00 lakhs.

Area Oriented Fuel Wood and Fodder Project: This project is a 50:50 CSS project and is implemented in degraded forests and private wastelands for meeting the requirements of fuel wood and fodder of the state. In the 9th Five Year Plan the financial outlay of the project is Rs. 693.00 lakhs of which 50 per cent is funded by the Government of India and 50 per cent by the State Plan.

Development of National Park and Wildlife Sanctuaries: The Government of India is also funding schemes for development of Kanchenjunga High Altitude National Park and 6 wildlife sanctuaries in the state on yearly basis.

Eco-Development of Wildlife Sanctuaries and National Park: This scheme funded by the Government of India is implemented on the fringes of the wildlife sanctuaries and National Park through active participation of the local people. This scheme is aimed at providing assistance to the people living on the periphery of the sanctuaries and national park to as to obtain cooperation and help in management of the protected areas.

National Environment Awareness Campaign: The Ministry of Environment and Forests, Government of India provides financial assistance in organising environmental awareness among the local mass. Such campaigns are organised by involving the local NGOs by providing financial assistance to them.

Catchments Area Treatment Plan of Hydroelectric Projects: The Department has been implementing two catchments area treatment projects. One such project is being implemented in South hand West District in the catchments of Rangit Hydroelectric Project. The total financial outlay of the catchments area treatment plan is over Rs. 1300.00 lakhs and is being implemented from 1995-96 and is proposed to be completed by 2001-02. Another project on North and East District, viz. Catchments Area Treatment Plan of Teesta Stage V Hydroelectric Project is being implemented with the financial target of Rs. 2420.25 lakhs for a period of 9 years commencing from the year 2000-01.

Soil and Water Conservation: Soil and water conservation works are being carried out in 30 identified watersheds in the state. The works include vegetative engineering, low cost engineering structures in land slide affected areas and a forestation works in geologically fragile areas of the state.

Awareness Camps, Workshops and Trainings: The department has been organising and conducting awareness camps to educate the common mass towards protection of forests and environment in the state and the country. Workshops are also being organised to obtain maximum participation of the local people in implementing different schemes of the department for sustainable development of the people of the state. Training Programmes are also being organised from time to time to impart training to the staff as well as to the Village Forest Committees and Watershed Associations for effective implementation of the schemes for socio-economic development of the people of the state.

Industries

With the changing scenario of economic, political and social aspects of life, there is pressing need for accelerating the pace of industrial development of the state. There is sharp increase in the numbers of educated youth searching for the employment and the problem has been augmented by the migration of the people from rural areas to urban areas looking for better jobs and living conditions.

The Department of Industry has been playing a pivotal role in implementing various developmental schemes and solving unemployment problems to some extent by providing employment and extending necessary assistance for self-employment through its various undertaking and agencies. Though the state has limited natural resources and skilled manpower and the topographical location of the state also hampers the establishment of large industrial unit. Keeping in view of facts, there is need for formulation of effective industrial policy with long-term solution of this phenomenal problem.

However, the Department of Industry through its undertaking and agencies has shouldered the responsibilities of removing this problem and also envisages a better tomorrow for its people. Some of the biggest achievements of the department during the recent year are summed up as follows:

Revival of Government Food Preservation Factory (GFPF): One of the biggest achievements of the department is the revival of GFPF. The industrial unit, which was handed over to one private party, was closed due to mismanagement rendering its employees jobless. However, the government realised its importance and took over the management of units and at present the factory is doing very well.

Its products are not only famous but have very high market demands, at present its products available in the markets are, fruit juice, orange squash, passion fruit squash, tomato ketchup, tomato puree, orange marmalade, mixed fruit jam, synthetic vinegar, mango pickle, etc. with brand name of Sikkim Supreme. It has also decided to launch new products like Dalley chillies pickles, Dalley chillies with bamboo shoot pickles, mixed pickles, pine apple squash, orange juice in 800 ml cans, etc., by February 2001. In view of its demand and better quality products, the government has plan for further expansion and modernisation of plant and machinery and in such event there is ample scope for further employment of manpower.

Sikkim Jewels Limited: Sikkim Jewels Limited was established in the year 1972 to cater the demand of Watch jewels and Cup jewels, initially with the capacity of 2.00 lakhs of Cup jewel and 3.00 lakhs of watch jewels per month. Now its capacity has increased to 3.00 lakhs of Cup jewels and 32.00 lakhs of watch jewels per month. The company has also consolidated its position in the market for Watch jewels, Cup Jewels and Rotors Magnets.

The Company has sold jewels worth Rs. 1,54, 86,000 from April 2000 till December 2000, against the total sale of Rs. 131 lakhs during 1999-2000. The Company has orders worth Rs. 130 lakhs in hand to be dispatched by December 2001. It has also received orders for 120 lakhs nos. of jewels worth Rs. 123 lakhs for next year, *i.e.* for 2001 from foreign clients which is net increase of 400 per cent in export market and in domestic market also it has orders in hand worth Rs. 72.00 lakhs.

SITCO: The Sikkim Time Corporation was established during 1976 with assembly of Mechanical watches for HMT. The company has expanded and diversified its business into manufacture of mechanical watch crown, semiconductors and manufacture of digital and analogue watches over the years. Its products with brand name "SITCO" has very good market demand for its watches. As of now the company has employed 318 employees in the factory.

Speaker Manufacturing Unit: Apart from its usual business of watch making SITCO has reached another milestone with the foundation stone laying of its Speaker Manufacture Project by the Hon'ble Chief Minister of Sikkim, Shri Pawan Chamling on 13th Dec. 2000. The unit will produce 10,000 speakers per day for both B/W and colour TVs. Speaker manufacture, being a labour intensive one is ideally suited for a place like Sikkim. The project cost (excluding working capital) is Rs. 300.00 lakhs and the annual sales realisation (at full capacity) will be Rs. 516.00 lakhs. The unit will give employment to 92 local people at full working capacity.

Sikkim Precision Industries Ltd.: The Sikkim Precision Industries Ltd. (SPIL), Namchi, was first conceived during March 1998, when the Hon'ble Chief Minister desired that a project be identified and established at Namchi for the industrial development of South and West Sikkim and for providing gainful employment to the people of these districts. Consequently a high tech. project suitable for Sikkim was identified and it was decided to establish the new Public Sector Company to undertake the project. Thus the Sikkim Precision Industries Ltd. (SPIL) was set up with MD, SITCO being appointed as its Managing Director and given the overall task of implementing the project. Thereafter the land for the project site was acquired at Gurpisey, Namchi and M/s Tata Consultancy Services (TCS) appointed for preparation of the Detailed Project Report (DPR). The DPR was submitted by TCS in Nov. '98.

The foundation stone for the project was laid by the Hon'ble Chief Minister of Sikkim Shri Pawan Chamling on 4.12.1998. The Project site was relocated to Boomtar in March, 2000 since it was found that infrastructure development costs will be too high given the different terrain of the site Gurpisey.

The unit specialises in the production of 'Power Device' in collaboration with M/s Bharat Electronic Ltd. of Bangalore. The civil construction of the project was started at the new site from July 2000 after the Board of Directors of the Company directed the construction be undertaken directly by the Company for faster and cost effective execution. At present the site levelling works have been completed and the construction of the main factory building is under way.

Sikkim Temi Tea: Sikkim Temi Tea located at Temi-Tarku, South Sikkim, is situated between the elevation range of 4,800 ft to 6,000 ft, covering an area of 173 hectares. It is famous for its quality products, which is known not only in India but also in abroad. The unit is major source of employment for the local people and also one of the important revenue earner for the government.

Its annual turnover during the year has exceeded 100 MT. It has a/so added Rs. 235 lakhs in the state exchequer as revenue and has set the target of Rs. 240 lakhs as total earning for this financial year, i.e. for 2000-01. Apart from providing employment and generating revenue, it is providing assistance to private tea growers of the state for establishing tea gardens. Under this Programme approximate 6 lakh tea sapling has been already distributed free of cost to various tea growers' society and private parties.

Under the assistance of Temi Tea Board; tea growers' society like Sang-Martam Tea Growers' Cooperative Society has started flourishing, which with further generate additional income as well as employment opportunities to the local people of that areas.

Consultancy Services: The Department of Industry also provides Consultancy Services to the aspiring Industrialist/entrepreneur for setting up own unit through Small Industries Service Institute (SISI) Government of India, Tadong and Sikkim Consultancy Services (SICON), Gangtok. It has set up 'SICON' or Sikkim Consultancy Services at District Industries Centre (East and North) at Gangtok where free consultancy services are provided to unemployed youth for setting up their own unit and establishment for providing 'self-employment' and employment to other unemployed.

Prime Minister Rozgar Yojana: Rural Artisan and Small Scale Entrepreneur have been continuously trained by the Department within four districts in collaboration with SISI, SICON, Nationalised Banks, SIDBI, etc. Under PMRY Scheme altogether 567 numbers of beneficiaries were provided financial assistance during the last six years.

Small Scale Industries Registration: During the last six years the department has granted 238 Provisional Registration and 96 Permanent Registration Certificate to Small Scale Industries and Tiny Industries. The department of Industry is putting every effort to implement the policy of government for the betterment of its people. It is also striving hard to figure Sikkim in the industrial map of country.

SIDICO: Sikkim Industrial Development and Investment Corporation Ltd. (SIDICO) set up in the year 1977 is a state level principal financial institution engaged in promotion, financing and development of industries in tiny, cottage, hotels, small and medium sector in the state of Sikkim. Besides, the corporation has also been providing soft loan/seed capital assistance and participating in the share capital in its selective venture projects. Financial assistance is made available by the corporation for fixed assets such as land; building, land and machinery, etc., with an ultimate objective of setting up of industries in the state.

Since the corporation was facing financial crises, during the year 1995-96, the corporation was restructured and all the liabilities on account of refinance availed from IDBI/SIDBI were settled. During the last five years from 1995-96 to 1999-2000, the corporation sanctioned loan amounting to and.10.35 crores to 2,147 beneficiaries and the recovery for the same period was and.12.66 crores which itself was record.

Directorate of Handicrafts and Handloom (DHH): Progress made during the last six years in the Handicrafts and Handloom Sector. Seven new training centres were opened in 1919 where training in various crafts are imparted. The rate of stipend for the trainees has also been increased from Rs. 200 p.m. to Rs. 300 p.m., and Rs. 250 p.m. to Rs. 350 p.m. A new Block Printing Section was started and in house printing of various multicraft items is carried out.

Infrastructure development by way of construction of a three storeyed building at Gangtok, a two storeyed building at Lindong in Dzongu, a four storeyed-building at Namchi. Further, a three storeyed building was purchased from HUDCO at Melli.

New District Handicrafts and Handloom Centre, Namchi: The development of these permanent infrastructures has created enough working space for further development and growth, as well as created a conducive working environment. Modernisation of looms was carried out by purchase of cart iron looms, which has resulted into production of better quality carpets.

Introduced 'Hire Purchase Scheme' for issue of Handicrafts and Handloom items to the State Government Employees on monthly instalment basis. This scheme has been a great success and has resulted into high sales revenue. Craft Fairs are organised at Gangtok as yearly feature and have been participating at various fairs in the state as well as at the National Level.

Animal Husbandry: Cattle, buffaloes, yak, sheep, goats, pigs, mules and ponies are the important domestic animals of Sikkim. Poultry birds are also domesticated in different parts of the state. Buffaloes and cattle are mainly limited to the tropical humid belt and temperate zone. In the higher cold areas, Yak is the important animal. Government of Sikkim has established a separate department of animal husbandry.

During the first three plans the animal husbandry department formulated a scheme to meet the increasing demand for meat and dairy products, poultry birds and eggs. Veterinary health services were made available in villages and like farmers, those interested in animal breeding and poultry farming were trained at different stations in India. Exotic breeds of sheep that thrive well under the vagaries of climatic conditions prevailing in Sikkim were introduced in the state.

Small Scale Industries

For a long time the skeletal means of transport and communications, lack of sources, of fossil fuel and non-exploitation of water as a source of power, best utilisation of forest and mineral wealth, dearth of entrepreneurs and feudal government's half-hearted measures, the establishment of even medium and small-scale industries could not be expected. Moreover, in feudal countries the autocratic rulers could meet their comforts and luxuries by even huge doses of imports but hardly any of them thought of founding and developing industrial units to provide succour to a section of their subjects. Sikkim has been no exception to this practice.

In Sikkim during the period of first three economic plans apart from some were nail and tannery units, a distillery unit and a fruit preserving plant each were set up at Rangpo and sangtam respectively. The distillery as well as stannaries were set up in the private sector but the brewing and distilling unit was established in the public sector.

This unit of Sikkim has earned an enviable position for producing finest grades of whisky, brandy, gin and rum. On the recommendations of the National Council of Applied Economic Research the tea plantations were promoted and a modern tea processing factory has come up at Temi.

A small scale Industries Corporation has been set up in Sikkim which has based its policies, plans and projects on the following guidelines:

- The construction of industrial estates at district headquarters at the first instance and thereafter creating industrial estates in other urban areas also.
- To develop, expand and strengthen the existing small-scale units so as to keep them economically viable at all times.
- Extending all type of facilities, subsidies and assistance to potential entrepreneurs.
- Granting protection to all new ventures in all respects.

After about a decade and half (since merger) the process of industrialisation in Sikkim is seen to be gradual but steady. Some relatively medium scale units are fast coming up in the region which are likely to generate employment opportunities for many people.

It is quite satisfying to narrate that as against the target of 40 units to be established during 1985-86 all the forty were set up. During the next year 42 units against the projected 40 units were established. In the year 1986-87 a equal number of units had come up till November, 1987.

The Sikkim Time Corporation Limited has implemented the discrete silicon semi-conductor project. This Corporation has already been assembling HMT watches besides manufacturing quarts clocks and watch crowns. SITCO has been consistently establishing new records amongst all the 13 watch assembly units of HMT Limited around the country. SITCO maintains its lead in terms of productivity, *i.e.*, 23.2 watches per operator per day.

During the year 1986-87 SITCO achieved a remarkable target by way of assembling 4,18,000 watches. This is the highest number ever assembled in the country in any of the watch assembly units. In its own manufacturing programme of wrist Watches SS Crowns, SITCO has manufactured and sold 1 million crowns to HMT Limited and other watch makers throughout the country. Today SITCO stands at the top not only amongst all the assembly units of HMT limited in the Country, but also amongst all the Industrial units of the state.

Yukshom Breweries Limited, one of the large Industrial units, has already gone into commercial production. The other large unit, Sikkim Vanaspati Limited, started production in 1988. Scan Industries Private Limited, Dunzong, Rubber Industries Private Limited and Sikkim Mineral Private Limited have also gone into production, Metalex Industries Private Limited (PP Casps), Labbot Private Limited (glass bottles) and Sikkim Anti-Feed (Cattle feed) went into production during 1989-90.

Recently the Industrial Development Corporation and Industrial Finance Corporation have been merged together to constitute Sikkim Industrial Development and Investment Corporation Limited. An Industrial Training Institute was set up at Rango in 1976 to provide trained personnel to different industrial units. The Department of Industries, in coordination with the Sikkim Rural Development Agency conducts various training programmes to train rural youth, such programmes aim at motivating, enthusing and training the youth to set up artisan Oriented Industrial Units.

The SIDICO during its existence of over a dozen of years has helped many Industrial Units. Major among these have been aluminium conductor manufacturing unit, NDPE bags manufacturing unit, Colour photo laboratory, Bottle manufacturing units, Biscuits manufacturing unit, Talcum Powder Unit, Leather Goods Manufacturing Unit, Cold—storage Project, Barbed wire manufacturing unit, etc.

Manufacturing

In a state like Sikkim which suffers from physical constraints and other limitatings neither large-scale industries can be so viable nor the state can expect even the medium and small scale industries to expand at a very rapid face. Nevertheless, as detailed below some handicrafts as well as small scale and cottage industries have shown appreciable progress.

Handicrafts

Since time immemorial, the tiny and mountainous state of Sikkim has been known as a repository for some handicrafts produced by artisans and craftsmen who never obtained any formal training in institutes imparting such training. In fact such artisans and craftsmen inherited the related skills in their own families wherein they were born and brought up. Spinning of wool and weaving woollen fabrics, making of carpets, druggets, rugs and preparing bamboo ware have been dominating carpets in the region. Even during the economic plans initiated and completed in the pre-merger period the Sikkim government paid special attention towards the promotion and development of handicrafts in Sikkim.

In fact the people of Sikkim had been very much impressed from the Gandhian ideals who throughout his political career had stressed upon village uplift and for achieving this goal he had advocated the development of handicarfts and cottage industries which supplemented and complemented the earnings of an average ruralite. In the year, 1957, the Government of Sikkim established the Palden Thondoup Cottage Industries Institute at Gangtok.

Apart from training the traditional craftsmen on scientific lines the Institute also imparts training even to raw hands in the arts of carpet making, weaving of woollen and cotton fabrics, traditional religious painting (on walls, fabrics, card boards and wood), toy making, doll making, bamboo work, coir work, embroidery, dying ceramics, carpentry, silversmithy, black smithy and manufacturing of hand-made paper, etc.

During the second plan period (pre-merger period) the batik and tailoring sections were also added. Nearby 200 persons have also been provided employment by the Institute. Besides running training as well as refresher courses for the traditional artists and craftsmen the Institute also produces high-quality goods for the home as well as foreign markets and thus provides a source of revenue earning to the State Government.

The popular government after coming into power took some concrete steps for promoting the cause of handicrafts so that besides providing succour to the artisans and artists the promotion of cottage industries helps in the raising of general standards of the people. For a pretty long time only the traditional arts were attended to and the Government Cottage Industries Institute at Gangtok also lent a helping hand in furthering the cause of handicrafts and cottage industries.

An overwhelming majority of the people (particularly the traditional craftsmen) living in far-flung areas and remote villages was unable to be benefited from these attempts. Hence, it was felt in the concerned quarters that there was a need of expanding the net of these institutes by way of starting their branches in the isolated remote and peripheral villages.

Resultantly first such branch was established at Lachung in January 1976. Obviously the handicrafts and cottage industries earlier pursued on crude lines got the much-needed support for their development and expansion. Some of the traditional weavers, after having lost the Tibet market for the procurement of fine wood, had gone in the background. Through the Institute and its branches special efforts were made to procure equally qualitative wool to be made available to such artisans on cheaper as well as subsidised rates.

The State Government also arranged an exhibition-cum-sales programme at the Central Cottage Emporium at New Delhi for the first time in November-December 1975. It has now become an annual and regular feature. With such steps the Sikkimese traditional arts and crafts have already regained their lost glory and the days is not far off when the persistently consistent efforts of the government by way of ameliorating the economic plight of the artists and craftsmen shall achieve their right and allowed objective.

Trade and Business

The Sikkimese for a long time steeped low in the mire woven by poverty, ignorance and disease. During their entire recorded and known history barring a couple of rulers no King paid any attention for the social resurgence and economic uplift of the masses. With the beginning of present century when the Indian freedom fighters started paying equal attention towards the social as well as economic development of the Indian masses, a section in the Sikkimese population too started thanking in this regard.

When India became free and soon after the democratic setup switched over to the planned development, in the Indian protectorate of Sikkim also people raised very high hopes. During the times of Tashi Namgyal, few enlightened and dedicated Sikkimese raised the banner of revolt against the Chogyal and his apathy towards the basic needs of his subjects. Such a development was bound to open the eyes of the feudalistic theocratic monarch who earnestly desired to do some think for the people but never wished to part with the autocratic rule. Tashi Namgyal took up the issue with the then Prime Minister of India, Pandit Jawaharlal Nehru who had deep love for the people of Sikkim.

In a bid to help his neighbours, he started extending technical know-how and material help to Sikkim. Till the merger of Sikkim with the Union of India, she had already completed a Seven Year Plan and two Five Year Plans solely with the help of India. Till then India had spent millions of rupees for the socio-economic uplift of Sikkim and the enlightenment thus brought about among the masses enhanced their thirst and desire for property as well as democracy.

Thus, the struggle for throwing away monarchy and attaining merger with India multiplied manyfold. Although some people have scathingly attacked the merger of Sikkim with India, but it goes without saying that the tempo and degree of socio-economic progress made in Sikkim during the post-merger period is much more than the development which took place during the entire era theocratic monarchy.

Commercial Activities

The major products which are exported from Sikkim are large cardamom, apples, oranges, potatoes, wines (liquors, rum, brandy whisky, rums, etc., handicrafts, timber and assembled HMT watches, wall clocks, canned fruits. The main imports for Sikkim include cereals, other food stuffs, machines, tools, cotton pieces, cloth, drugs surgical equipment, chemicals, spare parts, vehicles, cycles and many other consumer goods. Before the occupation of Tibet by China, Sikkim had a flourishing trade relations with the formate. Pashmina was the major item of import from Tibet After 1962 when the Sino-Indian relations became highly strained and ultimately changed.

Since then the trade has primarily been carried out between Sikkim and other parts of India. In good old days the trade was carried on beasts of burden particularly the mules and ponies, but now the goods carrier fleet of SNT accomplishes this task.

With the increasing tempo of development and dawning awakening among the masses and the changing fashions the imports of beverages, cloth, cosmetics, electronic goods, electrical appliances, engineering goods, synthetic goods, chemical fertilizers, pesticides, insecticides, sanitary wares, hardware, etc. have increased manifold. Of late the export of tea from Sikkim has stepped up.

The tea produced in Sikkim is similar to the world-famous Darjeeling tea. Sikkim tea is sold in Kolkata. Auctions along with Darjeeling Tea and buyers from all over the world bid for the tea. Sikkim tea has fared very well in those auctions for the last three years. In 1985 it was No. 2 and in 1986 and 1987 No.1 in the Kolkata auctions for orthodox teas.

Agriculture

Agriculture as elsewhere in the country, is the mainstay of the people in Sikkim. Going by the history of civilization, after the stage of hunting and food gathering, man took to shifting cultivation and settled agriculture as his mode of earning. Industrial development has been the further stage of development.

All those societies which have been away from the modern developments in science and technology continue to be agro-pastoral societies and Sikkim still being at this stage can be no exception. Before it that the agricultural practices and patterns obtaining today in Sikkim are explained it is pre-requisitely essential to briefly narrate the paedologic (soil) conditions and state or irrigation in the state of Sikkim.

Soil

Sikkim being no exception, the soil conditions over the entire Himalayan belt are varied and diverse. Thus at micro level the soils in Sikkim depend upon the degree of glaciation, amount of river action, type and quantum of forest cover, degree of slope, temperature and aspect of the hill slopes. Nevertheless, elevation and forest covers are the most important factors on which the soils of an area or tract or pocket depend.

Other two factors of importance are aspect and degree of slope. By aspect it is meant whether the hill slope in north-facing or south-facing. The north-facing slopes in the northern hemisphere and particularly the Himalayan belt are less sunny and less moist than the south-facing slopes as a result of the apparent annual march of the Sun.

In the higher reaches, where the ground remains covered with perpetually frozen ice or where snow falls for a major period of the year, the soils found have been greatly affected by the past and current glacial action. In other words the soil morphology of these heavy snow receiving and perpetually snow-bound areas is determined by the Spatio-temporal impact of the glacial action.

In the southern-most zone of the subtropical wet forests the soils are leached because of excessive and down pouring rainfall. But on the rather hand the presence of dense deciduous and evergreen forests add a lot of humus to these soils as a result of the continuous decomposition of leaves, ferns and grasses. This factor also results in higher doses of oxidisation of these soils. In the zone of temperate forests, in the river valleys along the beds of the streams and rivulets are met the riverine alluvial soils.

Although on slopes these soils are thin but on terraced patches quite a thick veneer of these soils is found. However, in areas covered predominantly by pines and other coniferous trees the soils have turned highly acidic and podzolic. On the other hand in oak dominated patches brown soils have come to be developed. The steeper slopes, devoid of verdure and subjected to regular erosion the soils are immature. In fact the soils lying on these slopes do not get enough time to be matured and the next rains drain them away.

As staged earlier in higher reaches, which remain under the impact of moving ice and snow melt flow during warmer days, fluvio-glacial soils are found. In these glaciated areas the soils are dominated by boulder clays and outwashed silts. Nonetheless, for want of detailed and sufficient scientific study of these soils, which also remain inaccessible to the peasants, it is difficult to provide a detailed soil profile.

In the hilly State of Sikkim characterised by heavy rains it is expected that the problem of soil erosion should have assumed alarming proportions. But the presence of forest and grass covers have saved the soils from being subjected to excessive erosion. It is only on the precipices and bare slopes that soil erosion has assumed dangerously threatening postures.

Irrigation

Irrigation has become an indispensable agricultural aid these days particularly in areas of deficient and seasonal rainfall. In hilly areas at times, it becomes essential since because of steep gradients the rain water speedily drains away and at times it is needed for crops, hence only artificial application of water can come to rescue. In hilly areas it is physically impossible and ecologically dangerous to have big dams and vast reservoirs to work as sources of water supply to canals. Nevertheless, Kuhal, i.e., zigzag contour water channels, though with different nomenclatures, are used the worldover in tropical subtropical hilly areas.

The irrigation Department constructed 99 km long Kuhals during the year 1985 to 1988, whereas, in the year 1989 about 20 km long Kuhal construction was completed. The Richi-Aruba Kuhal (Eastern District), Satdule Kuhal (Western District), Sakyong-Santok Kuhal (Northern District) and Keojing Kuhal (Southern District) were among the major Kuhals which were repaired during 1988-89.

In fact the breeches in Kuhals and frequent silting of the channel courses often need repairs. During the year 1988-89, a budgetary provision of rupees 1.90 crore had been provided for irrigation. It had also been targeted to provide irrigation facilities to 1,200 hectares of cultivable land. In view of the appreciable success being achieved in expanding the irrigated hectarage the Government of Sikkim decided to provide irrigation facilities on a total hectarage of 21,000 hectares by 1981.

Farming

Agriculture has a long and winding history in Sikkim. It is gathered that the native of Yore in this region were not farmers. Gathering of wild fruits, edible roots and tubers provided them sustenance and they led an extremely primitive life. It were the Bhutia immigrants who gave sedentary farming and semi-nomadic pastoral activities to Sikkim. Bhutias cultivated only the relatively flat pieces of land found scattered in the bottoms of the river valleys. They were unaware about the use of manure.

Resultantly when they found that repeated village of land exhausted itself of its fertility they moved ahead in search of some other fertile and tillable pocket. It were only the Nepalese peasant immigrants which laid the foundations of settled or permanent agriculture in Sikkim. The Nepalese who by nature are sturdy, hardy, industrious and painstaking people, cleared large tracts of woodlands to expand the agricultural area. They were also adept in the art of creating terraced farms along the hill slopes. Thus they also initiated terraced cultivation in Sikkim.

Agriculture in Sikkim, among other things, is largely influenced by varied terrain and varying micro-level climatic conditions. Maize (corn) paddy, wheat and buckwheat are the principal cereals raised in Sikkim potatoes and cardamoms are the major cash crops. Under horticulture oranges and apples of different varieties are grown. In recent years attention has been paid by some progressive farmers to grow a variety of vegetables, banana and pineapple particularly for sale in urban areas.

Maize is the dominant crop of the foothill zone of Southern Sikkim. Higher temperature and a fairly good rainfall during the growing season, maize is sown in early summer and harvested towards the end of the summer season, since stagnating water damages the crop, it is mainly raised on slightly rolling fields on which drains are also laid out to prevent soil erosion. It is an exacting crop from two angles. On the one hand, it needs heavy doses of manures and fertilizers while on the other the processes of laying drains, weeding and thinning require plenty of human labour. About 56,000 hectares of cultivable land is devoted to maize farming every year in Sikkim.

Requiring plenty of heat, plenty of water, plenty of fertility, plenty of human labour (also which yields in plenty and can feed plenty of people) paddy is the second major crop of the region. It is mainly a crop of river valleys, where the annual floodings renew the soil fertility and supply of water for artificial irrigation whenever needed can be had during times of need. In fact a major chunk of the Kuhal irrigated hecterage is given to paddy cultivation particularly during the summer period.

On higher elevations where temperatures, rainfall and soil conditions favour, paddy is planted on terraced fields. Whereas in the river valley bottoms transplantation method is employed to avail higher per hectare yields in the terraced farms at higher elevations where plenty of water cannot be made available, mostly broadcasting method is used for paddy cultivation. The Department of agriculture demonstrated the raising if high yielding varieties even on terraced fields following the much publicised Japanese method. Paddy cultivation is done on about 15,000 hectares of land scattered in river valleys.

Wheat and barley are winter crops. Barley is mostly grown on lesser fertile and relatively more cold areas. With increasing degree of press cold towards north the growing period falls short. It is in these areas that barley and buckwheat are raised. Nonetheless, with the introduction for quick maturing varieties of wheat, barley and buck wheat are being gradually replaced by spring wheat in some of the areas. The cultivable area under barley and buckwheat has thus fallen from 2,000 hectares in seventies to 800 hectares in 1989. The hectarage of wheat, on the other hand, during this period had risen from 11,500 hectares to 13,000 hectares.

Cardamom, oranges and apples are the important cash crops which are sent outside the state also. Similar to all the mountainous areas of northern India the terrain and climatic conditions are suitable for horticulture in Sikkim also. Apples are raised in the colder areas located on higher elevations in central and northern parts of northern Sikkim and luscious oranges are raised in the warmer foothill zone of the state. Cardamom is exported even to some foreign countries. Keeping in view its importance as a foreign exchange earning crop, special attention is being paid to the cultivation of cardamom.

Prior to the merger of Sikkim in the Indian Union, the Government of India has been extending many facilities to Sikkim for the development of agriculture, horticulture and vege-culture. Thus, with the aid and advice of the Government of India, the department of agriculture was set up bin Gangtok. Improved varieties of seeds and fertilizers were distributed on highly subsidised rates to the Sikkimese farmers and trained personnel were posted at key stations to assist and guide the peasants on matters related to increased yields, production and variety of crops. The areas suffering from pests and insects were provided with pesticides and insecticides on quite cheaper rates. Demonstration farms were established at Laches (for horticulture and vege-culture) and Tadun g (for maize and vegetables). A nursery for providing better samplings of fruit plants was set up at Gangtok. Exclusively apple demonstration farms came up at Lacking and Lagyap. To encourage the horticulturists, a fruit-processing plant was set up at Singtam.

The Government of India felt that the training of some selected persons, on modern and scientific lines, in the fields of agriculture, livestock breeding, Agriculture and horticulture held the key for future prosperity in Sikkim. Thus a good number of progressive farmers were sent for training to different farm universities and agricultural research training centres of India. During the second plan an eighty hectare seed multiplication farm was set up for raising better seeds of paddy, maize and vegetables at Gyalshing. Another sixty hectare potato seed farm was set up in the western district. During the following plan the scheme of launching farm oriented courses was put into practice. The Gyalshing seed multiplication farm doubled its production while at Ribdi more varieties of seed potatoes were developed.

The popular governments besides taking steps to effect egalitarian land reforms, checking benami transactions and helping the small are marginal farmers have also been taking steps to develop agriculture in all its phases. In view of the fact that region has a very limited tillable hectarage along the hilly and sloppy terrain, attempts are being made to follow an intensive but careful approach for better land utilisation for realising maximum output. During the recent years, land use and cropping patterns as well as combinations have been modified to suit the typical agro-climatic and topographical conditions. The thrust during these years has been to promote the cultivation of crops like fruits, large cardamom, ginger, potato, flowers and off-season vegetables.

A production level of 120,000 tonnes of cereal and food crop production was achieved during 1988-89. The production is further being augmented by inducting more suitable varieties as well as high yielding varieties of pulses and oil seeds. The achievement related to the total production of oil seeds and pulses have been satisfactory. The production level of 250,000 tonnes is likely to be achieved during 1990-91 when the total production of food crops is expected to be around 128,500 tonnes. The anticipated production of large cardamom, potatoes, ginger and minor tuber crops is likely to touch the 60 thousand tonnes mark in near future.

The State of Sikkim has attained commendable production level for fruits and vegetables. The production by the end of 1989-90 was 48 thousand tonnes. The cultivation of flowers and off-season vegetables is being propagated among farmers with satisfactory results. The progress of improved seed production in Sikkim has been steady and continuously improving. It is anticipated to produce 4,000 tonnes of better seeds by the end of 1989-90 against the 1987-88 production of 3,400 tonnes. Two farmers training centres established in Sikkim have been extending regular facilities of training to farmers including farm—females on various aspects of agriculture with emulatable and laudable success. By the end of 1989-90 the target of training number of regional agricultural centres has been increased from 9 to 12, Regional subcentres 7 to 13 and the numbers of village level workers centres touched an all time high figure of 150.

Livestock

Domestication of cattle, sheep, goat pigs, ponies, mules and yaks (in the higher reaches) has always been a supplementary economic activity of the farming class in Sikkim although there have been exclusive livestock breeders also in the state. Buffaloes and cattle are mainly limited to the sub-tropical zone and the mild temperate zone in central Sikkim, although in this zone the number of buffaloes falls and toes of sheep, ponies and mules rise progressively. In the extremely higher reaches of the State Yak is the most important animal.

The separate department of Animal Husbandry was started much before the merger of Sikkim in the Indian Union on the counsel of the Indian government. The Government of India has realised that in a hilly and inaccessible region like Sikkim agriculture alone was not in a position to provide succour to everybody. Mixed farming amply supplemented by horticulture was the only answer. Immediately after the setting up of a separate department, a number of livestock dairy farms and poultry farms were started. Two demonstrative sheep farms (at Dentam and Lachen), two poultry farms (at Tadung and Gyalshing) and a piggery at Gyalshing were set up. Apart from increasing the flock of sheep at the Dentum Farms, with a view to obviate wool shortage, a new sheep breeding centre was established at Zemu in the Lachen area.

During the first three plans the department tried to increase the production of milk, meat and eggs to cope with the progressively rising demands. New varieties of poultry birds like Leg Horn, White Cornish and Rhode Island-Reds were introduced to improve the poultry stock. Besides getting the prospective livestock breeders in different centres in India, veterinary health services were provided in many villages. To improve the sheep stock as also to raise wool production exotic breeds of sheep that thrive even under vagaries of weather were introduced in the state.

For rejuvenating the apple and orange orchards, a number of demonstration plots were started. And such plots were allotted to small and marginal farmers under the SFDA Project. The same project also envisaged the provision of milk cattle to such farmers who could use the soil growing the fruit trees as grazing grounds. Subsidies were also provided to these farmers to improve and augment their stock. The setting up of a milk chilling plant at Gangtok was a major breakthrough in the field of dairy farming. Notwithstanding these steps, the popular governments over the recent years have taken some viable and concrete steps in different fields related to animal husbandry.

The main thrust has been to strive for improving the standard of living of people especially the rural poor by inspiring and encouraging them to domesticate and rear high yielding breeds of cows, goats, sheep, pigs, poultry birds, etc., etc. In keeping with the National Policy, the major objectives during the Seventh Plan had been to create more facilities and infrastructure for motivating farmers to take up animal husbandry as a major occupation to generate incremental incomes and also raise the productivity. Nine veterinary hospitals (Deorali, Manga, Gyalshing, Rhenock, Chungthung, Soreng, Dentam and Singtam), 61 veterinary dispensaries (about half of them operating in rented buildings) and 36 stockman centres have been opened for the promotion of livestock farming.

One artificial insemination centre (Deorali), 35 such subcentres, one Bull rearing farm (Gyalshing), 3 piggery farms (Karfektar), 5 poultry farms (Tadong, Gyalshing, Rhenock, Karfetakar and (Mangan), 2 goats farms (Mangalbarey and Karfetakar), 5 fodder see farms (karfetakar, Tadong, Rabongla, Manalbarey and Pangthang), 59 registered milk produces societies, 77 unregistered milk producers societies, 11 poultry demonstration farms, one cheese plant (Mangan), one organic farm (Majhitar near Rangpo) for processing hides, skins, bones, hooves, etc., into manure and gelatine, one modern slaughter house (in Rangpo) and the Sikkim Livestock Development Corporation are those concrete steps recently taken which will go a long way in bringing about "White Revolution" in the state.

Horticulture

Sikkim is a tiny Himalayan State. It has net cultivated area of 79,000 hectares and the irrigated area is negligible, hence farming, in the state is practically rain fed. The State being hilly, the agro-climatic condition ranges from sub-tropical in the lower valley to alpine in the upper reaches.

Sikkim is the natural home for about 475 species of orchids found in various climatic condition from warm and humid hills to snow peaks. Therefore, agro-climatic condition of Sikkim is suitable for growing varieties of orchid as well as temperate flowers like Lillylium, Antherium, Carnation, Gerbera, Glaxonia, Gladiolus, Begonia, Ornamental foliage, ferns and host of other flower varieties.

Over 80 per cent of the population of Sikkim directly or indirectly depends on farming activities. The development measures of the "GREEN REVOLUTION' implemented in other Indian States were not successful in the Himalayan Region, because adequate fertilizer were never available on time, irrigation could not be developed and soil are very fragile. Population growth and consequent fragmentation of farm land in Sikkim has cost reduction in per capita holdings.

This reduction has forced farmers to cultivate cash crops such as potato, ginger and mandarin orange, which have cost rapid nutrient depletion of the soil. Instead, production of another cash crop, Large Cardamom a plant native to the Sikkim Himalaya has been a boon to the people of Sikkim. Large Cardamom is a perennial cash crop grown beneath the forest cover on marginal land. Hence, it is well fitted in the agro-forestry system of land use. Thus the cardamom plantation has a considerable contribution towards preservation and protection of forest cover in Sikkim. This is the crop grown without the use of chemical fertilizer and pesticides. It is therefore, the total cardamom produced of Sikkim is pure organic. Apart from its high-income value and low demand in labour, large cardamom is also a low value and non-perishable crop. This is a great advantage in an area where accessibility and transportation are restricted.

Unlike farming system based on high input the existing crops production in Sikkim hills are unique and full fills the concept of integrated plant nutrient system. The cattle waste, forest litter, green leaves of trees and crop residues are the organic inputs to supplement the mineral fertilizer requirement of crops to obtain the desire yield level.

In the Sikkim hills farmers considers cropland not as a discrete independent system but as a subsystem of complex ecosystem consisting of croplands, animal husbandry, forest and Human beings. Remoteness, inaccessibility difficult terrain, fragile ecosystem, environment risk and uncertainty are the measure barriers in the farm production system operating with the low external inputs in Sikkim Hills. The farming is rain fed, use of mineral fertilizer in the hills practically nil and FYM and compost are use as measure source of nutrient to support crop production. The principal horticultural crops grown in Sikkim include Large Cardamom, ginger, turmeric, oranges, apple, pear, off-season vegetables flowers like gladiolus, orchids, lilies, gerbera, carnation, antherium for both cut flowers and planting materials. Large Cardamom occupies the largest area of about 24 thousand hectares of total cropped area. Ginger is the very important cash crop of Sikkim. It is grown by all section of farmers including tenants, sharecropper, and small marginal SC and ST farmers. Approximately 15 to 20 thousand tones of good quality ginger is annually produced and marketed outside the state. The ginger available in Sikkim is less fibrous with high moisture content and suitable for manufacture of ginger products like preserve, candy, crystallised ginger, ginger biscuits and so on.

Since spices like ginger and cardamom are available in adequate quantity in Sikkim, it may be possible to establish an oil and oleoresin extraction unit. The end users of oil and oleoresin will be the pharmaceuticals, cosmetics, food, beverage processing, and perfume and fragrance industries. A study on oil extraction of cardamom has been already done under Indo-Swiss Project Sikkim and information is available. It is reported that the Large Cardamom oil is comparable to the small cardamom oil. To support the horticultural crop production in Sikkim Indo-Swiss Project is operating. The areas of intervention by the ISPS Project are (a) ginger disease management, (b) to improve the quality of cardamom by developing improve curing system and (c) development of marketing for horticultural produce. Under the ISPS Project through the consultancy service of TERI a technology called "Gassifier System of Cardamom Curing" has been developed. To make available the system to the cardamom growers a fabrication unit of the gassifier system is required to be set up. The existing practice of grading and packing in gunny bags needs to be replaced with marketing of cardamom with polishing, grading and packing with a presentable form. Among the fruits grown in Sikkim Orange is the important crop in respect of area and production. The orange industry in Sikkim is suffering a set back because of the dieback disease.

To revive the crop we have initiated rejuvenation programme supported by the replantation scheme, with budded plants on trifoliate and rang pur lime rootstock. The planting materials are being produced both in Government farms and farmers field under the supervision of Horticulture Officers. The other fruits grown are apple, pears, litchi and passion fruits. There is good scope of seed production of various vegetables like broccoli, cabbage, cauliflower, beans, peas, etc. We are prepared to tag up with private firms having expertise in seed production to take up joint venture project on vegetable seed production. The share of the State Government may be in the form of land and manpower both skilled and unskilled. Sikkim grows a special chilly locally known as 'Dalle Khorsani'. It has good aroma with considerable pungency. Efforts are being made to tag with private firms for setting up processing unit.

The current status and potentiality of the important horticulture crops is given below:

Sl. No	Unit	Crops	Production On 31.03.2001	Production Potential
1.	000'T	Cardamom	3.60	5.00
2.	000'T	Ginger	20.00	40.00
3.		Fruits	10.00	20.00
4.	000'T	Vegetables	20.00	50.00
5.	000'T	Potato	24.00	40.00
6.	000'T	Turmeric	0.60	10.00
7.	000	Flowers		
		a. Cut Flowers	Nos 500	Nos 3000
		b. Planting Material	1000	3000

With large number of educated persons coming out who will look for a lucrative and decent profession, floriculture is likely to be an alternative. The important flowers, which are already adopted, are gladiolus, carnation, gerbera, orchids and zanthadesia. The effective boost under the floriculture Programme has been with the extension of CSS. The Namli Farm was declared as Model Floriculture Centre under CSS for production and distribution of flower seeds and planting materials.

A joint venture agreement with M/s Natsyn Flora, Chennai, has been signed for production of cut flowers of cymbidium orchids for export. Under the project the cut flowers production is anticipated to start by 2005.

Sikkim suffers from horticulture research backup, as there is no Agriculture College or University with the exception of ICAR subcentre and Spices Board. The facilities available with these institutions are being utilised for the benefit of the state. In addition to this department of Horticulture has initiated research work on ginger disease management and cardamom curing with Indo-Swiss Project. Adaptive trials of the horticulture crops in the government farms and also in farmers field.

The upgrading knowledge and skill of Horticulture manpower in various fields are being fulfilled by providing them training within the state by inviting resource person from outside or by sending them for higher studies leading to degree/diploma in specialised field. Crop production technology are being transferred to the farmers field through a system of training, audio-visual aids, printed materials, group meeting, field days, exhibition, crop competition conducted tours, exposure trips including field demonstration and group discussions.

Forestry

The forests cover nearly 30 per cent area of the state and have immense economic value for the region. During feudal regime no steps were taken to utilise the forest wealth or to conserve it. The popular government has not only started schemes of reforestation and afforestation but has also made serious attempt to conserve the wealth of green gold. Trees of ornamental value and ecological importance are being planted over vast areas. The setting up of a saw mill at Rangpo and experimental floatation of logs along the Teesta river are some of the new steps in this regard. A paper plant is fast coming up at Mille under the aegis of the Hindustan Paper Corporation. The paper mill shall be manufacturing condenser tissues and carbon paper besides common grade paper.

The Forest Department has developed gardens of medicinal herbs to raise the production of such plants as Ipecac, Rauvoulfia Serpentina and Lycopodium. The nearest Ipecac garden, from Gangtok is situated at Saramsa. For the proper management of the forest wealth many local people were sent for training to the Indian Forest Research Institute, Dehra Dun.

The Programmes related to soil conservation and pisciculture also fall in the jurisdiction of the Forest Department. The department has taken up with success the experimental schemes to propagate fishing in Sikkim. Three experimental fish farms have been established at Gangtok, Rhinchenpong and Lachung which rear Mirror Crap fish for which fingerlings were initially obtained from the state of Himachal Pradesh.

Transport System

The mountainous terrain with gradients landslides, screes, landflows, snowfall and heavy rainfall are some of the serious bottlenecks which ilupede the road building activity in the state. The feudal rulers neither had the will nor funds for connecting the capital city of the state with as many places as possible. For obvious reasons there are no railway lines in Sikkim. Although some perennial rivers flow though the state yet their turbulent nature and steep gradient prevent them form being navigable.

In the year 1954 there was only one 80 km (50 miles) long Trunk Road which connected Gangtok with the border town of Rangpo, linking Sikkim with the state of West Bengal. During the plans three types of roads, viz., motorable roads, Jeepable roads and bridle paths continue to be constructed in different parts of the state. During the first plan 68 km motorable and 120 km, jeepable road lengths were added.

In the next plan, 80 km and 92 km lengths of motorable and jeepable roads were constructed. These road lengths, however, did not include the National Highway and the Border roads exclusively result by the Government of India. By the end of the Third Plan Period the road lengths maintained by the Central Government and the State Government measured 282 km and 280 km respectively. Most of the roads are concentrated in southern Sikkim and a thinner road net is found in the eastern section. The northern and western parts of the state are the best accessible parts of the region. The Sikkim Nationalised Transport established in 1949 plies its vehicles on all the roads. About 250 buses ply on different routes.

To cope the increasing demand, the SNT has started 85 bus services, on reciprocal basis, to the adjoining areas of West Bengal. The SNT has to maintain its fleet in good condition for the transportation of essential commodities and defence equipment. However, with the present fleet of about 160 trucks and tankers the SNT finds it difficult to cope with the situation.

For better management and for providing better office accommodation the Yatayat Bhavan at a total cost of Rs: 40.34 lakh was recently constructed on the SNT campus. The SNT also maintains an outbooking agency for the persons desirous of travelling by railway outside the region.

9

Polity

Flanked by Nepal on the east and Bhutan on the West, with the highlands of Tibet in the north, Sikkim is like a lively painting framed with care. It merged with India in 1975. Covering an area of 7,096 sq km, Sikkim has a population of 5,40,493. Sikkim is noted for her floral wealth and an estimated 4,000 varieties of flowering plants and shrubs are found here. Its dense forests abound with all kinds of fauna — the black and brown bears, the barking deer, the musk deer, the samber, wild boars and leopards. Spread below the Kanchenjunga (8,603 m), the third highest mountain in the world and revered by the Sikkimese as their protective deity, Sikkim is situated in the eastern Himalayas.

State Symbols

State day	May 16 (day of accession to India)
State animal	Red Panda
State bird	Blood Pheasant
State tree	Rhododendron
State flower	Noble orchid

Government and Politics

Like all states of India, the head of the State Government is a governor appointed by the Central Government. His/her appointment is largely ceremonial, and his/her main role is to oversee the swearing in of the Chief Minister. The Chief Minister, who holds the real executive powers, is the head of the party or coalition garnering the largest majority in the state elections. The governor also appoints the cabinet ministers on the advice of the Chief Minister. Sikkim has a unicameral legislature like most other Indian states. Sikkim is allocated one seat in each of both chambers of India's national bicameral legislature, the Lok Sabha, and the Rajya Sabha. There are a total of 32 state assembly seats including one reserved for the Sangha. The Sikkim High Court is the smallest high court in the country.

In 1975, after the abrogation of Sikkim's monarchy, the Congress Party got the largest majority in the 1977 elections. In 1979, after a period of instability, a popular ministry headed by Nar Bahadur Bhandari, leader of the Sikkim Sangram Parishad Party was sworn in. Bhandari held on to power in the 1984 and 1989 elections. In the 1994 elections, Pawan Kumar Chamling from the Sikkim Democratic Front became the Chief Minister of the state. The party has since held on to power by winning the 1999 and 2004 elections. It won all the 32 seats of the state assembly in 2009.

Political Parties

Political parties in Sikkim participate whole-heartedly in the assembly and the parliamentary elections of the state. There are both national level and state level political parties in Sikkim, although current position of the state shows a clear preference for the regional parties over the national level parties.

In the early days of the democracy in the state of Sikkim, the national level political parties started to make their presence felt more strongly in this picturesque Himalayan state. The Indian National Congress had the greatest influence of all other national political parties at Sikkim in that time, as it is now. The other national level political parties did not share the wide popularity that INC enjoyed. However, many of them have become proactive to increase their influence in this region.

The state level political parties of Sikkim enjoy great popularity in the state. In fact, Sikkim is one of those few states where the state political parties enjoy popularity and power that is much higher than the high profile national political parties. There are many state and regional political parties in Sikkim. The history of the Sikkim political parties features a number of switches of loyalties, cessations and merges. Not all of them managed to have equal significance in the state's political scenario. However, Sikkim Democratic Party (SDF) enjoys great popularity in the state and continues to be the ruling party of the state for the last two assembly elections.

National Political Parties

National political parties in Sikkim have had a telling presence in the political scenario of the state right from the time of the state's inclusion in the Indian democracy in 1975. Indian National Congress was the greatest presence of all national political parties at Sikkim in the state at that time and still continues to be so. Bharatiya Janata Party also has a presence in the state, though it is not that prominent as of now. The situation is similar for the Communist Party of India (Marxist) (CPM) as well. However in Sikkim, national political parties have always played second fiddle to the state and regional level parties.

Indian National Congress

The Indian National Congress, the most important of all national political parties in Sikkim, started its journey in the state with great success. Soon after Sikkim was given the status of a state within the Indian democracy, Indian National Congress in Sikkim emerged as the most prominent national party. It won the assembly elections in 1977. Thereafter, the regional issues dominated, ushering in the age of great success for the state level parties in Sikkim. However, the presence of Congress as the most prominent of the national level political parties in Sikkim continued. Congress managed to win only one seat in the 2004 assembly elections, having participated in 28 of the 32 constituencies. That was a temporary setback in the electoral profile of the party in the state. However, INC is keen to regain its lost ground and is continuously strengthening its organisational infrastructure in the state.

Other National Political Parties

Other national political parties in Sikkim include the Bharatiya Janata Party (BJP) and Communist Party of India (Marxist) (CPM). However, they have only a kind of fringe presence in the state. BJP competed in four constituencies but did not succeed in winning any of them; CPM participated in only one assembly constituency, but with no success. However, both these parties are trying to better their performances next time around.

State Level Political Parties

State level political parties in Sikkim plays crucial roles in the political scenario of the state. The role that Sikkim state level political parties play in the politics of the state is rarely seen anywhere else in India. The way the national political parties were virtually washed away in the 2004 assembly elections attest to the popularity that the state level political parties of Sikkim enjoy among the inhabitants of the state. Sikkim Democratic Front (SDF) is the single largest of the state level political parties in Sikkim.

Sikkim Democratic Front (SDF)

Sikkim Democratic Front (SDF) is the single largest state level party in Sikkim. It has met a success in the assembly elections of 2004, that is almost unbelievable for a state level party in India, where the national parties dominate the political scenario by and large and the state level parties are left to play only fringe coalition roles. SDF is a bright exception to the general trend. The party has its headquarters in Umbrella Upper Deorali in Gangtok of East Sikkim. Shri Pawan Kumar Chamling, the reigning chief minister of the state is at helm of the party. SDF met with resounding success in the 2004 assembly elections, winning as many as 31 out of 32 seats and going up to form the government.

Sikkim Himali Rajya Parishad

Sikkim Himali Rajya Parishad or the Sikkim Himalayan State Association is one of the major state level political parties of Sikkim. SHRP operates from its head office at Metro Point at 5th Mile Tadong in Gangtok of East Sikkim. The party operates under the presidentship of the party president Dr. AD Subba. In the 2004 assembly elections, SHRP teamed up with BJP, INC and a few other regional parties to form the Sikkim National Liberation Front. It stood fourth in the only assembly constituency in which it fought.

The Constituencies

State constituencies of Sikkim are the very backbone of the democratic governance of the state. Ever since Sikkim became a part of the Indian democracy in 2005, the various state constituencies of Sikkim have been ascertained and thereafter been fiercely fought by both national and state level parties. The politics of Sikkim have seen a prominent presence of the state and regional parties, much more than is generally found in other parts of India. 32 assembly constituencies and one parliamentary constituency form the Sikkim state constituencies.

Parliamentary Constituency in Sikkim

Sikkim has only one parliamentary constituency, which is one of the most prestigious of the Sikkim state constituencies. The Sikkim parliamentary constituency sends a representative from the state to Lok Sabha of the Indian legislature. Therefore, election here is very fiercely fought by the various national and state level parties of the state. Even this constituency among the Sikkim state constituencies, has seen a dominance of the state level parties, with Sikkim Democratic Front winning it for the last four times.

Assembly Constituencies of Sikkim

There are 32 assembly constituencies in Sikkim. These state constituencies at Sikkim elect candidates for the unicameral legislative council of the state. The elections in the assembly constituencies are some of the most fiercely fought polls in Sikkim. In the 2004 assembly elections, Sikkim Democratic Front made a clean sweep of the polling results, succeeding in all but one assembly constituency in the state. These state constituencies in Sikkim are divided into general, SC and BL seats, reserved for candidates belonging to the above categories.

State Legislature

Sikkim legislature is a unicameral body. Just like the legislature structure of India, Sikkim legislature comprises of a legislative assembly with the speaker responsible for conducting the proceedings of the house. The governor is appointed by the centre and is the representative of the president in the state. Legislature of Sikkim operates for a term of five years, like everywhere else in India. However, there can be special occasions when the legislature can be dissolved.

Governor and Speaker

The governor is the head of the state legislature at Sikkim. Although the post is largely ceremonial in profile, yet there can be times when he has to take important decisions regarding the operations of the state legislature. Shri V. Rama Rao is the present governor of Sikkim. The speaker is the second most significant person in the legislature in Sikkim. He is vested with the responsibility to conduct the proceedings of the legislative assembly and guide the debates and discussions initiated by the members of the Legislative Assembly towards a fruitful end. Shri Dawa Norbu Takarpa is the speaker of Sikkim legislature and he is assisted by deputy speaker Shri Mingma Tshering Sherpa.

Leader of the House and Secretary

The chief minister of the state usually does the role of the leader of the house. He represents the ruling party or the ruling coalition, whichever the case may be. He guides the members from his party and also the members from the opposition towards a fruitful completion of the issues brought up in the house. Shri Pawan Chamling is the present Leader of the House in the Sikkim legislature. He is assisted in his legislative duties by Shri Ran Bahadur Subba, the minister of Parliamentary affairs. The secretary Shri T. K. Chankpa, is an important part of the legislature in Sikkim.

Government and Administration

State Administration

The courts of illakadars were neither honorary nor stipendary ones, as they kept to themselves half the court fee realised and the fines imposed by them. Thus every illakadar was *ipso facto* the courts of original jurisdiction of the respective illaka. Sufficient care was taken to limit the rights of landlords for over-assessment. Thus, if a rayot felt that he had been over-assessed, the case was investigated by the three kazis, lamas or thikadars in any of the above four classes.

Besides, these judicial powers, the illakadars were given a number of administrative powers. Firstly, they were the agents of government at the local level. They were the middlemen between the government and rayots and were responsible for the collection of revenue of their illaka which included a fixed sum on account of land rent and household tax; secondly, they were to maintain the registration of births and deaths in their illaka; and lastly, whenever the government felt the need to undertake any work in certain areas the concerned illakadars were not only notified about it but required to undertake it.

For example, we find that in 1908-09 the durbar decided to plant road side trees along all roads to provide shade for the travellers, the responsibility for undertaking the work was shouldered by the illakadars. Despite the government's effort to put some restraints on the landlord's right of overassessment, in the absence of any provision for people's participation this aspect remained a farce and the lot of the peasants was never redeemed. The government, in fact, continued to receive complaints from rayots against their landlords for over-assessment. In each case, the complaint was submitted for enquiry to a 'Panchayat' consisting of two landlords and an intelligent rayot. In some cases, the findings of panchayat were favourable to the rayots.

The notification of 1906 was, in fact, an effort to give legal status to the already existing illaka system, rather than to introduce a system of self-government. No doubt, this 1906 notification paved the way for decentralisation but a true spirit of democratic decentralisation was yet to develop in this tiny state. The nature of the state was highly feudalistic and the wishes of the people did hardly articulate.

Up till 1935-36, there were 104 illakas in Sikkim. There were three classes of illakadars, *viz.* (1) leased out illakas, (2) illakas under direct management, (3) monasteries.

There were 91 illakas under the first type and the system of collection was that the lease-holder would pay annually certain fixed sum on account of land rent and household taxes on the 15th January and 28th of February respectively every year. Illakas under Class II were those which were under direct management of the state. There were eleven illakas under this class which were placed in charge of different managers who credited into the state treasury from time to time, the entire revenue collected by them under different heads as they came in. Under Class III were monasteries. There were seven illakas under this class. These monasteries paid annually on the 28th of February certain fixed sum on account of household tax only. They did not pay land rent which they recovered from the rayots and utilised it for religious purposes in the monasteries.

Of the Illakadars in the state, twenty-one were Kazis, six Bhutias, eight Lepchas, thirteen Nepalese and one domiciled plainsman.

Besides these prevailing social systems that had bound every Sikkimese, it is interesting to note that in 1910, a different council development to try cases of British Indian subjects. The 'Indian Panchayat', as it was called, was located at Gangtok consisting of four Indians (one as president) one Nepali and one Sikkimese as members. The Indian Panchayat was empowered to try petty civil and criminal cases in which British subjects were defendants.

- *Bhutias:* a term applied to all Tibetans of Sikkim who are not kazis.
- *Lepchas:* a tribe said to be original inhabitants of Sikkim.

In the preceding section we have seen that though administration was decentralised, little thought was given to the spirit of popular participation and of interlinking of different layers of government. During the forties, there was an epoch-making turn of events in the history of this Himalayan state.

The inspiration for these turn of events was drawn chiefly from the struggle for Indian independence. Soon after the independence of India three political parties" sprang up in Sikkim. On December 27, 1947, these parties formally merged together and formed a new patty, the Sikkim State Congress.

The abolition of landlordism became the cardinal aim of this party. As an institution the system was beset with a number of flaws; the existence of civil-cum-criminal power (in Adda Courts) was a glaring one. The landlord's court had undoubtedly served a good purpose inasmuch as it proved to be less expensive to the villagers, as the petty cases could be tried by illakadars within their illakas, but this very judicial power had become one of the most potent weapons in the hands of illakadars to make rayots subservient to their will.

Local Self-government

Sikkim's history is shrouded in mystery. What little information we can have is through the interpretation of various legends, folklores and anecdotes. Originally, Sikkim had been the land of the Lepchas. The Tibetans came to Sikkim later. In the 15th and 16th centuries, as a result of religious strife between the rival sects in Tibet, the fugitives (Nyingmapa sect) found shelter in Sikkim and next in the process of migration came the Nepalese, who had actually started trickling down in the 19th century only.' Thus three tribes — Lepchas, Bhutias, and Nepalese are the inhabitants of Sikkim. While discussing the evolution of Panchayat system in Sikkim, it is important to bear in mind the system that was prevalent in the 19th and the early 20th centuries upon which the present system of self-government is founded.

Like in any other traditionalist society, in Sikkim too, the internal administration was feudal in character. This feudal class wielded both judicial and administrative powers within the limit of their estates or illakas. For the regulation of the intra-village affairs, the mondals were appointed by these illakadars! Their main function consisted in the maintenance of law and order and collection of land revenue. The Panchayats, in those days, were the products of disputative exigencies only. Whenever any quarrel occurred the panchayats were formed to decide the case.

However, side by side with this system, a unique system of self-rule was prevalent in two villages of Lachung and Lachen in North Sikkim. They had very unusual and almost communistic government of their own, even in those days, when the rest of the people of Sikkim were groaning under the yoke of feudalism.

On every occasion the whole population used to meet in a panchayat or council where they would sit in a circle for consultation.' This traditional institution of local self-government was called *Zumsha* or assembly of people. The Pipon (the village headman) was elected by adult members drawn from each of that family for 'a term of two years. The Pipon would nominate two Gyapons (assistants) to assist him in performance of his functions. Besides, there was another assembly of influential village elders, Gyemmi, for aiding and advising the Pipon in functions involving the community interest. Its members were nominated by the Pipon.

The system had worked so well among these Lachungpas and Lachenpas that J. C. White, the first political officer in Sikkim, in massive administrative development and change he brought about in the country, allowed it to continue with slight modification only.

With the intrusion of the British in the administration of Sikkim, a new era of administrative change ushered in. Prior to this, the administration was in confusion. On the condition of Sikkim, J. C. White observed.

Chaos reigned everywhere, there was no revenue system, the Rajah taking what he required from the people, those nearest the capital having to contribute the largest share while those more remote had toll taken from them by the local officials in the name of the Rajah, though little found its way to him, no court of justice, no police, no public works, no education for the younger generation.

In the absence of any codified laws and regulation, the Kazis, lamas and thikadars were in the habit of levying fines and illegal cases and in various ways oppressing their rayots." Thus, in 1906, as per the political officer's notification, attempt was made for defining and limiting the powers of the Kazis, lamas and thikadars.

With the introduction of this notification of 1906 the centuries old illaka system was at least given an official recognition and powers of illakadars defined. The notification sought to give judicial powers to the illakadars. In general, all the illakadars were given the power to try petty cases of cattle trespass, petty land disputes and debt cases of value not more than Rs. 10 with fine to the extent of Rs. 5 (cl. 2). The illakadars were divided into four classes according to the judicial powers they were invested with (cl. 3).

Thus, Kazis, lamas and thikadars with first class judicial powers acquired the powers to try ordinary civil and criminal cases and to fine up to Rs. 100 or imprisonment for one month, within the limit of their illaka. If the sentence of imprisonment was passed the prisoner was to be confined in jail at Gangtok. The second class illakadars were granted the powers to try ordinary civil and criminal cases and to fine up to Rs. 50. In the same manner, the third and fourth class illakadars were empowered to try ordinary civil cases and to fine up to Rs. 25 and Rs. 15 respectively.

The notification, however, specifically, maintained that all serious criminal cases were to be tried in the courts of political agent (cl. 4) and everyone had the right of appeal to the courts of His Highness the Maharajah and of the political agent [cl. 6 (a)].

Rule of Law

While there is class conflict in West Bengal, caste conflicts in Bihar, UP, religious bigotry and violence in Punjab and communal riots in Ahmedabad and Maharashtra, three major groups co-existed in Sikkim for the past 200 years.

Lawyers and judges complain they have no work as civil and criminal disputes are few. Everyone brews 'chang', the locally fermented drink from millets, but there is no drunkenness on the streets. Prostitution is unheard of. But a woman has the full freedom of separation or remarriage. It is common among the Bhutias of Tibetan origin to marry a widow with a child without any stigma. Stepsons and stepdaughters have as much right to the property as one's own sons or daughters.

The Bhandari Government claims that its clamp-down on smuggling has protected the state's economy and stopped immigration from neighbouring Nepal.

Effects of Gorkha Movement: The Chief Minister, who is very much concerned because of the entry of displaced persons from Darjeeling into various places in Sikkim as a sequel to the Gorkhaland movement, said that the state's law and order situation was not only under control but conducive to initiate development programmes.

Though, Mr. Bhandari had asked Mr. Subhash Ghisingh to normalise the situation in Darjeeling district as, because of the agitation in Darjeeling Sikkim's supply line is being threatened. He made it clear to Mr. Ghisingh that any extreme movement in Darjeeling district would affect Sikkim economically and he would not support it.

Political circles made it clear that Mr. Bhandari was seeing a threat in the rise of Mr. Ghisingh as a contender to the leadership of the Nepalese-speaking people. However, according to Mr. Bhandari, the demand for Gorkhaland is not merely a demand of the Nepalese. It is the demand of all those who are permanently settled in Darjeeling. The people of Darjeeling are entitled to a legitimate share in economic and political benefits within the framework of the Indian Constitution. The Darjeeling agitation came as a boon to him as the tourist traffic for Darjeeling, Kalimpong and Kurseong had to be diverted to Sikkim.

The Achievements

The pipeline of funds from the Centre, says India Today, May 15,1985 has also had a visible impact on the state's development, as borne out by indicators:

- Ten years ago there were 264 educational institutions in the state; today there are 761. One result: the number of persons employed in agriculture declined;

- Power generation has risen more than five times to a capacity of 17 MW compared to 2.5 MW at the time of merger: Result, Sikkim sells surplus power to neighbouring

West Bengal and from a handful, no fewer than 181 villages of a total of 405 have electricity.

- In the Sixth Plan period, 350 km of new roads were hewn out of the mountains.

- Irrigated area has doubled to 8,000 hectares.

- Sikkim's gross product, the value of total production in the state has risen about 50 per cent in five years to Rs. 37.4 crore in 1983-85.

Not surprisingly, save for settlements of migrant Nepalese labour, Sikkim shows few signs of the crushing poverty that scar so many other parts of India. Most of the people have land and Sikkim being the largest producer of cardamom which always has a ruling price, the people are not badly off. The growth of population is also less than many other Indian States as a large section of the tribal people still practise polyandry. With billowing expectations and conflicting sectarian aspirations the Sikkimese polity today is an unstable raft on which few politicians can balance successfully.

But no leader, not even Mr. Bhandari, seems to be sure where he stands today. At one end is the rising clamour of the majority Nepalese who feel they are still being suppressed, still being denied opportunities commensurate with their efforts and number or the other are the insecure Lepcha and Bhutia tribals craving for a leader to protect their interests. And on top is the omnipotent Centre demanding obeisance to national integration and unity. Freed of the monarchial strait-jacket but pinned by this Trinity, Sikkim, 12 years after its merger with India is prospering but still far from being the "happy house" its name implies.

10

Tourism

- -

Tourism is one of the most important economic sectors of the state, the wealth of natural resources the third highest mountain in the world, the rich flora and fauna, cultural festivals and festivities and a rich tradition are some of the tremendous potentials that is available in Sikkim for the promotion of tourism. Due to lack of large and medium industries, tourism is one of the most sustainable industries in the state thereby creating tremendous opportunities in terms of revenue generation and employment opportunities. With these potentials, the government has not lagged behind and has therefore declared tourism is one of the topmost priorities in the overall developmental scenario of the state.

The Tourism sector is strategically placed in the socio-economic development of the state thereby giving each and every citizen an opportunity to avail of the facilities. In order to bring about a long-term perspective plan on the development of tourism sector, the Department has prepared a perspective plan for 15 years beginning 1997-98 and terminating in the year 2011-12.

Sikkim is a land of immense scenic beauty, natural charm and a variety of fauna and flora. The third highest mountain in the world Kanchenjunga (8,586 metres) is situated here. 'Sikkim' commonly attributed to the Tsong word 'Su-Khim' means New or Happy House. Sikkim has a lot of open monasteries, chortens, flying prayer flags and lofty stupas all giving a tinge of mysticism. Siliguri junction (114 km from Gangtok) and New Jalpaiguri Junction (125 km from Gangtok) are the two closest railway stations to this Himalayan state of India.

Bus service for Bangkok is available from Darjeeling and Kalimpong also. Calcutta is the starting point for travel by air. Indian Airlines operate a regular scheduled flight between Calcutta (Dumdum airport) and Bagdogra. A Dakota service between Calcutta and Ambri is also available. The entrance to the state of Sikkim is at the border town of Rongpo, which is located in the Teesta valley. Rongpo is a small town famous for the liquors and wines produced here.

It is a great market for oranges. Some of the important tourist centres are: Gangktok, Bakkhim — a natural garden, Yoksum — meeting of three great Lamas, Dhubdi monastery, Tashing Monastery, Rumtek monastery, etc. There are 200 monasteries in Sikkim. Kanchenjunga National Park is one of the highest national parks in the world and includes the world's third highest mountain (Kanchenjunga). The Yak and the musk are the animals found in Sikkim. There are over 4,000 species of plants.

Sikkim state lies in Northeastern India. On the southern slopes of the Himalayas Sikkim is bounded on the north and northeast by the Tibet Autonomous Region of China, on the southeast by Bhutan, on the south by West Bengal and on the west by Nepal. The area is 7,096 sq km. One of the highest regions in India, Sikkim is traversed by the main range of the Himalayas and by several spur ranges.

It is entirely mountainous, with one-third of the land covered with dense forests of sal, sambal and bamboo, which are mostly inaccessible and unexploited. Kanchenjunga (8,598 m/28,209 ft) one of the highest peaks in the world lies in Sikkim. Sikkim receives heavy rainfall. The perennial river Teesta, and its tributaries, which are fed by both snow and rain, waters it. The climate ranges from tropical to alpine. Generally the lowlands are hot and humid, the hills are temperate, and the mountains are permanently covered with snow.

Average January temperatures in Gangtok, a hill city, range from 4° to 14°C 39° to 57°F); in May the average temperatures range from 14° to 22°C 57° to 72°F). Annual rainfall varies from about 1,300 to 5,000 mm (about 50 to 200 in), depending on the altitude and region of the state. Sikkim has a single-chamber legislative assembly with 32 members. The state sends two members to the Indian National Parliament: one to the Rajya Sabha (Upper House) and one to the Lok Sabha (Lower House). Local Government is based on four administrative districts. Gangtok is the Capital of this hilly state.

Gangtok: Gangtok is the capital of Sikkim. Its name means the 'High Hill'. Situated at a height of over five thousand feet above sea level, the city looks to be tucked away in a cloud sprawling over a hill. Kanchenjunga, renders a spectacular view from Gangtok, with its magnificent snow and ice scenery. Some of the important sites of the city of Gangtok, like the Palace, Palace Chapel Tsuklakhang, the Deer park, Institute of Tibetology and the Namgyal chorten are located on the spine of the ridge.

Tusklakhang: Tusklakhang Royal Chapel is situated on a level ground in the palace complex. On all corners of the chapel are located the formidable heads of snow lions-wood sculpture in relief. Inside the chapel is depicted the magnificent wood work, highlighted by the massive Buddhist murals that adorn the walls. An eternal butter lamp lights the floor to ceiling altar, housing the deities and the scriptures. Tsuklakhang is the venue of all important festivals and festivities. The warrior dances to worship Kanchenjunga, the Black Hat dance to celebrate Sikkimese New year's day, etc. are all celebrated in this chapel. Earlier the coronations of Chogyals, Oath taking by counsellors and royal weddings were celebrated inside the chapel.

The Research Institute or Namgyal Institute of Tibetology: This institute is on the top of a hill. It was established to promote research on Tibet and Mahayana Buddhism.

The Namgyal Institute of Tibetology has come to be known as the highest seat of learning among the Mahayana scholars. The institute was inaugurated by Late Pandit Jawaharlal Nehru on October 1,1958. The Institute is dedicated to the cause of advancement of Tibetan studies. Located in serene surroundings, the institute has its interiors lavishly decorated with great murals and ornate wood carvings and altars holding the images of the Buddhas, the Bodhisattvas and the Tantric deities.

The cabinets of the halls contain a vast library of Tibetan deities. It contains a greatest collection of books on Mahayana Buddhism. The museum of the institute contains another asset of Mahayana. More than two hundred icons, prized objects of traditional art, ritualistic chortens, brass bells, Dorjis (thunder bolts), Rosaries, thangkas (hand painted scrolls woven or applique) are the main collections of the museum which have won international acclaim for the institute.

Government Cottage Industries Institute: The multi craft institute originally named after the last Chogyal Palden Thondup, is an academy of craftsmanship. The locally made handicraft products are sold at the institute. Foremost among the institute's products are the beautiful hand woven woollen carpets with traditional Sikkimese motifs and unique designs and combinations of rich colours.

These attractively designed carpets are in great demand in Sikkim and abroad. The handsome woollen textures are durable, plush and are dyed not with synthetic dyes but traditional vegetable Sikkimese dyes. The designs vary from sophisticated harmonising tones to the brilliant rioting of vermillion against intense blues.

Another exclusive product of the institute is the Sikkimese table locally called as Choktse. These foldable Choktse are prepared in varying designs and dimensions. The Sikkimese hand made paper is another product of the institute demanded inside and out side the state. The traditional Sikkimese weaves and woollen blankets which can be designed into bags, shawls, jackets, opulent Sikkimese thankas (traditional tapestry), leather works, dolls, variegated applique work, batiks, an exquisite selection of dolls and a variety of fashionable garments for modern people are the other displayed specialities of the institute.

Gate Ways: The Gateways for Gangtok city have been designed in a very attractive and artistic manner. There is a strange enchantment and charm about these gates. The gate that spans the entrance to Tashiling the secretariat has a beauty of its own. The Sikkimese art and the minute skill depicted by the Sikkimese artists are visible on these structures.

Deer Park: On the southern fringes of Tashiling, overhauling a valley that drops a sheer thousand metres below, is located the Gangtok's Deer Park. There is an image of Lord Buddha enshrined in the Deer Park in his preaching posture. The park is a sanctuary for deer, brought from Sikkim and other neighbouring lands and symbolises the quest for peace and harmony between neighbours. To walk around, to the soothing ripples of the Rongnek stream added with the charming site of spotted deer and long horned antelopes would really prove to be a prized walk.

Orchid Sanctuary: Orchid Sanctuary is situated below the Namgyal Institute of Tibetology. A large variety of orchids ranging from the commonest variety to rarest ones are found in the sanctuary. Sikkim is renowned for rich and numerous varieties of orchids.

Khabelongstok: At a distance of about 21 km from Gangtok is located a historic Kabi or Khabelongstok the venue where blood brother hood was sworn between Khye-Bumsa, the renowned ancestor of Namgyals, the former ruling house of Sikkim and Thekong Tek the then and last Lepcha chieftain amid sacrifices and the looming form of the revered and sacred Kanchenjunga. A memorial stone adorns the place as a testimony to the historic and sacred agreement. Prayer flags stand guard on the hill above and people from all corners of the state come with offerings of flowers to pray at the sacred spot.

Monasteries: Sikkim's monasteries are institutes of scholars and saints dedicated to the spreading of noble teachings of Lord Buddha. The monasteries of Sikkim apart from being the places of religious discourses, worship and meditation are the store houses of many hand written religious books and murals, the part and parcel of Sikkimese cultural heritage.

Dube-De Monastery is the oldest monastery of Sikkim. It was built over the cell of the hermit where lama Lhatsun Chenpo lived and meditated. Under his direction the Sangla Choling monastery was also built at the same time. He also built the Tashiding and Pemyangtse monasteries. All these purmonasteries are leading monasteries of Sikkim.

The Tashiding Monastery in Sikkim is second in importance to the premier and largest monastery of Pemyangtse. The legend goes that Guru Padmasambhava (Rimpoche) shot an arrow into the air and said that he would meditate at a place where the arrow fell. The arrow fell on the hill where Tashiding stands today. Tashidings fame has spread far beyond the frontiers of Sikkim. Till 1959 it was an important place of pilgrimage for Tibetans. The Buddhists from other parts of India, Nepal and Bhutan consider it as Mecca. Every pious Sikkimese wishes to die and to be cremated at Tashiding.

Monastery at Pemayangtse (Perfect Sublime Lotus): This monastery is situated 120 km west of Pemayangtse. Opens from sunrise to sunset. This is the second oldest monastery of Sikkim. The monastery was constructed in 1705 AD. The original building was designed on the Tibetan monastery pattern. But now the main building has completely been rebuilt in concrete and also painted in Sikkimese style. But the original carved altar, thrones, old images; old painted banners and the ritual objects have been left intact to maintain the continuity with the past.

The walls and the ceiling of the large Dukhang (Prayer Hall) have numerous thangkas and wall paintings. There is an exceptional collection of religious art works including an exquisite wooden sculpture on the top floor depicting the heavenly palace of Guru Rimpoche. The monks' quarters build in stone and wood is sited at the side of the monastery. This is the headquarters of the Nyingmapa sector. The monks have been recruited here from the leading families of Sikkim according to Nyingmapa tradition.

According to the tradition, only unmarried Bhutia monks with no physical blemish can live at this monastery. They are mostly drawn from the elite Bhutias. Since its inception the monastery has been closely associated with the royal family. Only the head lama of this monastery was permitted to enthrone the erstwhile Chogyals. The lamas of this monastery once completed the chronicle of Sikkim and kept the hand written manuscript in the library of the monastery but unfortunately it was destroyed during Gurukha invasions. Only two pages of this manuscript could be spotted by Hooker at a later stage. Rumtek, Gangtok Chhulakhang, Rinchinpong, Talung, Enchey, Lingtam, Namchi and Singtam are other renowned monasteries of Sikkim.

Rumtek Monastery: This monastery stands, 24 km away in picturesque environs on the lower valleys of southwest Gangtok. It is the headquarters of Kagyu (black hat) order of Tibetan Lamaistic Buddhism. It has the typical monastic paintings and intricate woodwork.

After 1959 the older Sikkim monastery perched on the spur of the hill has recently been renovated but without interfacing with the original traditional architecture. The new monastery of Gelwa Karmapa has been patterned on the Lama series of Tibet. Karmapa Lama after his self-exile from Tibet lives here.

The Enchey monastery is located on the Gangtok, Nathu La road just about three km from the capital city. Most of the monasteries in Sikkim belong to the Nyingmapa sect of Lamaism. The Pemyangtse governs all the Nyingmapa monasteries. There are separate monasteries for Lepchas at Lingtam, Jikim and Fagye also managed by the Pemyangtse. Nuns reside in very few monasteries of Sikkim and that too in diminishing numbers. On the walls of the monastery are painted the four religious Kings, the Masters of four main directions as mentioned in the Mahayana scriptures. In the almirahs, are placed the hand written manuscripts of many religious books.

Some of the important achievements made in the field of the tourism sector is as follows:

Relaxation of Entry Permits: Relaxation of entry permits to foreign tourists has been made to a large extent. Foreigners are now permitted to avail of the inner line permits from any of the Indian Missions abroad and any Tourism Offices located in the four metropolitan cities and at the Border Checkpoint at Rangpo, East Sikkim. The State Government has also facilitated the extension of inner line permit to foreigners for a total period of 45 days at an interval of 15 days each, which can be now duly extended by the Superintendent of Police of all the four Districts of Sikkim. Earlier the entry of foreigners for adventure tourism has been restricted to not less than four pax. This has now been relaxed to a minimum of two pax.

Single Window Clearance: The Department of Tourism has initiated a single window clearance for investors that want to invest in Sikkim in the travel trade business, hotel/ resorts, by acting as a facilitator to expedite the projects. The department of Tourism would take the responsibility of identification of the land, registration of the Company and all other related matters concerning setting up of such projects in the state of Sikkim.

Samdruptse Project: The State Government has embarked on a very ambitious Programme of implementing the project of constructing a 108 feet statute of Lord Guru Padmasambhava at Samdruptse in South Sikkim at a total cost of Rs. 6.00 crores. The project is being speedily implemented and the necessary infrastructures such as road, water, site levelling, etc., have already been completed. The Government of Sikkim has entrusted the religious aspects of the construction of the statue, the design and its dimensions to Ven. Dodrupchen Rimpoche. To facilitate tourists moving up from Namchi to Samdruptse and in order to give them a panoramic view of Namchi town the Department is in the process of installing a ropeway from Namchi to Samdruptse.

Tsomgo Lake: Tsomgo Lake, which is situated at an altitude of 12,400 feet *en route* to Nathula Pass, has been developed into a very popular tourist spot. The department has completed the construction of the Alpine Cafeteria and toilet facilities for the benefit of the tourists and is in the process of completing a designated car parking area for 200 vehicles and a Yak yard. Together with these construction of shopping complex is also being undertaken. The cost of the project is Rs. 203.00 lakhs.

Artificial Lake at Uttarey: The Department with a view to establish a new destination in West District as a means for gradual dispersal of the tourist has proposed the development of an Artificial lake at Uttarey, West Sikkim at an approximate cost of Rs. 200.00 lakhs. Rural Development Department has been given the responsibility for preparing the project report by the government, which will then be submitted to the Ministry of Tourism, Government of India for seeking central assistance.

The area has been surveyed by the Mines and Geology Department and has certified the stability of the land for resurrecting the old dried out lake. This will enhance the tourism potential in West Sikkim immensely. Compensation for land has been made.

Nathula: The Nathula Pass was opened for the first time for the domestic tourists from September, 1999. The tourists were allowed to visit four days in a week @ Rs. 300 per person. Better facilities like PHC, STD booth, and parking facilities have been provided which the Union Minister for Communication Shri Ramvilas Paswan inaugurated.

The amenity is expected to facilitate the tourists and the Army to make phone calls to their relatives from a place located at a height of more than 14,000 ft. A noble thought in itself.

Tourist Toilet: Out of thirteen tourist toilets sanctioned during 1999-2000 at an estimated cost of Rs. 2.18 lakhs each, five toilets located at Singtam, Rumtek, 3rd mile and 17th Mile and Namchi have been completed. These toilets will be made operational on pay and use basis. The rest located at Temi and Bermiok in South District and Phensang, Phodong, and Mangan in North District will be completed within the shortest possible time. These will provide added facilities to tourists.

Chungthang: Construction of Tourist Lodge at Chungthang, North Sikkim has been approved and sanctioned. The Buildings and Housing Department are taking up the construction. During the financial year 2000-01 has prioritised several schemes under the Centrally Sponsored Schemes incorporating projects like angling, computerisation, wayside amenities, refurbishment of monasteries, tourist lodges, lake development, development of water falls, trekking routes, improvement of old heritage bungalows, tourist toilets, etc. involving a sum of Rs. 552.76 lakhs as the central financial assistance against the total sanctioned projects for Rs. 720.49 lakhs. The remaining cost of the project is to be met from the Pan as the State Component.

Development of Saramsa Garden: Development of Saramsa Garden which is known to be a very popular picnic spot and recreational centre having various species of plants and trees located at 45 minutes drive from Gangtok is being developed into a beautiful garden. A green house to various species of orchids and an open air theatre is also constructed, for staging the cultural show of the state and a car park has been constructed.

The entry to the garden is through a beautiful traditional gate that has been provided. Beautification of the garden and car park has also taken up. The plan is in consonance with the blue print prepared by the Tata Consultancy Services.

Development of Namli Tourist Centre: The Tourist recreational complex at Namli in East Sikkim is being developed into a tourist complex having facilities like parks, gardens, angling, walk around to and water sports which would be connected with Saramsa Garden and therefore making the entire area into a integrated tourist development complex. This will be an added tourist attraction to both domestic and international tourists plus local people as it is within a driving distance from Gangtok the Capital of Sikkim.

Tourist Information Centre at Namchi: As Namchi is now developing into a very popular tourist centre and with the completion of the Guru Padmasambhava Statue at Samdruptse, it is expected that this will be one of the most sought after destinations particularly from the pilgrimage tourism point of view. Apart from this the adjoining areas are being developed into a beautiful trek route from Mehnam to Tendong and Damthang. In order to facilitate flow of the tourist traffic a Tourism Information Centre has been completed and put into operation.

Teesta Tea Tourism Festival: For the last two years Sikkim has been hosting for four days the Teesta Tea and Tourism Festival in a very big way. During the event tourists from abroad and India visit Sikkim to savour the rich cultural and traditional heritage of the state in its entire splendour. Traditional dances are performed at the monasteries, archery competitions are held, a carnival of the rich cultures of three ethnic communities is put on display and last but not least an all India River Rafting competition is held on the Teesta and Rangit Rivers; this has now become an annual feature.

Flower Festival Gangtok and Namchi: As Sikkim known to have a wide variety of species of plants and flowers. Sikkim is the home to the rare species of rhododendrons, orchids, primulas and host of other flowers, which is exhibited throughout the year at the annual flower festival that is being held in Gangtok, for the benefit of the tourists. This has been a very popular attraction to the tourists. To further and promote the rich floricultural aspect of the state, a similar flower festival is held once a year in Namchi the headquarters of South District.

Sight Seeing by Helicopter: Apart from connecting Gangtok the capital of Sikkim to Bagdogra with regular flights to Delhi and Calcutta, the Helicopter Service has become a boon to the tourism industry in Sikkim. With the introduction of the service, Mountain Flights Gangtok-Singtam-Geyzing-Yuksom-Dikchu-Gangtok, Gangtok-Mangan-along the Teesta river to Chungthang-Lachung-Yumthang-Gangtok-Mangan-Chungthang-Lachen-Zemu Glacier-Green Lake-Lachen-Gangtok, it has become a very special treat for the tourists visiting Sikkim. Mountain flights are very popular and are not conducted in other parts of the country. Apart from this the Helicopter Service also conducts charter flights to all the four Districts of the State.

Marketing Strategy: The Department has taken up aggressive marketing strategy in India and abroad to promote Sikkim as tourist destination. In India the Department has participated in fairs like Travel and Tourism Fair, Delhi, Mumbai and Ahmedabad, SATTE at Delhi and India Expo at Delhi and abroad the Department has sent delegations to ITB Berlin and MART in London.

Apart from this the Department had hosted a number of renowned foreign and Indian Publishers and Travel Writers to Sikkim part from renowned television networks to cover the various facets of the tourism industry in Sikkim. This has been a tremendous success in terms of the in crease in the arrivals of the tourists both of domestic and international.

Aero Sports: The Department with the assistance of Alpha Aviation Ltd. Recognised by Government of India is in the process of setting up a Aero sports club in Sikkim in order to assist all the youth of Sikkim in the fields of Aero sports in Sikkim, so that they could embark on this adventure as a full time profession. The Department is acting as a facilitator in terms of organising training Programmes and also leasing out equipments to interested parties.

Human Resource Development: The Department has prepared many projects in human resource development and has organised various seminars, workshops having faculty members brought from outside the state as keynotes speakers in the field of the Tourism Industries for imparting training Programmes to the local youths, travel operators, hotel and restaurant operators and taxi drivers, etc. This is with the intention of inculcating a spirit of professionalism so that we are geared to take on any category of tourists that is intending to visit Sikkim be it Indian or foreign.

Strengthening of Infrastructures: The Department has strengthened infrastructures in terms of upgrading facilities at Siniolchu in Gangtok, Hotel Mt. Pandim in West Sikkim, Rangpo Tourist Centre at Rangpo, wayside amenities at Chungthang, Kabi, Rumtek and also in the process of constructing wayside amenities at Temi Tarku, Singshore, Toong, Melli, Tashiding. This will be an added facility to the tourists visiting the tourist circuits on these routes. Apart from this the Department is also having a base camp constructed at Yuksom, which is under progress, having a designated parking area, toilet facilities, trekkers hut and camp sites. A Tourist Information Centre is also coming up at Gyalshing the Headquarters of West Sikkim and a tourist lodge is being constructed at Tashiding in West Sikkim and Assangthang in South Sikkim. All these projects have been duly sanctioned by Ministry of Tourism, Government of India. Many more projects are on the pipeline and negotiations are on with a number of investors for setting up hotels and resorts in Sikkim, for which land has been identified and the process of signing a MoU is under way.

National Award: The Department of Tourism, Government of Sikkim takes the privilege of mentioning that it has been the recipient of the National Award given by the Ministry of Tourism, Government of India for the best performing State in the North Eastern Region for two consecutive years. This is proof enough to indicate the seriousness and the priority that has been set by the Government of Sikkim in furthering the promotion of Tourism in the State with the aim and object of making it as one of the premier destinations in the country in the near future.

Tourism Development

The State had a tremendous potential on two counts: tourism and power plant. Pointing to the revenue potential in tourism, the Chief Minister opined that the central ban on foreign tourism in Sikkim was hurting the state. The need to develop the northern and western areas of Sikkim for internal tourism for which funds are not forthcoming yet. The Government has approached the ITDC for setting up a hotel in Sikkim.

A senior official of the Tourism Directorate of Sikkim says: "In some way we are better off without foreign tourists as the vices such as drugs and other that go with it could affect our simple people badly". But the Chief Minister felt that certain amount of flexibility in having tourists would help the state's economy. The Tourism Department and the Department of Forest have a large number of guest houses, bungalows and tourist lodges which could be better utilised for internal tourism with relaxation of the rules.

The State Tourism Department is confident that Sikkim can earn a lot of foreign exchange through tourism for it happens to be the only State, where there are monasteries representing all the four seats of Mahayana Buddhism. It has ample facilities of organising trekking trips to the foothills of the Kanchenjunga which in Tibetan means the mountain with a wide waist but in Lepcha language the mountain of five jewels, river rafting tours on Teesta and Rangeet or from the Himalayan ranges.

Sikkim has the highest altitude national park in the word, the Kanchenjunga National Park stretches from 8,000 ft to 28,000 ft and abounds in some of rarest species of animals such as the musk deer and the red Panda. The Government plans to have rubber boats for "shooting the rapids" in western Sikkim and skating on the frozen lakes in the north during the winter.

Development of new tourism centres has been given priority in Sikkim's plan. The existing recreational spots are being proposed to be developed as tourist centres. The Tibetology Institute Complex, Orchid Sanctuary, Rumtek Monastery, Cheeklakhang Enchey Monastery as well as the Phodong Monasteries, Deer Park, Yuksam, etc. are perennially popular.

Tourist Attractions

In its scenic beauty, physical charm, floral diversity, faunal variety, colourful people and theological spectacle no other hill state of India excels Sikkim. The Himalayan States of Jammu and Kashmir, Himachal Pradesh, Arunachal Pradesh, Meghalaya and the Himalayan sections falling within the state frontiers on which millions have been spent for development are no match for the natural pristine beauty which reins in every nook and corner of Sikkim.

Had the erstwhile feudal authorities made efforts to develop some of the scenic spots and opened the region to tourists from any part of the world, today it would have been number one in its tourist attractions. The bashful beauty of an unknown lake, the timid thrust of an unnamed mountain, the sunny sweetness of unexpected flowers, wonderful orchids, multicoloured Chirping birds, stately trees, quashing streams, velvet-carpeted verdure, snow-capped hill ranges, zigzag serpantine bridle paths are surely to become the cynosure of the tourists, Sikkim on the whole is natural beauty personified and its scenic charm extends many catchy haunts for the tourist. For tourists and visitors travelling by train from other parts of the country Siliguri Junction and New Jalpaiguri Junction (both in the northern neck like part of West Bengal) are the two closest railway terminal for this fabled Himalayan State.

The former junction falls at a distance of 114 km from Gangtok while the letter is 125 km from it. From both these places bus services for Gangtok are available. Those who wish to enter Sikkim after visiting Darjeeling and Kalimpong can avail the bus services initiating from these centres. For the visitors travelling by air, Kolkata is the nearest (Dumdum) airport. A scheduled flight is operated between Kolkata and Bagdogra From Bagdogra the tourists have to avail the bus service. A Dakota Service between Kolkata and Ambri (138 km from Gangtok) is also available.

The tourists enter the region through the border town of Rangpo, located in the Teesta Valley. As soon as the tourists enter here the region deeply steeped in religion he is welcomed by stupas, monasteries, pagoda-like structures, prayer flags and prayer wheels. The pagoda-like roofs and painted turquoise of the buildings apprise the visitor that he had reached the state which has a distinctly different architecture than one left behind by him. Rangpo is a small town, known all over the country for the wines, liquors and brews produced here.

It is also a great market centre for oranges which arrive here on beasts of burden from all parts of the state. It is strange but true that the town is dominated by the Marvari traders and businessmen. From Rangpo the visitors arrive by meandering road in the town of Singtam. Gangtok is a town settled on an isolated ridge appearing like confetti spilled over a giant knee.

The important buildings in Gangtok have been constructed on the spine of the ridge which is taken as very sacred feature. The palace, palace chapel Tsukiakhang, the deer park, the Namgyal chorten dedicated to Guru Rimpoche and the Namgyal Institute of Tibetology, etc. are all located on this spine located at an elevation of five thousand feet (about 1650 metres) above the mean sea level, the city looks too tucked away in a cloud sprawling over a hill. The streets and lanes of the city are a blend of different ethnic groups. Majority of the people sport mongoloid physical features but the dresses and jewellery worn by them make them distinct from each other. The gay silks of the Bhutias, heavy necklaces of the Nepalese and harmoniously muted colours of the Lepchas make them appear differently. The Tibetans of older generation wearing turquoise earrings as the swagger through the Crowded Bazars are vignettes to be cherished. The peak Kanchenjunga which depicts magnificent snow scenery gives a spectacular view from Gangtok.

The early dawn appears romantically pink and orange hued in this town. The massive coppery clouds render it plumed while the lighting extends it a faintly luminous version.

Like the changing designs of a kaleidoscope the mount Kanchenjunga changes its view from time to time and in different weathers. The following places are of tourists and academic interest in Gangtok and its surroundings.

Namgyal Institute of Tibetology

On a hillock below Gangtok amidst the stately trees of Oak, ash and biron is situated the prestigious Institute. The beautiful and imposing structure of the Institute surrounded by verdure is a magnificently splendid instance of the traditional Sikkimese architecture. The foundation stone for this rare institutes was laid down by the 1989 Nobel Peace Prize Winner Dalai Lama on February 10, 1957 when before his exile in India, he still occupied the coveted position of the spiritual head of Tibet. The Institute was inaugurated and thrown open for theologists and religion-based academicians by no less than a person like Pandit Jawaharlal Nehru who besides being an astute politician, efficient statesman, lover of art and bearing was a scholoastic luminary.

The primary objective of the Institute is to promote the cause of Tibetan studies. Placed in serene environment, the interiors of the Institute have been lavishly decorated with large murals, on rate wood carvings, and great altars holding the idols of Lord Buddha, Bodhisattvas and tantric deities. A library consisting of a vast variety of books, "encyclopaedias," reference manuals and manuscripts in huge cabinets is also attached to the Institute.

There are about 32 thousand volumes, mostly xylographs, translated versions of the original teachings of Lord Buddha, and manifold works of distinguished Buddhist scholars from all parts of the country. The collection pertaining to the titles on Mahayana is the largest in Asia and in all probability in the world too. The museum section of the Institute is equally rich and great asset for the organisation. Prized objects of traditional art, dorjis (thunder bolts) of different shapes and sizes, more than 250 icons, ritualistic chortens, brass bells, rosaries, thankas (land painted woven scrolls) are those major collections which place the Institute among the such best organisations.

Tusklakhang

The royal chapel, popularly known as Tusklakhang is located on an elevated but level surfaced, plateau like, ground in a palace complex itself. Although the mists, blowing of long trumpets, Chortens, fluttering praying flags, lofty stupas, vast open monasteries afford an atmosphere of mysticims still further heightened by cirmson robed lamas and humble nuns everywhere but a visitor from outside can confirm it by simply visiting this religious place. A leading repository of a sizeable collection of the sacred Buddhist scriptures, the chappel till recently had been both a worship hall and a venue for religious congregations.

The chappel's architecture consistent of sheer great facade broken by magnificent portal and is one of the finest examples of the traditional Sikkim architecture. In all corners of the chapel building have been seated the formidable heads of snow loins wood sculpture in relief. Inside the building the visitors finds unique and magnificent wood work, highlighted by the huge Buddhist murals adorning the walls of the hall.

An eternal butter fuelled lamp lights the floor of the ceiling of the altar, housing idols-goddesses and sacred scriptures. The reverential calm the prevails inside is pervaded by the scents of kindled juniper. Tusklakang continues to be a venue of all important festivals; religious, cultural or social. The New Years Dance, *i.e.,* Black Hat Dance, Warrior Dance to worship Kanchenjunga, etc. are all performed and celebrated in the Chapel. Earlier the coronation ceremony of the Chogyal, the royal wedding, path taking ceremonies were all celebrated inside the Chapel.

Orchid Sanctuary

The orchid sanctuary, peculiar to Sikkim in South Asia, is located in the Gangtok just below the Namgyal Institute of Tibetology. Ranging between the commonest variety to the rarest among rare variety of orchids have been preserved in the orchid sanctuary. The world over the tiny Himalayan State of Sikkim is known for having the largest variety of orchids otherwise existing in different micro, climatic subdivisions.

But all of these varieties are kept alive in this sanctuary with the help of certain artificial devices. A keen and investigative visit to the sanctuary is sufficient to convince a visitor that how adept is the Almighty Designer who weaves different floral patterns and gives different colours and hues to the so far known 631 varieties of orchids.

Gateways: The State of Sikkim is also known for gateways erected at the entrances to many urban settlements in general and the capital town of Gangtok in particular. No efforts have been spared by the Sikkimese artists to make these gateways attractive and imposing. The gateway spanning the entrance to the Civil Secretariat, *i.e.,* Tashling has a beauty and charm of its own. The minute skill and deftness of fingers and comprehension of natural patterns by the local artisans and craftsman are amply exhibited on this gateway alone.

Deer Park

The deer have a special place in Buddhism and thus it has been quite essential for the Chogyals to maintain a deer park. The Deer Park of Gangtok has been created to the south of the Secretariat. On the southern fringe of the Tashing, overlooking a valley that drops a thousand metres below, is situated the Deer Park which is one of the greatest and fascinating attractions to a visitor. The visit reminds us of Sarnath (in the vicinity of Varanasi) where Lord Buddha after getting his first sermon amidst frolicking deer. And such a feeling dawns after one has slighted the image of Lord Buddha in preaching posture enshrined in this Deer Park. The image in fact is the true replica of Lord Buddhas preaching posture enshrined in the precincts of the Bodh Vihar at Sarnath.

In the Deer Park at Gangtok the precept of the reversed Buddhist saint Scholar Shantideva, for a moment, lifts up every visitor. The saying runs as under:

"Shower forth, Ye Heavens, sweet rain in season dive. That Mother E: the rich harvest swell in ample stream, Hold fast, O' King, the path of Righteousness That World on World may rise to Bliss Supreme."

The park is no doubt a sanctuary for deer brought from different parts of Sikkim and any other part of the earth. Yet it symbolises the quest for harmonious peace and reciprocal brotherhood among neighbours. The enthroned statue of Lord Buddha faces the Civil Secretariat as if it is sermonising the powers that be inside to dispense impartial justice to all irrespective of their colour, creed, and conviction.

The statue perpetually calls upon the employees of the Secretariat to do their sacred duty in such a way that the evil vanishes and the righteousness comes to reign in all parts of the land of gods and goddesses. In the evening, a visitor in the calm atmosphere of the park feels a strange but satisfying invoilable tranquillity. A leisured but thoughtful walk around the soothing ripples of the Rangtok stream added with the charming sight of spotted deer and the long harped antelopes would be highly rewarding for the visitor.

Cottage Industries Institute

The multicraft Institute which was originally named Palden Thondup Institute for Cottage industries, after the name of the last Chogyal is in fact an academy of artistanship and craftsmanship wherein more than 250 dedicatedly devoted trainees produce cottage crafts of authentic Sikkimese designs and patterns. The locally produced handicraft goods were also sold through the Institute till recently.

Foremost among the products of the institute are the beautiful hand woven woollen carpets which carry traditional Sikkimese motifs, unique designs, fascinating patterns and very soothing colour combinations and blends. These artistically produced carpets not only attract the visitors but are in great demand within Sikkim as well as outside the state.

The institute has also started producing some other woollen goods which are durable, plush and they are dyed not in synthetic colours but traditional vegetable colours manufactured in Sikkim. The designs range between sophisticated harmonising tones to the brilliant rottings of vermillion against intense blues. Another exclusively indigenous product of the Institute is a Central Table locally called *Choktse*.

This table, worthy of being placed in every drawing room is much liked by all. It is a folding table and it has been made with a view that these tourists who wish to carry the souvenir should be in a position to do so with perfect ease. These tables are manufactured in different shapes, different sizes and in different patterns and designs. The Sikkimese hand-made paper is yet another souvenir liked by every one and produced by this institute. The Sikkimese are very expert weavers who weave large blankets which can later on be turned into shawls, jackets, bags, opulent Sikkimese thartkas (traditional tapestry), battiks, dolls and some other usable articles.

Khabelongstock

At a distance of 21 km from the capital town of Gangtok is located the historical site of Kabi or Khabelongstock. It is that place where the historic agreement of blood brotherhood was arrived at between Khye Balsa, the remotest ancestor of the Nagyal and Thekong Tek the then Lepcha Chief amidst ritual sacrificings and the looming form of the awe inspiringly revered and sacred the Bhutias continued for centuries.

A memorial stone still adorning the spot bears testimony to the historic agreement arrived at. No wonder besides the Lepchas and the Bhutias even tourists entering this region love to visit this place as pilgrims. Prayer flags and chortens stand guard on the hillock where people from all corners of the state come with offerings of flowers to pay their homage at this sacred spot.

Rumtek

Rumtek is that place, at a distance of 24 km from Gangtok, where are situated two important monasteries of the Kagyappa sub-sect of the Mahayana Buddhism. The harmonious sounds given out by the prayer chanting lamas, the crymbals, drums, reeds and trumpets appear to welcome one and all even before the monasteries are sighted by the visitors. The older monastery for Kagyappa lamas perched on the spur of the Rumtek hill was renovated during the seventies of the last century, of course, with least interference with the original but traditional structure.

The monastery has been designed after the Lamasary pattern of Tibet. The Karmapa Lama of Tibet lived here for the rest of his life after his exile from Tibet. On the way to Rumtek, the tourists can also visit the Enchey monastery situated on tile Gangtok Nathu La road just a distance of three km from Gangtok. All these worth-visiting and rewarding monasteries in Sikkim are institutions of Scholarship and Saintliness, dedicated to the spread of noble teachings of Lord Buddha.

Now, when even the remostest settlements of the state are being connected by roads, one may visit Yamthang Lachen, Lachung Tsunthong, Yuksonl, Chewabhanirange, Bentam, Barang, etc., etc., places which find mention in the Sikkim. Chronicles. Although many places offer very attractive sites yet there is dearth of tourist facilities. Nonetheless, the State Department of Tourism is at the job and it is expected that not in a very far future many other parts of the state shall be thrown open to tourists and visitors.

Bibliography

Acharyya, S.K. and K.K. Ray: *Geology of Darjeeling Sikkim Himalaya: Guide to Excursion*, New Delhi, 1977.

Arora, Vibha: *Gandhigiri in Sikkim*, Economic and Political Weekly, 2008.

Awasty, Indira: *Between Sikkim and Bhutan: The Lepchas and Bhutias of Pedong*, Delhi, 2004.

Bastola, Yadab: *Young Warriors*, The Kathmandu Post, 2009.

Basu, Amitabha/Das, Swapan K./Majumdar, Partha P.: *Demography and Demographical Genetics of Two Isolated Mountain Villages of Northern Sikkim*, Eastern Himalaya, Journal of the Indian Anthropological Society, 1982.

Basu, N.K.: *Assam in the Ahom Age*, Calcutta, 1970.

Basu, Saikat.: *The Land of Arresting Beauty: The Tourism Scene*, Focus on Sikkim, Frontline, 1997.

Bell, Charles A.: *Administrative Report of the Sikkim State for 1912-1913*, Government Press, Calcutta, 2001.

Bhadra, Madhumita: *Sikkim: Democracy and Social Change*, Minerva, Calcutta, 1992.

Bhadra, Ranajit Kumar, Bhadra, Mita: *Plantation Labours in North-East India*, N.L. Publication, Dibrugrarh, 1997.

Bhagabati, K. Abani and Kar, K. Bimal: *Survey of Research in Geography on North-East India 1970-1990*, Regency Publication, New Delhi, 1999.

Bhandary, Shashi Ram: *A Novel embody in Nepal's Tourism*, Today, 2000.

Bhanja, K.C.: *Wonders of Darjeeling and the Sikkim Himalaya: Accounts All Authentic*, Gilbert & Co., Darjeeling, 1945.

Bhasin, Veena: *Transhumants of Himalayas: Changpas of Ladakh, Gaddis of Himachal Pradesh and Bhutias of Sikkim*, Kamla-Raj, Delhi, 1996.

Bhattacharjee, D.S.: *Society in Sikkim: The Changing Scenario*, The Administrator, 1994.

Bhattacharjee, J.B.: *North East Indian Perspectives in History*, Vikas Publishing House, New Delhi, 1995.

Bhattacharya, Aparna: *The Bhutia-Lepcha Women of Sikkim: Tradition and Response to Change,* Indus, New Delhi, 1994.

Bhattacharya, Bimalendu: *Sikkim: Land and People,* Omsons Publication, Delhi, 1997.

Bhattacharya, Pranab Kumar: *Aspects of Cultural History of Sikkim: Studies in Coinage,* Calcutta, 1984.

Bhattacharyya, N.N.: *Religious Culture of North-Eastern India,* Manohar Publishers & Distributors, New Delhi, 1995.

Bhaumik, Subir: *Insurgent Cross Fire: North-East India,* Lancer Publishers, New Delhi, 1996.

Bhuyan, B. C.: *Political Development of the North East,* Omsons Publications, New Delhi, 1989.

Blandford, William T.: *Account of a Visit to the Eastern and Northern Frontiers of Independent Sikkim,* With Notes on Zoology of the Alpine and Sub-Alpine Region. Journal of the Asiatic Society (of Bengal), 1871.

Brownrigg, H.S.: *Routes in Nepal, Bhutan, Sikkim, Tibet, Burma and between Assam and Burma,* Calcutta, 1878.

Campbell: *Papers on the Valley of Chumbi,* Journal of the Royal Asiatic Society, , 2001

Chakravarthi, K.R.: *Government and Politics in Sikkim,* Indus, New Delhi, 1994.

Chandra, P.R.: *Sikkim: Its Old Laws and Customs,* North Bengal University Review, 1981.

Chattopadhyay, Suhrid, Sankar, Talukdar, Sushanta: *Testing Ground: The Elections in West Bengal, Sikkim and the Seven North-eastern States have become Crucial in the Final Power Game,* Frontline, 2009.

Chaube, S. K.: *Hill Politics in Northeast India,* Orient Longman Limited, Patna, 1973.

Chaudhuri, A.B.: *Himalayan Ecology and Environment,* New Delhi, 1992.

Chaudhuri, Kalyan: *A Coup in Sikkim: After 15 Years, Bhandari Bites the Dust,* Frontline, 1994.

Chettri, Nakul: *Assessment of Natural Resources use Patterns: a Case Study Along a Trekking Corridor of Sikkim Himalaya,* India, Resources, Energy, and Development, 2006.

Choedon, Yeshi: *Impact of Modernization on Society and Culture of Sikkim,* Har-Anand Choegyal, Lisa, 1991.

Chopra, P.N.: Sikkim, S. Chand, New Delhi, 1985.

Chorlton, Windsor: *Felsbewohner des Himalaya: Die Bhotia. Amsterdam,* Time-Life Books, 1982.

Cintury, Chandrakala: *The Vow Fulfilled: Saga of Sidkeong-Alexandra Historic Association,* Indus, New Delhi, 1994.

Clarke, C.B.: *Botanical Notes from Darjeeling to Tonglo,* Botanical Journal of the Linnean Society, 1876.

Coelho, V.H.: *Sikkim and Bhutan,* Vikas Publication, Delhi, 1970.

Cohen, Stephen Philip: *Security Issues in South Asia,* Asian Survey, 1975.

Das, B.S.: *Sikkim's Identity as an Indian State,* Indus Publishing Company, New Delhi, 1992.

Das, Gurudas: *Research Priorities in North-East India: With Special Reference to Arunachal Pradesh,* Regency Publications, New Delhi, 2002.

Dash, A.J.: *Bengal District Gazetters: Darjeeling,* Calcutta, 2001.

Datta, Amal: *Sikkim Since Independence:* (a study of impact of education & emerging class structure), Mittal Publication, New Delhi, 2001.

Datta, Karubaki: *Religion and Society in Tibet, Bhutan and Sikkim: a Bibliographical Study,* Gyan Publishing House, New Delhi, 2001.

Datta, P.S.: *North East and the Indian State: Paradoxes of a Periphery,* Vikas Publishing House, New Delhi, 1995.

Datta-Ray, Sunanda K.: *Smash and Grab: Annexation of Sikkim,* Vikas Publication, New Delhi, 1985.

De, R., and J.R. Kayal: *Seismotectonic Model of the Sikkim Himalaya: Constraint from Microearthquake Surveys,* Bull. Seism. Soc. Am., 2003.

De, R.: *A Microearthquake Survey in the Himalayan Foredeep Region, Sikkim Himalaya,* J. Geophys, 2000.

Dhamala, K. Ranju Rani. *A Socio-economic Study of the Pemayangtse Monastery of Sikkim,* Gyan Publishing House, New Delhi, 1991.

————: *Emerging Pattern of Political Leadership in Sikkim,* Occasional Paper, 1986.

Doig, Desmond: *"Sikkim, Tiny Himalayan Kingdom in the Clouds, "* National Geographic, CXXIII, 1894.

Dutta, Ashish: *Eastern Himalayan Traveller's Guide: Darjeeling-Sikkim-Kathmandu- Bhutan,* New Delhi, 1994.

Gammie, G.A.: *The Vegetaion of Temperate and Alpine Sikkim,* In H.H.Risley, The Gazetteer of Sikkim, Bengal Secretariat Press, Calcutta, 1894.

Gangopadahyay, Niladri Sekhar: *Insurgency and Media: A study on Tripura,* Nabankur, Agartala, 2002.

Garden, E.: *Nepal, Sikkim and Bhutan in Pictures,* I.B.H., Calcutta, 1972.

Gassah, L. S.: *Research Priorities in North East India: With Special Reference to Mizoram,* Regency Publications, New Delhi, 2001.

Gibbons, Bob and Bob Ashford: *The Himalayan Kingdoms: Nepal, Bhutan & Sikkim*, New York, 1983.

Gopalkrishnan, R.: *Insurgent North-Eastern Region of India*, Vikas Publishing House, New Delhi, 1995.

Gorer, Geoffrey: *Himalayan Village: An Account of the Lepchas of Sikkim*, Michael Joseph, London, 1967.

Goyal, Narendra: *Political History of Himalayan States: Tibet, Nepal, Bhutan, Sikkim and Grover*, Jain Brothers, New Delhi, 1966.

Gulati, M.N.: *Tibetan wars through Sikkim, Bhutan, and Nepal*, Manas Publications, New Delhi, 2003.

Gupta, Ranjan: *Sikkim: The Merger with India*, Asian Survey, 1975.

Gurung, Chanda: *Case Study in Darjeeling District and Sikkim*, ICIMOD, Kathmandu, 1999.

Hazarika, Niru: *Profile of Youth Organisations in North East India,* V. V. Rao Institute of Micro Studies and Research, Assam, 1998.

Hooker, J.D.: *A Lofty Mountain on the Confines of Nepal and Sikkim*, Journal of the Asiatic Society of Bengal, 1849.

—————: *Himalayan Journals - Or: Notes of a Naturalist in Bengal, the Sikkim and Nepal Himalayas, the Khasia Mountains etc.*, John Murray, London, 1969.

Humboldt, B.A.: *Physical Geography of Sikkim-Himalaya*, Hook. J. Bot., 1851.

Jain, Ajit Prasad: *Sikkim: Retrospects and Prospects*, New Delhi, 1973.

Jha, S.K. and S.N. Mishra: *Sikkim: Government and Politics*, New Delhi, 1984.

K. Warikoo: *Society and Culture in the Himalayas*, HarAnand, New Delhi, 1995.

Kandell, Alice S. and C.Y. Salisbury: *Mountaintop Kingdom Sikkim*, Vikas Publication, New Delhi, 1977.

Kazi, Jigme N.: *Inside Sikkim Against the Tide,* Hill Media Publications, Gangtok, 1993.

Kotturen, G.: *Folk Tales of Sikkim*, Sterling Publication, New Delhi, 1979.

Kumar, B.B.: *Tensions and Conflict in Northeast India*, Cosmo Publications, New Delhi, 1995.

Lacaita, C.C.: *Sikkim including the Kalimpong District*, Botanical Journal of the Linnean Society, 1916.

Lall, Vinay D.: *Human Settlement Strategy for Sikkim: Status, Policy, and Action Plan*, Society for Development Studies, New Delhi, 1991.

Lama, Mahendra P.: *Sikkim: Society, Polity, Economy, Environment*, Indus, New Delhi, 2001.

Mackenzie, Alexander: *The North East Frontier of India*, Mittal Publications, New Delhi, 2001.

Mahendra P. Lama: *Sikkim: Problems and Prospects of Development*, Manas, New Delhi, 1992.

Male, P.F.: *Sikkim*, Oxford, Calcutta, 1971.

Malla, Shashi P.B.: *The Himalayan Kingdoms, Nepal, Bhutan and Sikkim: The Politics of Survival*, C.N.R.S., Paris, 1978.

Marshall, Julie G.: *Britain and Tibet 1765-1947 : a Select Annotated Bibliography of British Relations with Tibet and the Himalayan States Including Nepal, Sikkim, and Bhutan*, Routledge Curzon, London, 2005.

Mathew, K.M.: *A Bibliography of the Botany of Sikkim*, Bulletin of the Botanical Society of Bengal, 1970.

Nag, Sajal: *India and North-East India: Mind, Politics and the Process of Integration 1946-1950*, Regency Publications, New Delhi, 1998.

National Bureau of Soil Survey: *Master Plan for Irrigation Development, Sikkim*, Govt. of Sikkim, Agricultural Finance Corporation Ltd, Report, 1994.

Nembang, Saroj: *The Kirat Limbus of Sikkim: A Brief Sketch*, The Town Press, Siliguri, 1992.

Nuh, V. K.: *Struggle for Identity in North-east India: A Theological response*, Spectrum Publications, Guwahati, 2001.

Pakem, B.: *Insurgency in North-East India*, Om Sons Publications, New Delhi, 1997.

Porter, A.E.: *Census of India 1931: West Bengal and Sikkim*, Usha Publication, New Delhi, 1987.

Raina, V.K., and B.S. Srivastava: A Reappraisal of the Geology of the Sikkim Lesser Himalaya, *Stratigraphy and Correlation of Lesser Himalayan Formation*, K.S., 1980.

Rao, P. Raghunadha: *India and Sikkim*, 1814-1970, Sterling Publication, New Delhi, 1972.

Risley, H.H.: *Gazetteer of Sikkim*, Bengal Secretariat Press, Calcutta, 1894.

Ronaldshay, Lord: *Himalayan Bhutan, Sikkim and Tibet*, Delhi, 1977.

S. K. Chaube: *The Himalayas: Profiles of Modernisation and Adaptation*, Jalandhar, Sterling Publishers, New Delhi, 1998.

Sarma, Nilotpal: *Plainsmen in Sikkim and their Occupational Structure*, Indus, New Delhi, 1994.

Schaefer, Ludwig: *A Sikkim Awakening*, Himal, 1995.

Sengupta, Nirmalananda: *State Government and Politics: Sikkim*, Sterling Publication, Bangalore, 1985.

Sharma, S. K. and Sharma, Usha: *Documents on Sikkim and Bhutan*, Anmol Publications Pvt. Ltd., New Delhi, 1998.

Sharma, Suresh Kant: *Encyclopaedia of Sikkim and Bhutan*, Anmol Publication, New Delhi, 1997.

Singh, K. S.: *People of India: Sikkim*, Seagull Books, Calcutta, 1993.

Sinha, A.C.: *Youth Movements in North-East India: Structural Imperatives and Aspects of Change*, Indus Publishing Company, New Delhi, 1994.

Smith, W.W. & Cave, G.H.: *The Vegetation of the Zemu and Llonakh Valleys of Sikkim*, Records of the Botanical Survey of India, 1913.

Srivastav, Nirankar: *Survey of Research in Economics on North East India 1970-1990*, Regency Publications, New Delhi, 2000.

Syiemlieh, R. David: *Survey of Research in History on North-East India 1970-1990*, Regency Publication, New Delhi, 2000.

Tarapot, Phanjoubam: *Drug Abuse and Illicit Trafficking in North Eastern India*, Vikash Publishing House, New Delhi, 1997.

Taylor, David and Malcolm Yapp: *Political Identity in South Asia*, London, 1979.

Temple, Richard: *Travels in Nepal and Sikkim*, Ratna Pustak Bhandar, Kathmandu, 1977.

Thomas, C. Joshua: *Dimensions of Displaced People in North-East India*, Regency Publications, New Delhi, 2002.

Verghese, B.G.: *India's North East Resurgent: Ethnicity, Insurgency, Governance, and Development*, Konark Publishers, New Delhi, 1997.

Virk, D.S.: *Sikkim Tibet 1903-1908*, New Delhi, 1989.

White, J.C.: *The Book of the Law*, The Gazetteer of Sikkim, Bengal Secretariat Press, Calcutta: 1894.

————: *Himalayan Bhutan, Sikkim and Tibet*, ESS Publications, Delhi, 1977.

Yonzone, G.S.: *Science and Technology Education in Sikkim*, Indus, New Delhi, 1994.

Young, Lincoln J.: *Agricultural changes in Bhutan: Some Environmental Questions*, Geographical Journal, London, 1991.

Index

D

Dalai Lama, 39, 56, 57, 58, 59, 60, 62, 141, 206.

Damber Singh Degree College, 46, 145.

Dance, 41, 42, 43, 44, 126, 132, 197, 207.

Dasain, 44, 125.

Deer Park, 196, 198, 204, 205, 207, 208.

Dhanwar, 155.

Dikchu, 26, 116, 117, 202.

Drukpa Tseshi, 45.

Dzongkha, 149, 152, 153.

E

Economic Development, 74, 116, 119, 128, 161, 165, 172, 195.

Economy, 1, 15, 16, 20, 21, 49, 65, 67, 68, 75, 85, 88, 111, 159, 161, 193, 204.

Education, 32, 45, 46, 48, 66, 67, 86, 87, 124, 139, 140, 142, 143, 144, 145, 146, 148, 152, 154, 160, 192.

Education System, 143.

Election, 5, 79, 87, 89, 159, 188.

Electoral System, 91.

Ethnic Group, 107, 151, 153, 155.

European Commission, 134.

Executive Council, 69, 78, 79, 86, 89, 90.

F

Farming, 6, 15, 16, 18, 34, 35, 125, 164, 169, 175, 176, 178, 179, 180.

Festival, 11, 41, 42, 43, 44, 45, 125, 131, 132, 136, 202.

Flora and Fauna, 9, 24, 30, 31, 36, 37, 119, 120, 195.

Forestry, 117, 118, 164, 180, 182.

G

Gangtok, 1, 3, 4, 5, 7, 8, 9, 18, 19, 20, 21, 24, 26, 27, 30, 31, 33, 34, 35, 36, 37, 41, 43, 45, 48, 49, 50, 54, 55, 56, 57, 65, 66, 69, 71, 72, 76, 78, 79, 81, 82, 84, 87, 90, 96, 98, 99, 118, 120, 121, 122, 124, 129, 132, 133, 134, 135, 140, 143, 144, 147, 158, 160, 167, 168, 169, 171, 172, 177, 179, 183, 187, 188, 190, 192, 195, 196, 197, 198, 199, 201, 202, 203, 205, 206, 207, 208, 209.

Geology, 7, 116, 117, 142, 200.

Glaciers, 6, 25, 26, 36, 37, 38, 105, 106, 110, 111, 115, 118, 129.

Gorkhali, 151.

Government, 3, 4, 5, 7, 10, 11, 15, 16, 17, 18, 20, 21, 24, 30, 36, 45, 46, 48, 49, 52, 57, 60, 64, 68, 69, 70, 71, 72, 74, 76, 77, 80, 81, 82, 83, 84, 86, 87, 88, 89, 90, 91, 92, 93, 94, 95, 96, 98, 99, 100, 102, 108, 116, 118, 119, 120, 123, 126, 128, 133, 134, 135, 137, 139, 140, 142, 143, 145, 149, 152, 153, 157, 158, 159, 160, 161, 162, 163, 164, 165, 166, 167, 168, 169, 171, 172, 175, 177, 178, 181, 182, 183, 185, 187, 189, 190, 191, 192, 193, 195, 196, 197, 200, 203, 204.

Governor, 4, 57, 63, 64, 65, 66, 84, 92, 93, 142, 185, 188, 189.

❏❏❏

www.ingramcontent.com/pod-product-compliance
Lightning Source LLC
Chambersburg PA
CBHW061830260326
41914CB00005B/943